THE OVERSEAS CHINESE

Ethnicity in National Context

edited by

Francis L.K. Hsu
EMERITUS
DEPARTMENT OF ANTHROPOLOGY
NORTHWESTERN UNIVERSITY

and

Hendrick Serrie
DEPARTMENT OF ANTHROPOLOGY
ECKERD COLLEGE

University Press of America, Inc.
Lanham • New York • Oxford

Copyright © 1998
University Press of America,® Inc.
4720 Boston Way
Lanham, Maryland 20706

12 Hid's Copse Rd.
Cummor Hill, Oxford OX2 9JJ

All rights reserved
Printed in the United States of America
British Library Cataloging in Publication Information Available

Library of Congress Cataloging-in-Publication Data

The overseas Chinese : ethnicity in national context / edited by
Francis L. K. Hsu, Hendrick Serrie.
p.   cm.
Includes bibliographical references and index.
1. Chinese—Foreign countries. 2. Chinese—Foreign countries—
Social conditions. I. Hsu, L.K. Francis. II. Serrie, Hendrick.
DS732.093 1998   305.895'1—dc21   98-18865 CIP

ISBN 0-7618-1163-X (cloth: alk. ppr.)

∞™ The paper used in this publication meet the minimum
requirements of American National Standard for information
Sciences—Permanence of Paper for Printed Library Materials,
ANSI Z39.48—1984

Dedication

This book is dedicated to our wives

Vera and Gretchen

and to our children

Eileen and Penny, Karim and Keir

Contents

Chapter 1
The Overseas Chinese:
Common Denominators of a Changing Ethnicity
    by Hendrick Serrie and Francis L. K. Hsu   1

Chapter 2
The Chinese in Calcutta:
The Reproduction of Hakka Identity
    by Ellen Oxfeld   13

Chapter 3
The Chinese in Northern Thailand:
A Preliminary Perspective on Kinship and Ethnicity
    by Ann Maxwell Hill   43

Chapter 4
The Chinese in the Philippines:
From Aliens to Cultural Minority
    by George H. Weightman   65

Chapter 5
The Chinese in Brisbane:
Segmentation and Integration
    by Lawrence W. Crissman, George Beattie and James Selby   87

Chapter 6
The Chinese in New Zealand:
Persistence, Change and Innovation
by Charles P. Sedgwick 115

Chapter 7
The Chinese in New York City:
Kinship and Immigration
by Bernard Wong 143

Chapter 8
Chinese Immigrant Children in New York City:
Bicultural Conflicts
by Betty Lee Sung 173

Chapter 9
Chinese Around the World:
The Familial and the Familiar
by Hendrick Serrie 189

References 217

Index 227

Chapter 1

The Overseas Chinese: Common Denominators of a Changing Ethnicity

Hendrick Serrie
Francis L.K. Hsu

Introduction

Immigrants from China have made their home in many countries of the world. In the process of adapting to different national host cultures, they have retained or modified some elements of traditional Chinese culture and have eliminated others. There are cultural denominators that identify Chinese culture everywhere, while at the same time Chinese ethnicity varies with the unique features of each host nation. The articles in this book describe, compare and analyze a wide array of Chinese communities: in East, Southeast and South Asia, in Europe, and in North and South America.

Serrie has examined thirteen monographs of mainland, "offshore," and overseas communities in a synchronic comparison of recruitment principles and purposes of Chinese social organizations. Crissman, Beattie, and Selby; Sedgwick; Weightman; and Wong add a diachronic dimension to their analyses, noting the changing laws affecting Chinese immigration to Australia, New Zealand, the Philippines, Peru and the United States, and showing the demographic consequences and changing social groups. Oxfeld, Hill and Sung focus on particular segments of Chinese communities, namely Hakka tannery entrepreneurs, Yunnanese mothers, and Chinatown teenagers, in Calcutta, northern Thailand and New York City, respectively.

Psychocultural Orientations

Several scholars relate their findings to the psychocultural orientations discerned in traditional Chinese culture by Hsu. In *Under the Ancestors' Shadow* (1948) Hsu described the importance of patrilineal kinship for the Chinese. In *Americans and Chinese* (1953) he contrasted the kinship orientation of Chinese culture with the orientation towards individualism and contractual associations in American culture. In *Clan, Caste and Club* (1963) he contrasted these Chinese and American orientations with the orientation towards religious and occupational castes in (Hindu) Indian culture.

Hsu then developed the hypothesis that the dominant dyad or two-person relationship in Chinese culture is father-son, and that the psychocultural attributes of continuity, inclusiveness, authority and asexuality that inhere in this relationship permeate other aspects of Chinese society and culture. In contrast, in American culture the dominant dyad is husband-wife, and its inherent attributes of discontinuity, exclusiveness, volition, and sexuality are pervasive in American society and culture (1965; 1968; 1971; 1972; 1974).

In an analysis of thirteen Chinese communities around the world, Serrie concludes that many of the functions of Chinese social organizations, whether or not they are structured on the basis of kinship, express the Hsu attributes of continuity, inclusiveness, authority, and asexuality.

Wong demonstrates that, while the dominant dyad of the New York Chinatown "incomplete" family was father-son, it was complemented by a mother-child dyad back in China. The father-son dyad is also dominant in the "non-residential extended family," which owns and operates a business. But among the families of professional Chinese,

American-born Chinese, and well-off or well-educated New Immigrants, the dominant dyad is husband-wife. Finally, it is Wong's observation that among poorer New Immigrant families, the children — who are more familiar with American culture — tend to dominate their parents.

Sung shows Chinese adolescents in New York City to be family-oriented and situation-centered — another of Hsu's terms — and to have conflicts with American teenage attitudes of resisting authority, expressing sexuality, and emphasizing individuality.

The Familial and the Familiar

Following Hsu, Serrie finds that the principles of recruitment in overseas Chinese social groupings indicate a preference for patrilineal kinship. In their early decades, however, overseas communities had too few kinsmen to replicate the traditional lineage structures of the mainland. Serrie finds that overseas Chinese communities extend the principle of kinship, substituting the "familiar" for the "familial" in widening circles of identification until sufficient numbers for a viable organization are reached. The principles of kinship, surname, residence, and origin are invoked not only in order to achieve critical mass for an organization, but may also serve to subdivide an aggregate of people too large to maintain kin-like face-to-face relationships within the organization.

The outermost boundary of familiarity is Chinese ethnicity, and the next outermost boundary is that created by the different Chinese languages. Oxfeld's research on the Chinese in Calcutta indicates that they are separated into three groups based on language and locality: the Hakka, the Cantonese, and the Hubeinese.

Kinship-Oriented Social Organization

Serrie's synchronic analysis of a global sample of Chinese communities yields three types of social organization. First, there is the more or less traditional rural village or town of old China, Hong Kong, and Taiwan, structured according to ties of kinship, residence, and contract, in order of decreasing importance. Second, there is the overseas urban minority community, organized on the basis of surname as a substitute for kinship, origin as a substitute for residence, and contract.

Third, there is the marginal mainland or overseas community, where the Chinese are so few in numbers or scattered so thinly across the rural or urban landscape, that formal social organizations are minimal and organized solely in terms of contract.

Weightman's research on the present-day overseas Chinese in Manila indicates a postwar strengthening of kinship-based organizations. The patrilineal extended family and the lineage or clan are common; the concentration of a few surnames is very dense; exogamy prevails in multiple surname groups as well as clans; and even Chinese Christians continue memorializing their ancestors.

Wong relates the different types of family structure in New York City to changing United States immigration policies. The exclusionist laws of 1882 and 1924, which prevented both the importation of Chinese women and the intermarriage of Chinese men with white women, maintained a Chinatown of bachelors and "incomplete families" composed of fathers united with sons old enough to leave their mothers, who remained in China. The repeal of these laws during World War II, and the passage in 1945 and 1953 of acts permitting entry and citizenship for war brides, refugees, and "stranded professionals," saw the rise of conjugal or nuclear families. The 1965 amendments establishing clear preference for skilled persons opened migration to entire families and to individuals who joined "enlarged families." These post-1965 New Immigrants also established "nonresidential extended families" in order to jointly operate a single business.

Segmentary Sociopolitical Organization

The articles on the Chinese of Australia and New Zealand build on Crissman's segmentary model. This points to the internal division of the Chinese community, first along dialect lines and next along lines of locality or surname, in order to achieve effective self-government without creating formal governmental institutions requiring hierarchical administration and representational politics.

Sedgwick sees the segmentary system as a series of changing responses, not only to the sociopolitical environment of New Zealand, but to international concerns focusing on mainland China, and to an internal cycle of corporation-fragmentation within the Chinese community itself.

In both countries, the rise of Communist China has required that the overseas Chinese maintain a low political profile, and athletics has emerged as a nonthreatening and major expression of Chinese ethnicity. (This is in pronounced contrast to the Chinese in New York City, who, according to Sung, experience feelings of inadequacy and ambivalence about sports.) Sedgwick observes a new parallel segmentary structure built on sports organizations or Christian churches alongside the older social divisions pertaining to the original homeland in China.

In Australia, Crissman, Beattie, and Selby plot the influx, since World War II, of Chinese students, refugees, and other immigrants from Southeast Asian countries, arriving with education, business and other professional skills, and capital for investment. Similarly, they plot the rise of younger generations of Chinese born and raised in Australia, also possessing superior education, business or professional skills, and capital for investment. These traits that pave the way to economic success are accompanied by a much more hospitable external social climate and a high degree of integration. A new segmentary system has emerged here also, but the subdivisions of the postwar immigrant Chinese are established, not on the basis of their original ancestral homeland in China, but on the basis of the countries of their own birth and childhood: Malaysia-Singapore, Vietnam, Papua New Guinea, Indonesia, and Hong Kong.

Self Ascription vs. Ascription by Others

Ethnic identity is created, not only out of a group's own sense and definition of itself, but also by the sense and definition that the outside host society has of it. Oxfeld sees Chinese ethnicity in Calcutta as dialogical or reflexive; it is generated within the Hakka community and, at the same time, is reinforced by Hinduism, with its ideas of ritual purity and caste, and by Indian politics, which includes Chinese Indians in the lingering resentment felt toward the Peoples Republic of China.

Indian economy and society target enterprises and occupations such as the Hakka Chinese tanneries as unclean and the province only of untouchables. Dietary differences, in which Chinese are accustomed to eating beef, which is forbidden by Hinduism, and pork, which is forbidden by Islam, as well as frogs, snakes, and the like, also isolate the Chinese. Even though they hold Indian citizenship, the Chinese in Calcutta feel insecure in their host culture. During the 1962 war between India and China, thousands of Chinese Indians were deported or put in concentration camps.

The Chinese who operate tanneries in Calcutta are relegated to the periphery of society. This is expressed territorially by the location of their tanneries on the outskirts of the city, and socially by the strict boundaries on social interaction between Chinese tanners and non-Chinese Indians. They interact only in economic or bureaucratic contexts and maintain strict social boundaries with employees, business associates, and occasional friends who are not Chinese.

Yet while the Hakka Chinese are peripheral to Calcutta society, Oxfeld observes that they express their own sense of centrality, placing non-Hakka persons at the periphery. They use the Chinese word *ren*, meaning "person," only with regard to fellow Hakka Chinese. They apply the word *lao*, meaning "bumpkin," to other Chinese in Calcutta who are not Hakka, e.g. the Cantonese and the Hubeinese. The word *gui*, meaning "ghost or devil" is reserved for all non-Chinese, which are divided into *wu gui*, "black ghosts" such as Hindu and Muslim Indians, and *fan gui*, "white ghosts" such as Europeans.

The Host Culture Environment

The political and social environment of the national host culture has been a major factor in defining the social organization of all overseas Chinese communities, as well as determining the course of assimilation or separation of the Chinese and host people.

Weightman describes the Chinese in the Philippines, a country with Hispanic colonial traditions and a brief period of American control prior to independence. Here, despite the strong antipathy towards Chinese, intermarriage during the Spanish period produced a group of Filipinized Chinese mestizos who were absorbed as part of the new elite. By contrast, until recent times the exclusionist laws of the American government have made Philippine citizenship impossible for most Chinese immigrants and have given rise to the separated Chinese community of today.

The historical contrast between Anglo exclusionist approaches to immigrant Chinese in Australia, New Zealand, the Philippines and the United States, on the one hand, and the Hispanic assimilationist approach in the Philippines, on the other, is reinforced by Wong's remarks on the rapid assimilation of the Chinese in Lima, Peru.

Wong shows the Chinese in Lima to be least concerned with patrilineal kinship or surname, in comparison with the Chinese in New York City or Manila. Despite the Hispanic tradition of the Philippines, the present-day Chinese in Manila are far more active in the maintenance of lineage or clan and surname organizations than are the Chinese in New York City. Weightman would attribute this to U.S. exclusionist policies, which overshadowed the Hispanic tradition during the period of American control of the Philippines, combined with anti-Chinese propaganda under the Japanese occupation during World War II and the rise of Philippine nationalism afterwards.

Assimilation and Intermarriage

However secure adult immigrants may feel about their ethnicity in whatever alien context they may find themselves, children born and raised in the new cultural environment will find their own ethnicity to be complex and problematic. There is the pull towards the culture of their parents, the source of life and care; but there is also a push towards the culture of their peers, especially when it is the source of friends, future spouses, and employment.

Assimilation and intermarriage go hand in hand. Through history the disposition of the Spanish to marry Chinese is in vivid contrast to the racist separatism of the English-speaking peoples. Since the 1960s the rise of a well-educated, capitalized Chinese business and professional class, combined with racial and ethnic egalitarian movements, has produced a change in Anglo racism, such that intermarriage between Chinese and Anglos has become commonplace. At the same time, in Southeast Asian countries nascent national chauvinism and xenophobia against the Chinese, combined with their status as an economically advantaged minority, has produced new barriers to assimilation. Ironically, it is resulting in a "Chinese brain drain" from those countries to such Anglo countries as Australia, Canada, and the United States.

In Thailand, Hill contrasts the overseas Chinese from Kwangtung and Fukien provinces, who are intermarrying and may be assimilating, with the "overland" Chinese from Yunnan province, who tend not to intermarry and are less assimilated to Thai culture. Although Yunnanese youth sent off to high school or university become enamored of Thai culture and attempt to reject Yunnanese culture, they must ultimately return to it in order to obtain the only employment available to them, usually in the Burma-Thailand trade that is controlled by the Yunnanese. Moreover, while the Kwangtung and Fukien Chinese have difficulties in finding spouses among their own groups in the urban areas of Thailand, the Yunnanese have sufficient young women available for marriage, all raised in a strict, conservative Chinese tradition and prepared to do the same for their own children.

The Australian-born Chinese in Brisbane are further assimilated. A majority have intermarried with whites and the use of Chinese language in the home has declined. In the mid-70s they expressed opposition to the admission of Chinese refugees from Vietnam, their common Chinese origin notwithstanding.

In New York City, Chinese range along a continuum of assimilation. Working with Chinatown adolescents, Sung probes the psychocultural conflicts inhering in growing up with two ethnic referents. In opposition to a home life that stresses dependence on the family, respect for authority, reporting misbehavior, academic achievement, and thrift in all things, the schools and neighborhoods tend to value individualism, physical and verbal aggressiveness, demonstration of affection and other feelings, erotic dress and behavior, frank sexual expression, and excellence in sports.

Sung reports teachers pointedly underlining American values to Chinese children practicing otherwise, and schoolmates and neighborhood white, black and hispanic children attempting to interact in ways that are normal to them and idealized in the mass media. Because many aspects of the American way of life are attractive to Chinese children, the opposition between Chinese and American values and behavior poses choices to Chinatown adolescents that are painful and sometimes immobilizing. If we follow Wong's analysis, almost all available good jobs will lure these children out of Chinatown when they are grown, and they will join those affluent Chinese who straddle both cultures and marry partners of whatever ethnicity they choose.

India stands in sharp contrast to other host nations. The religiously defined, occupationally based, hierarchical, hereditary caste system presents a fundamentally different kind of social reality that allows cultural and ethnic groups and subgroups a means of coexisting and preserving their ethnic distinctions indefinitely through time. According to Oxfeld, the Hakka Chinese are the only immigrant group that rejects the caste system. They focus strictly on the accumulation of wealth within an entrepreneurial ethic as the determinant of status differences within their own enclave.

Rejecting the fundaments of Hindu society, however, increases Hakka Chinese insecurity about their situation in India. Oxfeld reports that, starting the late 1970s, Hakka Chinese from Calcutta began emigrating to Europe, Australia, and Canada, especially to the city of Toronto. In Toronto, the pattern of Chinese settlement is widely dispersed; no occupation is monopolized by Hakka Chinese, and what were considerable financial assets in India convert to modest Canadian sums. Hakka children attend public schools, not private Hakka-run schools as in Calcutta, and Hakka children show signs of embracing Canadian culture.

The Practical and the Primordial

Some scholars (e.g. Glazer and Moynihan 1975:19) see ethnic identity in terms of primordial identifications and powerful emotions generated by a sense of shared physical and cultural traits. Oxfeld presents the Calcutta Chinese in terms of a contextual approach to ethnicity, and suggests the supposed dichotomy between the two approaches can be resolved by understanding that the enculturational experience of childhood is deeply internalized in every individual and leads to the compelling emotional identifications so often associated with ethnic identity in adulthood. Sung shows that in a radically different cultural environment, Chinese immigrant children are painfully conflicted as they experience opposing enculturational contexts. And Wong points out that within the American context, Chinese children, with their surer knowledge of the host culture, are often dominant over their immigrant parents.

Ethnicity, like nationalism, does not last forever. For any group, it lasts only for as long as it is needed. The primordial aspect of ethnicity, then, must be contrasted with its pragmatic aspect.

The purpose of culture is to provide human beings with an extra-somatic substitute for instinct. Each specific culture offers to its members an accumulation of ready-made solutions for coping with a particular natural and social environment. When the environment changes, the culture must change or survival is threatened.

Ethnicity, which is never a complete culture in itself, is even more susceptible to change than the host culture matrix of which it is a part. Just as nationalism arises when one nation state encounters cross-cultural difficulties in its efforts to survive and prosper with other nation states, so ethnic identity arises when an immigrant population of one culture confronts cross-cultural difficulties in its efforts to survive and prosper in a different host culture.

The struggle for survival engages humans in competition for scarce resources, a struggle that is made more efficient by the formation of groups. When relatively few human groups occupy a materially abundant environment there is little likelihood of intergroup competition and hostility arising. But as human populations multiply and resources become ever more scarce, conflict, increasingly violent, is likely to occur. Groups in competition and conflict are not always culturally distinct. But when they are distinct, ethnic identity (within the nation state) and nationalism (between nation states) arises.

As the Chinese emigrated overseas, they produced Chinese minority cultures in interaction with various host environments. Early waves of Chinese immigrants intermarried and merged with their majority peoples, for example in Thailand, the Philippines and Peru, renouncing their Chinese ethnicity as they incorporated into the national elite. Other intermarried Chinese produced culturally mixed groups, such as the Peranakans in Indonesia, the *luuk ciin* in Thailand, or the "Sinified mestizos" in the Philippines. Still other groups, like the Hakka Chinese in Calcutta and the Yunnanese Chinese in Thailand, maintained a cultural separation.

As we examine a variety of cases of Chinese communities around the world, we find almost any possible combination of Chinese and non-Chinese culture and almost any degree of cultural separation or assimilation.

According to Skinner (1968: 191-207), the Chinese diaspora excluded the mainland elite and was motivated solely by economic survival and the hope for wealth. The entrepreneurial ethic, so at odds with traditional Confucian values, became a dominant theme in all overseas Chinese communities. At the same time, many of the primordial elements of Chinese culture survived in radically differing overseas contexts. Organizing groups in terms of the familiar served to preserve the psychocultural orientations imbedded in traditional groups that on the mainland were narrowly based on the familial. The segmentary process served to subdivide groups as they became larger and thus to preserve the face-to-face, personal basis of community self-governance. Through groups based in the familiar, overseas Chinese are commonly found to monopolize specific occupational and enterprise niches. The emotional security that such groups offer is as much a practical tool for survival as are its economic functions. Chinese values, especially the values of thrift and education, are clearly linked to socioeconomic mobility.

The overseas Chinese have achieved a well-deserved reputation for economic, educational and social success. In some nations they are the target of envy and hostility expressed by the majority culture. But in overseas contexts that offer social acceptance, Chinese readily assimilate and intermarry, even when this results in the attenuation or disappearance of many elements of Chinese culture. Those Chinese elements that are not likely to disappear are the ones that will insure continued prosperity and happiness.

All but one of the articles in this book originally were published in *Family, Kinship and Ethnic Identity Among the Overseas Chinese*, Francis L.K. Hsu and Hendrick Serrie, (Eds.), *Journal of Comparative Family Studies*, Special Issue, 16 (2), 1985. (Reprinted by permission of *Journal of Comparative Family Studies*.). Ellen Oxfeld's article on the Chinese in Calcutta was first published in *Guest People: Hakka Identity in China and Abroad*, Nicole Constable (Ed.), 1996, Seattle: University of Washington Press. (Reprinted by permission of the University of Washington Press.) All articles have been revised.

I would like to thank Eckerd College and Lloyd Chapin, Dean of Faculty, for the hexennial leave in 1983-1984 that allowed me sufficient time to work on the first version of this book, and for the hexennial leave and financial support in 1997-1998 that has resulted in this second version. --HS.

Chapter 2

The Chinese in Calcutta: The Reproduction of Hakka Identity

Ellen Oxfeld

Calcutta is one of three major centers of the tanning industry in India, exceeded only by the cities of Madras in the south and Kanpur in the north. A small number of Hakka Chinese immigrants to Calcutta entered into the manufacture of leather during the World War I era. This occupation, considered to be polluting by high-caste Hindus and normally left to untouchables or Muslims, proved to be a lucrative source of income. Although the entire Chinese population of Calcutta consists of no more than eight thousand individuals, the Hakka now own and operate the vast majority of tanneries there, and their contribution to the Indian leather industry is far from negligible on a national scale.

This article is based on fieldwork conducted during the years 1980-82, and again in the summers of 1985 and 1989. It was first published in *Guest People: Hakka Identity in China and Abroad*, Nicole Constable (Ed.), 1996, Seattle: University of Washington Press. (Reprinted by permission of the University of Washington Press.)

The Hakka do not comprise Calcutta's entire Chinese population. Cantonese from Guangdong and immigrants from Hubei have also settled in Calcutta. The Cantonese, Hubeinese, and Hakka have each retained their native language, and each occupies a different economic niche. The Cantonese are primarily known as carpenters, while the major business of the small Hubeinese community is dentistry. The Hakka, in addition to their involvement in tanning, own and operate shoe shops, hairdressing salons, and restaurants. But the tanning industry still engages the largest number of Calcutta's Hakka population, and the Hakka community as a whole is by far the largest of the three Chinese subgroups.[1]

The Chinese tanning area is situated on the eastern periphery of Calcutta in an area known as Dhapa (also sometimes referred to as Tangra or Tapsia since it straddles two districts of those names). Approximately three hundred tanning businesses, the majority employing between five and fifty workers each, are found there. Housed in large concrete buildings of two and three stories, or small one-story structures with tile roofs, these factories are connected by a maze of unpaved, frequently muddy paths as well as open sewers through which the byproducts of the tanning process flow. The tanneries in this rust-colored industrial environment serve as both residences and factories for the Hakka.

This article investigates the constitution of Calcutta Hakka ethnic identity, utilizing as a starting point Orlando Patterson's definition of ethnicity as "that condition wherein certain members of a society, in a given social context, choose to emphasize as their most meaningful basis of primary, extrafamilial identity certain assumed cultural, national, or somatic traits" (1975:308).

I would add to Patterson's definition of ethnicity an insistence that ethnic identity is not simply a matter of how a group chooses to define itself, but also a question of the identity that others ascribe to it. The manner in which others view an ethnic group may play into the group's self-perceptions in a variety of ways. Group members may incorporate, reject, invert, or ignore the images others have of them. And the images others have of an ethnic group will in turn color the attitudes group members hold toward these others.

Ethnic identity is viewed here as dialogical or reflexive, in the sense that it is created, maintained, and reaffirmed through a continuous set of oppositions between one's own group and others.[2] To use Fredrik Barth's (1969) language, ethnic interaction creates ethnic boundaries, but the "stuff" these boundaries enclose, the particular diacritica utilized as ethnic boundary markers, can be discovered only by looking at particular contexts of interaction.

In the case at hand, three elements seem important in establishing and maintaining Calcutta Hakka identity: state and national politics, an ethnically differentiated and stratified economy, and a host society with a religious system based on the symbolic opposition of purity and impurity.³

I should make clear at the outset that although this article emphasizes the interactive nature of ethnic identity, it also acknowledges that the process of ethnic-identity creation is a historical one. In other words, an emphasis on interaction need not lack historical depth. Ethnic identities reproduce "differentiated social formations" (Bentley 1987:42), but changes in social conditions over time may create the need for either investing ethnic identities with new meanings or for dissolving certain ethnic categories altogether. Says G. Carter Bentley, in a recent article on ethnicity and practice, "As individuals develop new ways of dealing with a changing world, old truths erode; as what was formerly inconceivable becomes commonplace, degrees of sharing and affinity, hence ethnic identities, become problematic. At the least, under these conditions ethnic symbolism is likely to take on different meaning for differentially adapted segments of a population" (ibid.:43).

Focussing on what it means to be Hakka, and keeping in mind this potential of ethnic identities to transform themselves in response to changing conditions, I conclude this article with some questions about how the meaning of being Hakka may change for Calcutta Hakka who emigrate to Toronto.

Occupation and Ethnicity in Calcutta

Even before I came to Calcutta to do fieldwork, I was aware that it is a city in which ethnicity is a critical social, cultural, and economic force. Located in West Bengal, the great array and diversity of ethnic, religious, and caste groups that comprise Calcutta's population is due partly to its role as the preeminent city of Northeast India.

Despite its teeming population and well-publicized urban problems — poor sewage, overcrowded and polluted slums (*bustee*), multitudes of pavement dwellers, public transportation that is bursting at the seams — and despite the fact that Calcutta has now been overtaken by Bombay as a center of industry, the city continues to be a magnet that attracts migrants from not only the surrounding Bengali countryside, but also from the neighboring states of Bihar and Orissa, from more distant states within India (such as Gujarat, Punjab, Rajasthan, and Tamil Nadu), and from Bangladesh and Nepal. At one time Calcutta hosted a sizeable Jewish community and a smaller Armenian one. This continuous migration to Calcutta has been augmented by the great human waves associated with the partition of India in 1947 and by subsequent wars with Pakistan, culminating with the formation of Bangladesh in 1971, when millions of refugees poured into West Bengal and Calcutta. Indeed, in the years between 1881 and 1961, immigrants from outside West Bengal continuously comprised over 50 percent of the city's population (Chakraborty 1990:11).

Founded at the close of the eighteenth century by traders belonging to the East India Company, Calcutta eventually served as the capital of British India, until political agitation and unrest forced the British to relocate the capital to Delhi in 1911. Calcutta's predominance as a major port and center of trade, finance, and industry has continued since the days of the East India Company (Lubell 1974:3), and indeed the Calcutta region preceded other parts of the country in the process of industrialization (ibid.:14). Greater Calcutta is still the most populous city in India (Geib and Dutt 1987:32); in 1981 the population of its metropolitan district was 9.2 million, making it one of the ten largest metropolises in the world (ibid.:132). Furthermore, unlike Bombay and Delhi, no other major urban centers are found within hundreds of miles of Calcutta (Lubell 1974:2). Although the growth of the city is now said to be "merely" 25 percent per decade, or the same rate as India as a whole (Stevens 1983:3), the ethnic, caste, and religious diversity of the city continues to be a preeminent feature.

When I refer to ethnicity in Calcutta I refer to several types of groups. First, there are immigrants from outside South Asia, such as the Chinese and the Armenians. Second, there are people from South Asian countries other than India, such as Nepal and Bangladesh. Third, there are people from other Indian states, who speak languages other than Bengali. In addition, many of these groups, all of whom can be referred to as "ethnic" groups within Calcutta, are subdivided along caste and religious lines. Hence, Hindu Bengalis, as well as Hindu immigrants from other states in India, have a multitude of caste affiliations. Not only are most of these groups endogamous with respect to marriage, but, in addition, many are also associated with distinct occupational niches. Religion also divides the migrants. Migrants to Calcutta from the state of Punjab, for example, include Hindus, Muslims, and Sikhs.

The differentiation of groups in Calcutta is therefore based on several cross-cutting categories, including language, religion, caste, class, and regional origin. And each subdivision create by the combination of one or more of these categories tends to be associated with clusters of particular occupations. For instance, Hindi-speaking people include groups as varied as migrants from rural areas in Bihar and Marwaris, a trading people with origins in central India. While Biharis are industrial laborers and pushcart and ricksha operators, Marwaris are industrialists and businesspeople. South Indians, on the other hand, are commonly associated with clerical and administrative work (Bose 1968:39), while Sikhs are found in large numbers in the transport business (ibid.:38). Amongst Bengalis, who share language and ethnic affiliation, occupational differentiation is organized according to caste categories and/or regional origin. (Since Bengalis are native to Calcutta, one would expect a greater differentiation of roles within their group than among immigrants).

Even the leather business is organized according to linguistic, caste, religious, and/or regional categories. The Hakka buy rawhide from North Indian Muslims; they employ scheduled caste[4] Bihari migrants as laborers and Nepalese as guards; and they sell their leather to Punjabi Hindus, Muslims, and Sikhs.

While such ethnic variability might remind one of the ethnic diversity of American cities, such as New York, there is an important distinction. Although ethnicity is certainly a major component of socioeconomic status in American cities, particularly in the case of African American and Hispanic populations, there is a wide spread of income within each ethnic group. In Calcutta, however, as Brian J. L. Berry and Philip H. Rees point out in their study of the city's factoral ecology, the occupational differences *between* ethnic groups are greater than those *within* them. The only exception to this is among Bengalis, where castes are connected to occupational roles (1969:490).

One reason for the continuing importance of ethnicity in the social structure of Calcutta is the city's economy of scarcity. As Nirmal Kumar Bose stated, in reference to Calcutta, "Because there are not enough jobs to go around everyone clings as closely as possible to the occupation with which his ethnic group is identified and relies for economic support on those who speak his language, on his coreligionists, on members of his own caste and on fellow immigrants from the village or district from which he has come. By a backwash, reliance on earlier forms of group identification reinforces and perpetuates differences between ethnic groups" (1966:102).

To some extent, therefore, the Chinese are simply one of many groups in Calcutta affiliated with a particular economic niche. As with most ethnic, caste, and religious groups in this diverse city, the Chinese not only occupy particular economic roles, but are endogamous with respect to marriage and social life. On the other hand, their status as foreigners associated with a country that has been engaged in hostilities against India, combined with their association with a particularly degraded occupation (leather making), lend a certain uniqueness to their role and give them an outsider status greater in degree to that of other immigrants to Calcutta.

The Distinction Between Center and Periphery

Ethnic, caste, and religious distinctions play important roles in both the Indian leather industry and Calcutta's economy. However, in addition to the strong association between occupation and ethnicity, Calcutta also adds a geographic demarcation. Nirmal Kumar Bose (1966, 1968) examined this phenomenon extensively and charted in a series of maps the social, ethnic, and religious composition of Calcutta. He demonstrated that there was a tendency for higher caste and class groups to be associated with the center of the city, and for lower caste and class groups to be associated with the periphery.

The primacy of the central area in Calcutta has continued since British times and results from the interaction of both political and economic forces. When the British founded Calcutta, they built an imperial stronghold, Fort William, near the river and surrounded it with a large open area called the Maidan. They did so as a defensive tactic. The fort was so strategically placed that although British troops inside could easily see attackers (Lelyveld 1975:12), outsiders attempting to close in could not observe the fort until they were within firing range. The British residential quarter adjoined this protected area. Presently the Maidan functions as what the journalist Joseph Lelyveld calls "the city's lungs" (ibid.:12), the only open green space left. This area and bordering sections of the old native quarter continue to be prime real estate, partly because of their proximity to the open space of the Maidan, and partly because the major shopping district is located in this central area. Therefore, the high value of the center in Calcutta is closely linked to its original importance in securing British military, political, and economic power, and to its subsequent desirability for both residential and commercial use.

What is significant is that both spatial and occupational demarcations distinguish ethnic, caste, language, and religious groups in Calcutta. And these distinctions are reflected in and help maintain social separation. Calcutta is not a melting pot. Instead, each of the many groups maintains its separation from the others, rarely intermarrying and conservatively guarding its own customs and ways of life. For instance, Calcutta's schools cater to groups according to the language spoken. One finds Bengali, Hindi, English, Gujarati, and Chinese schools. Furthermore, many groups have their own associations, and few associations are based on a cross-ethnic membership (Tysen 1971). Indeed, in Calcutta questions of assimilation and acculturation are irrelevant. If the Chinese were to assimilate, for instance, with which group would they do so?

The existence of these relatively endogamous, occupationally demarcated, and geographically clustered subgroups, as well as the contrast between center and periphery, bear some resemblance, on a large scale, to the organization of Indian villages. But while in villages there is a division of labor based primarily on caste, in Calcutta the basis for this division has extended to include not only caste, but also language, religion, and regional origin.

As in a village, however, the economic interactions of groups have not broken down the barriers among them, which are reproduced through social and domestic organization. Indeed, the multitude of groups in Calcutta resemble the collectivities alluded to by Barth in his work on ethnic boundaries: "Their agreement on codes and values need not extend beyond that which is relevant to the social situations in which they interact" (1969:16). While many of these groups interact in the economic sphere, their separate ethnic identities remain unscathed.

Most striking, both the ethnic organization of Calcutta and the caste differentiation of Indian villages are reflected in an opposition between center and periphery. Just as low castes and classes are associated with the peripheral areas of Calcutta, in many Indian villages the untouchable outcasts are found in distinct quarters outside the village proper.[5]

Chinese Tanners: Peripherality and Impurity

One must be cautious not to stretch the analogy between village India and Calcutta too far, for the historical reasons behind the opposition of center and periphery differed in these two locations; the establishment of British military and commercial power was not a factor in the center/periphery distinctions in Indian villages, as it was in the colonially created city of Calcutta. In both cases, however, a knowledge of the values embedded in caste society is critical to understanding the contemporary social significance of these spatial oppositions, particularly the tanning community's location on the eastern periphery of the city.

The ideology underlying the Hindu caste system is based on a distinction between purity and impurity. Organic waste products are impure and so, therefore, are activities such as eating, sex, defecation, and menstruation. Furthermore, all people, animals, and things may temporarily undergo states of pollution through engaging in such polluting activities or through contact and interchange with others who are in a polluted state (see Kolenda 1985). All beings and things can be polluted, and may be hierarchically ranked according to their relative degree of pollution. Occupation is an important component of such ranking, since certain occupations, by their very nature, expose their practitioners to greater contact with pollution.[6] For instance, those who deal with human waste — such as sweepers, barbers, and launderers — are always in a more impure state than those whose occupations involve less contact with pollution, such as priests.

Significantly, none of the occupations engaged in by Calcutta Chinese — whether it be the hairdressing, restauranting, tanning, and shoemaking of the Hakka, the carpentry of the Cantonese, or the dentistry of the Hubeinese — is associated with high-caste activities in traditional Hindu thought. In a system in which status of groups is determined by the relative purity or impurity of their occupations, there is not doubt that tanning is viewed as one of the most supremely impure tasks. This is due to its association with dead cattle and the necessity of working with hides; death pollutes by making the entire body a waste product, and the association with slaughter of the sacred cow adds to the impurity.

It is not uncommon for immigrant minority groups throughout the world to engage in occupations that are denigrated by their host societies, or at least by the higher-status members of those societies. The Chinese specialization in vocations in India that are associated with lower castes — even untouchables — adheres to this pattern. What is fascinating, however, is the manner in which Indian society has incorporated the Chinese tanning community. The peripheral geographical position of the Chinese within Calcutta's urban space is in many ways analogous to that of an untouchable community within an Indian village.

The Chinese tanning community is in the eastern corner of Calcutta, adjacent to the city dump. The Indian residents of the areas surrounding it (Tiljala, Tangra, and Tapsia), come primarily from the *chamar* caste, a group traditionally considered untouchable and whose customary occupation was leather work (Bandyopadhyay 1990:79). The peripherality and isolation of the tanning district, as well as the association with an impure task, bring to mind the definition of untouchability employed by Louis Dumont:

> We shall define untouchability in the way that is most current by the segregation into distinct hamlets or quarters of the most impure categories. This feature is pan-Indian, as is the association with a religiously relevant function (quartering of dead cattle and consumption of meat, leather tanning, role in incineration or cleaning of rubbish and excrement, pig rearing and consumption of pork). (1970:134)

Of course, considerations of purity and impurity are not the only factors that prevented the Chinese from setting up their tanning operations nearer to the center of the city. The Chinese themselves emphasize other considerations in the selection of Dhapa as their site for tanning. Dhapa, formerly a marshy and swampy area, had the requisite amounts of available water, an essential for tanning. Furthermore, although close enough to the city to do business with buyers and suppliers, it was still relatively uninhabited and real estate was cheap. Conversely, Chinese shoe shops, whose original clientele was largely European and high-class Indian, had to be situated in the center of the city near the major shopping areas these groups frequented.

While several explanations can be found for the tanning community's peripheral location, there is not doubt that this geographic marginality and their degraded occupation have served to isolate the Chinese tanners even more than other Chinese subgroups in Calcutta.

Indian Views of the Hakka

It is important to point out that Indians, including Bengalis, are not aware of language differences within Calcutta's Chinese community. They usually refer to the Chinese as one group, and their attitudes seem to be influenced primarily by the Hindu religious ideology described above and by national politics, specifically by the fact that India and the People's Republic of China went to war in 1962.

There is not doubt that the Sino-Indian Conflict has been critical to Indian attitudes toward the Chinese. A common remark is that India was "stabbed in the back" by China, a reference to the fact that prior to the outbreak of hostilities, relationships between the two countries appeared congenial. While some individuals clearly differentiate between the Chinese who live in India and the People's Republic of China, others do not. One woman, for instance, told me that ever since 1962 she has regarded all Chinese as her enemies. And even those who were not alive at that time, or not old enough to remember the events, still seem to be affected by the conflict. Said one young man, "Everybody knows that China stole Indian territory, so Chinese can't be trusted."

At the time of the conflict, many Chinese residents of India were stripped of their Indian citizenship (this was done by a legally dubious promulgation declaring that no one could be an Indian citizen if their ancestors were citizens of a country engaged in hostilities with India). Chinese Indians who had become citizens of China when relationships between India and China were good were now even more exposed, since they were suddenly citizens of an enemy country. Several thousand Chinese Indians were rounded up and placed in a detention camp in the Rajasthan desert, where many remained for several years. An equally large group was deported to China.

However, while the loss of rights many Chinese experienced at that time is often one of the first items of conversation mentioned by Chinese, many Bengalis, as well as other Indians whom I met, claimed that they were not aware that the Chinese were deprived of their citizenship rights on account of the hostilities. When I raised the issue, some insisted that I had my facts wrong, or tried to explain it by saying that those who had lost their citizenship must have done something wrong. There were good Chinese and bad Chinese, one acquaintance argued, and if you were a good Chinese you would definitely be allowed to be a citizen.

But political history was not the only factor that influenced the way Indians, and particularly Bengalis, talked about the Chinese. Dissimilarities in diet were also frequently alluded to. In India diet is an especially significant marker of caste, ethnic, and/or religious affiliation. Chinese are set apart from both Hindus, who generally abstain from beef, and Muslims, who abstain from pork. In a situation in which diet is such a critical concern and symbol, it is not surprising that it is one of the most frequently mentioned items when ethnic groups discuss and define each other. The apparent Chinese willingness to eat almost anything was often cited as proof of their peculiarity. As a Bengali acquaintance put it, "They do eat rice [a staple of the Bengali diet], but I also heard that they eat frogs and snakes!"

To this focus on the impurity of food intake, a trait common to all Chinese from the standpoint of many Calcuttans, a view of the tanning area as particularly unclean was frequently added. While I was doing my fieldwork and my sister came to visit me for two weeks, she fell ill for a few days. This was a rather common occurrence for travelers, but many of my Indian friends were sure that these health problems resulted from being in the tanning district. Later, one of my friends wrote in a letter to my sister, "Next time you come . . . stay with us. It is difficult to stand Tangra [Dhapa] environment. Ellen has developed a bit of immunity."

In fact, for most Calcuttans, the tanning area is a place to avoid — a slightly mysterious, even dangerous location. One young college student, for instance, told of his reactions every time he passed the area on a bypass road bordering it. "Tangra is considered a rather unsafe area for a variety of reasons . . . the moment somebody mentions Tangra the two things you think of are Chinese, and you don't want to be there . . . and people are rather intrigued by the Chinese because they have, you know, they have their 'walled city' [an allusion to the appearance of the tanneries from afar] . . . there are these huge walls, and you can't see inside . . . people think it's mysterious, you don't know what is going on, you kind of wonder what happens there."

Although a range of feelings about the Chinese, and particularly about the Chinese tanning community, are expressed, such comments indicate that attitudes of hostility, avoidance, or at the very least, befuddlement are not uncommon. The conflict between India and China, Hindu ideas about purity and pollution, and the structure of ethnic relations in Calcutta, a city in which economic role and ethnic identity are closely correlated for all groups, all contribute to the maintenance of these ideas.

Hakka Views of Outsiders

The suspicion with which Indians view the Calcutta Chinese is reciprocated by an equally mistrustful attitude on the part of the Hakka toward outsiders. From the vantage point of the Calcutta Hakka, Indians, Westerners, and, to a marked but somewhat lesser extent, non-Hakka Chinese, are outsiders, and these distinctions are clearly revealed through Hakka terms for these groups. In fact, these terms are used in situations that, for an outsider, sometimes create almost ludicrous juxtapositions.

Several years after my introduction to the Calcutta Hakka community, when I was conducting research in Toronto, I met two sisters from the community who had recently immigrated to Canada. We got together on a Sunday afternoon for a reunion and decided to visit the CN Tower, the tallest structure in the city. I had my camera with me, and we all thought it would be nice to have a picture of the three of us in the vicinity of the famous structure. As a middle-aged, Caucasian man passed by, one of my friends shouted in Hakka to her sister, "Oh Look, there goes a *fan gui* [lit., "barbarian ghost" or "foreign devil"]. Let's ask him to take a picture for us!" The *fan gui* in question assented to our request and my friends thanked him cheerfully, remarking afterwards how nice it had been for him to help us out.[7]

Westerners are frequently called *fan gui* in the colloquial speech of the Hakka of Calcutta. Ghosts (*gui*) have frequently been associated in popular Chinese religion with outsiders and undesirables, such as bandits and beggars (see A. Wolf 1974), yet the term *fan gui* is used not only when consciously denigrating a foreigner, but also in neutral or even positive situations such as the one above. Like the residents of the immigrant Chinese community in California described by Maxine Hong Kingston (1975), the Calcutta Chinese use the word *gui* frequently when referring to community outsiders. Indeed, the Calcutta Hakka use the word for "person" (*ren*), only in reference to Chinese people. Thus, Chinese are called *Tang ren* (lit. "people of the Tang [dynasty]").

Yet when specific subgroups of Chinese are referred to, as opposed to the Chinese people as a whole, the Hakka also make important distinctions. When talking about themselves, they continue to use the appellation *ren*. Indeed, they usually refer to themselves as "people of Meixian," thereby distinguishing themselves not only from other Chinese, but even from Hakka who do not come from Meixian, Guangdong, from which all Calcutta Hakka originate. But the Calcutta Hakka use the word *lao*, translatable as "fellow" — a word connoting a vulgar person, a hillbilly or hick — when referring to the Cantonese or Hubeinese. Thus, a Cantonese is referred to as a *Guangfu lao*, rather than a *Guangfu ren*.

The Hakka distinguish between themselves and other Chinese groups in other ways as well. From their perspective, the Cantonese do not work as hard, are not as frugal, and, depending on the speaker, are either more Indianized or more Westernized than the Hakka; in all cases, the Hakka are portrayed as more loyal carriers of Chinese tradition than are other Chinese subgroups. "Those Cantonese," asserted one young Hakka man to me in denigrating tones, "they mix Hindi and English in with their Chinese." My first landlady in Dhapa, Mrs. Jia, liked to compare Cantonese and Hakka working habits, and would imply that Cantonese in Calcutta were less successful financially than the Hakka because they were overindulgent. "When Cantonese make money," she informed me, "they get lots of servants, east with ivory chopsticks, and use tablecloths, . . . but Hakka keep working hard."

The distinctions Hakka make between themselves and other Chinese in Calcutta are replicated in social organization. Lawrence Crissman (1967) has drawn attention to what he calls the "segmentary structure" of many overseas Chinese communities. These societies are divided into progressively segmenting subdivisions based on language, native place, and surname. It is only vis-à-vis non-Chinese that they present a united front. In the internal social structure of the Calcutta Chinese community, non-Hakka Chinese are definitely viewed as a category of outsider.

In referring to all other categories of outsiders, however, a much sharper distinction is made by the Hakka, since in these cases the word *gui*, rather than the less negative appellation *lao*, is used. Westerners are called *fan gui*, while Indians are usually referred to as *wu gui* (lit., "black ghosts" or "black devils"). When referring to an individual Indian man speakers will frequently append the word *gui* to his surname. Thus, Mr. Sen becomes Sen *gui*.

In their speech, therefore, the Calcutta Hakka differentiate themselves from two levels of outsiders: first, other speech groups among the Calcutta Chinese, and second, Indians and Westerners.[8] While Westerners are no longer highly visible or numerous actors within Calcutta's ethnic landscape, and therefore Hakka ideas about them are not constantly reinforced through interaction, this is not true of Indians.

Chinese interactions with Bengalis, for instance, often occur in settings that, for Chinese, reinforce negative stereotypes. Chinese are most likely to encounter Bengalis when they have dealings with government bureaucrats. Because many Chinese are still classified as foreigners, such contacts are not infrequent. Registering yearly with the Foreigners Office or making repeated applications for citizenship requires numerous meetings with government officials, and such interactions are seldom pleasant experiences. Indeed, one of the most frequent grievances I heard was that the only way to get anything done was to bribe an official. Less prosperous community members complained that because they did not have enough funds at their disposal to bribe effectively, they were at a perpetual disadvantage in securing citizenship papers, or in getting permits related to the conduct of their business, such as export licenses.

Bengalis also meet with government bureaucrats, of course, and they are not strangers to unmotivated, inefficient, or even corrupt officials. But since the officials are usually from the ethnic group to which they themselves belong, Bengalis will not conceptualize such interactions in ethnic terms. Rather, such behavior is often seen as a sign of the times (*shemoi kharap*, "times are bad") or as a symptom of bad government in general.

When Chinese encounter difficulties in their dealings with bureaucracy, however, they often blame the Bengali bureaucrats themselves, claiming that Bengalis are lazy and that the Bengali government workers will provide services only in return for bribes. Furthermore, they assert that because they are Chinese, they can be taken advantage of more than other groups. After a disappointing inquiry about a delay in the processing of his papers for a passport application, one Hakka acquaintance complained that you could get it done very quickly if you gave extra money to the official in charge. "They all need money for their daughters' dowries . . . and they know we can't object because we are Chinese."

The feeling that Chinese will never be treated fairly only because they are Chinese is quite pervasive. One year before I arrived, a band of *dacoits*[9] attacked a tannery. Three people were killed before the *dacoits* fled across the marshy area bordering Dhapa. Most Dhapa residents felt that the police had done nothing about the incident and had not tried to apprehend the culprits because the victims were Chinese. Ultimately the police did apprehend some people who they alleged were the perpetrators. Most Dhapa Chinese claimed that the matter was pursued only because they had complained to the Chinese Embassy in New Delhi and the embassy has interceded with the police on their behalf.

While Hakka interactions with Bengalis tend to occur in the bureaucratic sphere, their interactions with most other Indian groups are usually economic or commercial. Hakka tanners sell their leather primarily to Hindu, Muslim, and/or Sikh Punjabis, and they buy their rawhide from Muslims from Uttar Pradesh and/or Punjab. Most of their employees are Biharis of the *chamar* caste, as well as a smaller number of Nepalese and North Indian Muslims. Bihari women are employed as servants to wash clothes, do household work, or watch over small children (they do not cook since they are unfamiliar with Chinese cuisine, and their Chinese employers do not seem anxious to teach them — one of the many ways in which the ethnic boundary is maintained).

In short, Hakka interactions with Indians occur primarily in bureaucratic or economic contexts, where Indians are officials, workers, suppliers, servants, or customers. These contacts also require that the Hakka be conversant in a number of languages. In their interactions with tanning workers, rawhide merchants, and leather buyers, their primary language is Hindi. Hakka who run shoe shops in the center of the city may also need to know some Bengali. Those who run restaurants or beauty parlors may use a combination of Hindi, English, and Bengali. There are also generational differences with respect to these language competencies. Younger community members, who have attended English-medium schools, are more likely to be competent in English as well as Hindi. Older individuals, whose schooling was primarily in Chinese-medium schools, are still likely to know Hindi, which they speak with their employees; but they are unlikely to be competent in English.

Of course, the fact that Chinese interact with Indians primarily in the economic sphere does not mean that such interactions are totally impersonal or cold. For instance, in order to secure credit on favorable terms, the tanners go to considerable lengths to demonstrate their trustworthiness to their suppliers, particularly the rawhide merchants. Occasionally an extremely important supplier or buyer will be invited to a wedding feast. But attendance at a large life-cycle celebration, at which there are hundreds of guests, is the usual limit to the social intimacy that would occur between a Chinese and an Indian who had important business connections. Few outsiders ever have a chance to enter into close personal relations or interactions with the Chinese.

It is only in the English-medium schools, to which more and more young Chinese are being sent, that interactions that are not primarily economic or bureaucratic take place with different Indian ethnic groups. But even in these settings there is a tendency for Chinese to segregate themselves or to feel that they are excluded by others. One resident of Dhapa reflected on his years in an English-medium boarding school in this way:

> There would be a lot of name calling . . . even in teamwork you are more or less left to the last . . . mind you there were some pretty good [Indian] friends that I still keep in touch with now. . . . It's interesting . . . I would get along better with another minority, such as Anglo-Indian, you know, or somebody they would consider different, such as an Armenian.

While other young people from Dhapa talked of their experiences in English-medium schools in a more positive way, many emphasized that even if they had Indian friends, they would not bring them home. I observed that only on rare occasions did Indian school friends visit.

An Entrepreneurial Ethic

Hakka separation from other ethnic groups is facilitated by the interaction of caste, ethnic, religious, spatial, and economic organization in Calcutta. This separation is reflected not only in patterns of interaction and in Hakka attitudes towards outsiders, but also in the fact that Indian society has exerted so little influence on the substantive aspects of Hakka cultural values. Most non-Hindu minorities in India have been powerfully affected by the caste system. For instance, many tribal groups from the Indian subcontinent have been incorporated into the surrounding society as castes. They have attempted to raise their status not by rejecting Hindu practices, but by imitating higher-caste customs, such as abstention from eating beef. In so doing, they have indicated their acceptance of the basic premises of the caste system (Srinivas 1966:6). Furthermore, Indian Christians and Muslims, whom one might expect to have renounced caste as a result of their ideological traditions, have castelike divisions within their populations (Dumont 1970:206-7, 211). Even groups such as Parsis and Jews, who have immigrated to India from other countries, have come to replicate some elements of caste within their own group structures.[10]

Despite the all-encompassing nature of the caste system, however, none of the Cantonese subgroups in Calcutta has fallen into the patterns described above. They explicitly reject caste ideology in favor of a status system almost exclusively based on wealth. Thus, unlike certain Indian merchant communities (see Bayly 1983), the Calcutta Chinese have not tried to convert their wealth into higher status by entering into business activity that would be judged as more pure from the standpoint of the caste hierarchy. As pariah entrepreneurs, the Chinese have succeeded economically precisely because they have *not* assimilated caste ideology. One member of the community explained this to me in starkly sociological terms during the first few weeks of my fieldwork when he stated, "We don't have castes. Your blood doesn't matter. We have classes. What matters is how much money you make." Indeed, in this community, wealth is the chief measure of status, and owning one's own business is viewed as the best means of acquiring wealth.

This fact was clearly illuminated for me one day, shortly after I had settled into my Chinese landlady's house, when her nephew took me to visit and to introduce myself to some families in Dhapa. On the way home, he told me that under normal circumstances he would not even speak with the families we had just met. "They might know me as my father's son," he remarked, "because my father taught at the Chinese school for so many years. But they're rich people, and they only talked with me today because I brought you along."

This high priority accorded to the achievement of wealth as a measure of status is not atypical of other overseas Chinese societies. G. W. Skinner (1968) has discussed the importance of wealth in Southeast Asian overseas Chinese communities, as a criterion for leadership as well as a measure of status. As he points out, one reason that wealth is the primary component of status in these communities is that most Chinese emigrated in order to better their economic positions. "Unlike the Jews," says Skinner, "the Chinese went abroad in the first place specifically to make money, and unlike the Jewish *diaspora*, that of the Chinese excluded the traditional elite of their homeland. In consequence status for overseas Chinese was almost a direct function of wealth" (ibid.:195).

What is most critical here is that since status within the Calcutta Chinese community is based almost exclusively on wealth, there is no concept, as in caste ideology, that certain occupations or social groups can be compared in terms of relative purity and impurity. Nor is there any sense that social status can be inherited and is not dependent upon one's present social situation. Caste ideology ranks a multitude of endogamous groups in terms of their relative purity and pollution. Furthermore, one inherits one's caste; no matter how one may change one's life situation, one cannot change caste. Unlike other minority groups in India, the Calcutta Chinese have not adapted elements of caste ideology or practice.

Indeed, from the point of view of the Calcutta Hakka, any job is worthwhile if it is a profitable source of income. While tanning is viewed within caste ideology as a polluting occupation, one performed only by a particular untouchable caste, Dhapa Chinese consider tanning a good business because it is so lucrative.[11] Tanning is also viewed as far superior to while-collar desk jobs, where salaries rarely amount to more than a fraction of the earnings possible in even modestly successful tanning businesses.

In fact, running one's own business (in whatever line presents the most possibilities) is viewed by the Calcutta Hakka as the ideal economic activity and, unless circumstances make it absolutely impossible, as far superior to salaried employment. Not only do they see this as providing a greater income, but, in addition, they feel that one has more control over one's life. That business means family business is an assumption so deep that it is rarely discussed. But one need only look at the evidence to see that this is the case; of the 297 tanning businesses in Dhapa in 1982, only two were partnerships involving nonrelated individuals.

The high value placed on entrepreneurship as a way of life was one of the themes that was most frequently and explicitly articulated to me. For instance, one of my good friends and best informants, Mr. Zhou, was always perplexed as to why I would want to return to the United States to teach. One day, while discussing the advantages of business as opposed to salaried employment, he asked me, "If you wanted to start a business what would you do?"

"Well, I would borrow money and invest it," I replied.

"There you go, it's taking you so long to do your research, but you would know exactly what to do to go into business." As he shrugged his head, he added, "You'll never do well when you work for others!"

Indeed, for Mr. Zhou, it was difficult to understand why one would choose work other than business if given the option. In his view, salaries were fixed and limiting, while business opened up the possibility of multiplying one's resources exponentially through the application of one's own efforts. One of his favorite sayings, composed of four four-character phrases, was that there were four types of people: those who harmed themselves and others (*hai ren hai ji*); those who helped themselves but harmed others (*hai ren li ji*); those who harmed themselves to help others (*li ren hai ji*); and those who helped themselves while helping others (*li ren li ji*).[12] And, as if taken straight from Adam Smith and Jeremy Bentham, Mr. Zhou would then proceed to expound on the evident superiority of the fourth type — those who help themselves and thereby benefit others. This happy outcome, he would add, can most easily be achieved by engaging in one's own business.

A corollary of this preference for business was the assumption that no one with intelligence would wallow for long in the shadows of an employer. "You can never keep a good foreman," one factory owner told me, "because is he is any good, he'll start a business of his own."

Clearly, for both Mr. Zhou and other members of the Dhapa community, one goal of such business activity was to increase the material well-being of oneself and one's family. But it is not only the pursuit of a more comfortable life that makes wealth desirable in Dhapa — it is also the status that accompanies it and the ability to influence and to be respected by others.

The importance of wealth can be felt in many ways in the Hakka community. Whether an individual or family is *hen you qian* (very wealthy) or *mei you qian* (poor) is usually the first item mentioned in any discussion about them. The in-betweens excite very little comment. It is the wealthy who serve as community leaders — for example, as heads of business associations. Furthermore, community social life is focused on the ceremonies and celebrations that surround major life-cycle rituals, providing numerous opportunities for wealthy individuals to validate publicly their financial success. The wealthiest families stage more lavish and larger weddings and birthday celebrations than do other families, and the number of tables at a reception (ten people to a table) may be the talk of the town for several days before and after it is held (more than fifty tables is usually cause for extended comment). Likewise, the funerals of wealthy individuals are attended by larger numbers than are those of less prosperous individuals, even though the criteria that supposedly determine who should attend such functions are constant.

Indeed, because wealth is so critical to status, I had to quickly change my graduate-student ways of relatively frugal and simple living. When I first moved to my landlady's house, for instance, I walked to the local Chinese school where I taught English every morning. It was not far, not even a twenty-minute walk. But several Hakka acquaintances kept urging me to take a ricksha or buy a bicycle or motorscooter. Much to their relief, I finally bought a bicycle. They had worried that because I walked, people would think I was poor, and would look down upon me. Later, when my parents came to visit me in Calcutta, my landlady constantly reminded me to let people know that they were staying in the best hotel in Calcutta.

This emphasis on wealth does not exclude other characteristics from garnering status for a family or individual within the community. Nor does it mean that in all cases a wealthy individual will truly be respected. If community members feel someone gained wealth through cheating, or some other unfair means, they will certainly call him a "scoundrel" (*jian zei*) behind his back; and a person who is not rich, but who works loyally for his or her family will be granted a certain degree of respect. But no one denies the importance of achieving wealth as an ultimate goal, and many other qualities are valued precisely for the part they play in enabling a family to achieve prosperity.

We must not forget that in Chinese society, both on the mainland and overseas, monetary thinking and commoditization have a long history. As Hill Gates points out, late imperial Chinese society "included important capitalist elements. . . . The Chinese treated the major factors of production — land, labor, and capital — as commodities, with well-developed markets for each" (1987:260). Gates states that capitalism did *not* play a "hegemonic" role in late imperial China, because "capitalist elements were always subordinated to state control" (ibid.). Nevertheless, "a constrained but powerful capitalist worldview was reproduced constantly by the Chinese populace as an alternative to the bureaucratic/ feudal vision enshrined in the formal structure and practice of the state" (ibid.:261). That is, capitalism, in its more accessible petty-capitalist or small-scale owner production variant, appeared as an attractive alternative for working people, since it "offered a social model of upward mobility based directly on wealth rather than on connection with the state through the highly limited channels of degree- and office-holding" (ibid.).

Indeed, Chinese society has been monetized to increasing degrees since the eleventh century (Elvin 1973:149). It is a society in which even rural areas have been linked with a national market in some items for almost a thousand years (ibid.:106) and in which "increased contact with the market made the Chinese peasantry into a class of adaptable, rational, profit-oriented petty entrepreneurs" (ibid.:167).

Steven Harrell argues that there has long been a "Chinese entrepreneurial ethic, a cultural value that requires one to invest one's resources . . . in a long-term quest to improve the material well-being and security of some group to which one belongs and with which one identifies closely" (1987:94).

Even popular Chinese religious practice reflects a worldview thoroughly influenced by monetary thinking. After the introduction of Buddhism into China, the belief that a person's soul is reincarnated in another being after death became infused in popular Chinese religious thought. But in a Chinese variant, this belief took on a curiously monetary expression: souls are not just reincarnated, they need funds to do so. The urban Taiwanese whom Hill Gates studies, for instance, explained to her that souls en route to reincarnation borrow large sums from celestial treasuries. This money is "used to purchase a body for reincarnation, the rest defrays the cost of the individual's particular lot in life, a matter determined prior to birth. Some [,] indebted for large sums, will receive wealth, high rank, and other blessings in life while those who give less must live with correspondingly straitened means" (1987:268).

As a result, individuals are constantly attempting to pay off these debts throughout their lives. Burning paper money (paper representations of cash, not actual currency) to the gods is one way of paying off this debt, and even after one dies, one's relatives burn large amounts of paper money, for, as Gates explains, one needs to "pay off the account . . . if the spirit is to enter unencumbered into a new and presumably more fortunate incarnation" (ibid.). Thus, "we see the human body, the length of its life, and the quality of that life equated to specific sums of money — as extreme an example of the penetration of a money economy into human existence as metaphor can express" (ibid.:270).

Such religious practices are also quite common in the Calcutta Chinese community, where monetary symbolism is a pervasive part of ritual life. Indeed, among the Calcutta Chinese, the entire process of reincarnation is conceptualized in rather concrete terms in which large amounts of money and material goods are necessary for a fortuitous journey to reincarnation. In order to ease the heavenly travels of the recently deceased, paper replicas of the expensive accoutrements of modern living appear prominently among objects burnt as offerings (on one occasion that I witnessed this included a life-size three-dimensional paper Fiat car). The need for cash is emphasized as an essential element in almost all aspects of the afterlife.

"Suppose you live in India now, but after you die you come back as an African," my first landlady explained to me one day. "How will you get to Africa? By boat? By car? The best way is by airplane, but for that you'll need money, because the ticket is so expensive!"

Thus, in the case of the Calcutta Hakka we have a situation in which a high priority is placed on entrepreneurial thinking for reasons implicit in both their ethnic role in India and in a cultural ethos carried with them from their country of origin and perpetuated in their overseas environment.

This entrepreneurial ethic contrasts markedly with the values evident in other Hakka communities. For instance, in the Malay Hakka community described by Sharon Carstens (1996), people described themselves as having "no head for business," and the Hakka in Malaysia were weak economically relative to other Chinese groups. Similarly, Elizabeth Johnson (1996) cites Blake's (1981) description of the Hakka's "legacy of poverty" and comes to similar conclusions about the Hakka in Hong Kong.

Both Johnson and Carstens also suggest that the Hakka among whom they did fieldwork held an egalitarian ethic and that this may be connected to their poverty relative to other Chinese groups in the area. While Carstens suggests that Hakka experiences of poverty relative to other groups on the Chinese mainland may have influenced their adaptation to their overseas environment, my data on the Calcutta Hakka indicates that any notion of shared Hakka orientations embedded in deep-seated historical memory must be balanced by an awareness of the impact of the local context in which the particular Hakka community resides.

Hakka Identity and Women's Roles

Interestingly, the entrepreneurial ethic of the Calcutta Hakka has also influenced another feature of Hakka social organization — the sexual division of labor. Carstens (1996), Constable (1996), and Johnson (1996) all note the prominent economic role played by Hakka women in their communities. This role, they state, is frequently mentioned as a distinctive feature of Hakka culture by Hakka themselves, who often use it to contrast themselves with other local Chinese communities. In the Calcutta Hakka community women's economic roles, in the form of their active participation in the work of running family enterprises, are notable. And, as in these other cases, this is frequently commented upon by the Calcutta Hakka themselves, contributing to their own sense of a distinct identity.

However, unlike women's economic roles in the other Hakka communities, those of the Calcutta Hakka vary with the family's economic status. Women in families that own larger firms are much less likely to participate directly in the daily operation of their family businesses than are those in families with smaller firms. Furthermore, their access to property and income is not dependent on the degree to which they participate in family enterprise. For instance, in some families, women control the income generated by the sale of tanning waste products, but there is no correlation between this and their participation in the family business.

A woman who works hard in her family enterprise will enjoy the esteem and respect of her community and family. If her family's business is large and successful, she also has status as a member of a wealthy family, and she has access to certain resources within the business.[13]

Thus, the extensive role played by Hakka women in income-producing activities is also influenced by context. In this case, business participation decreases with financial success, suggesting that both Hakka identity and economic resources influence women's roles.

Conclusion: What Does it Mean to be Hakka?

Most of the material I have presented in this article can be understood in terms of a contextual, interactionist approach to ethnicity. For instance, language differences, one of the most irreducible mechanisms of maintaining ethnic distinctions, are reinforced by Calcutta's ethnically variegated economy and society, one in which there is only the organization of difference, and never a dominant group to which others can assimilate either linguistically or culturally. The fact that Cantonese and Hakka occupy separate occupational niches in Calcutta, for instance, certainly helps to maintain their differences. Likewise, the political situation and dominant religious ideology have deeply influenced Indians' ideas about their overseas Chinese population, and in turn, these ideas have indelibly affected Hakka attitudes toward outsiders.

A number of scholars who have written about ethnicity, however, have criticized this context-oriented approach, stating that it ultimately reduces ethnic groups to mere interest groups and that it underestimates the affective power of ethnic-group identity (see Glazer and Moynihan 1975:19). These scholars point out that "primordial" identifications, based upon shared physical and cultural traits as well as upon shared descent, often bind members of an ethnic group together (e.g., Isaacs 1975b).

Recently, however, the dichotomy between these approaches has itself been questioned. G. Carter Bentley utilizes Pierre Bourdieu's notion of "habitus" to explain the affective power of ethnic attachments. Habitus, he explains, is comprised of conscious and unconscious inclinations and outlooks inculcated and internalized from the earliest years of a person's life, and ethnic identity is integral to these. Bentley shows that it is precisely *because* of their power, because they are part and parcel of one's most strongly internalized behaviors, outlooks, and obligations, that ethnic bonds are so profound a force in the reproduction of social formations (1987:42).

Because ethnic identity is so fundamental in the formation of people's conscious and unconscious understandings of the world, Bently asserts, individuals may experience "crises of ethnic identity" when they undergo changed social circumstances (ibid.:43). In such cases they may respond with new formulations of ethnic identity, or they may reinvigorate existing notions (ibid.:43). For instance, in making sense of their situation, the Calcutta Hakka often draw upon the label that was originally applied to them by the Cantonese in Guangdong — that of "guest people."

"You know, we are the guest people, and we keep moving from place to place. We even did that in China," one friend in Calcutta told me. It was a refrain I heard frequently among residents of the tanning community.

But this term has continued potency for them not because of some primordial identification with past experiences, but because it describes their present situation, in which they are clearly an ethnic minority, and still on the move. Indeed, beginning in the late 1970s many Hakka began to emigrate from Calcutta to Europe, Australia, and particularly to Toronto. Emigrants point to a fear that new tensions between India and China will again threaten their security in India, and to a desire to diversify the economic activities of family members as reasons for their decision to leave India.

As one Hakka friend who had migrated from Calcutta to Toronto told me, "We look at what happened to the Sikhs [referring to Indira Gandhi's assassination in 1984 by a Sikh and the subsequent attacks upon and killing of Sikhs by angry mobs] and we think we are just as noticeable. If China goes to war with India again, it could happen to us."

In Toronto the Calcutta Hakka once again find distinctions between both Chinese and non-Chinese others to be socially significant. Toronto's urban geography, with its huge Chinatown and numerous Chinese-run businesses scattered throughout the city, serves as a daily reminder to the immigrants of their own aspirations to succeed in business, and of their present inability to do so.

For although the Calcutta Hakka are successful entrepreneurs in India, their Indian assets do not amount to much when converted to Canadian currency. Most end up working in factories, having — at least for the short term — postponed their entrepreneurial aspirations until they can acquire more capital.

Thus, in addition to comparing themselves with the multitude of non-Chinese groups in Toronto, Hakka from Calcutta frequently, and sometimes resentfully, contrast their situation with that of other Chinese immigrants. Wealthy immigrants from Hong Kong, in particular, are frequently the target of their comments.

But how will the Calcutta Hakka identify themselves and be identified as the length of their residence and their numbers increase in Toronto? Will the next generation still refer to themselves as "people of Meixian?" Or will they instead see themselves as descendants of Chinese Indians or as members of a more vague and amorphous category of Chinese Canadians? Will they speak Hakka at all? One Calcutta Hakka who had immigrated to Toronto hinted at the potentially shifting nature of Hakka identity when he said to me in the summer of 1986, "When we talk about home, we talk about Calcutta — it's still our root. For our father it's China, and for my children, it's Brampton [an area of Toronto]."

Given the extremely different realities of employment, education, and politics, one might hypothesize very dissimilar trajectories for Hakka identity in Toronto and Calcutta. The signs that this will be the case are already in place: the Calcutta Hakka immigrants in Toronto are employed in a variety of occupations rather than in a specialized ethnic niche associated with a degraded occupation; they reside in areas dispersed throughout the city, rather than in an isolated community at the periphery;

and their children, who are educated in Toronto's public schools, are beginning to use English rather than Hakka in interactions with their parents.

As Eric Wolf has stated in an analysis of labor immigration under capitalism, "Ethnicities rarely coincided with the initial self-identification of the industrial recruits, who first thought of themselves as Hanoverians or Bavarians rather than as Germans, as members of their village or parish . . . rather than as Poles, as Tonga or Yao rather than as 'Nyasalanders.' The more comprehensive categories emerged only as particular cohorts of workers gained access to different segments of the labor market and began to treat their access as a resource to be defended both socially and politically. Such ethnicities are therefore not 'primoridal' social relationships. They are historical products of labor market segmentation" (1982:381).

Notes

1. Although the Calcutta census has never broken down the Chinese population on the basis of language, the numerical dominance of the Hakka is evident. There are two Chinese schools for Hakka students and only one for Cantonese. Furthermore, the Hubeinese and Cantonese are frequently able to converse in Hakka, while few Hakka learn Cantonese or Hubeinese. Cantonese and Hubeinese informants assert that this is due to the fact that the Hakka now dominate Chinese life in Calcutta. Finally, the number of tanning businesses (approximately three hundred in 1980) clearly establishes tanning as the most important occupation of the Hakka. Only shoe shops come close (one hundred fifty in 1980).
2. Where one of these others is the state, as Stevan Harrell has so trenchantly demonstrated in a paper on Yi communities in Southwest China, the process by which groups create self-definitions is exceedingly complex (Harrell 1990b).
3. There is a vast literature that debates the origins of these distinctions themselves. Some argue that they serve to organize exploitative economic relations, and others that they are based on fundamental symbolic oppositions (e.g., Dumont 1970, Kolenda 1985, Mencher 1974). For our purposes here, we will simply note the influence of beliefs about purity and impurity upon Calcutta's Hakka. The debate about the origins of this system itself is far beyond the scope of this article.
4. The term "scheduled" caste is usually used to designate those groups who are known as "untouchables," i.e., with whom contact is considered especially polluting within caste ideology. The sociologist R.A. Schermerhorn points out that the term originated during the 1930s when the British desired to categorize for census purposes those castes with whom contact "'entails purification on the part of high-caste Hindus,' a dejure definition. Lists or schedules of such castes were drawn up for the purpose of singling out those groups suffering civil and religious disabilities" (1978:29). There are problems with this definition, since all castes are hierarchically ranked and contact between a relatively higher group and a relatively lower group — no matter what their particular identity — always entails the possibility of pollution for the higher group. Even among groups defined as untouchable, for instance, there is a hierarchy of relative purity. Nevertheless, the term is generally applied to those groups who in a particular region are defined as "the most defiled of all, the ones who can pollute all others" (ibid.:30).
5. Neither Indian cities nor villages are unique in terms of the significant symbolic role played by space within them. As Walter Firey pointed out

in a pathbreaking study, undertaken over forty years ago, of the city of Boston, "Space may be a symbol for social values" (1980 [1947]:169).
6. There is a broad and vigorous debate about the nature of the caste system in India, and the extent to which it is ideologically based. Some scholars, such as Dumont (1970) assert that the ideology of purity and pollution underlies and orders the social relations that can be observed among castes. Others, such as Mencher (1974), argue that this ideology is not shared by all castes. Still others, such as Marriott (1968), argue that the ranking of castes within villages cannot be explained solely in terms of relative purity and pollution, but must be derived by an analysis of transferal of different categories of food among castes. But while the degree to which the ideology of purity and pollution is universally shared, and the degree to which all occupations can be ranked according to it, has been disputed, no one would deny that work with rawhide and leather is considered within caste ideology to be an impure occupation associated with castes traditionally placed in the category of untouchable.
7. I usually spoke in Mandarin with my informants, many of whom had attended the local Chinese school, where Mandarin was the medium of instruction. Therefore, I use Mandarin transliteration for Chinese words in this chapter.
8. The definitions of Westerner and Indian are primarily cultural and contextual, rather than purely biological. This is illustrated by the fact that Chinese families that have had no sons will sometimes adopt babies of non-Chinese descent in circumstances in which it is not possible to find a baby of Chinese descent. These children are raised as Chinese and considered Chinese. On the other hand, the children of mixed Chinese-Indian marriages are not necessarily considered Chinese, even though they have some Chinese ancestry. They are usually classified, instead, according to the language they use at home.
9. *Dacoit* (armed robber) is a word commonly used in Indian English.
10. Parsis not only adopted caste notions about commensality, but also assimilated Hindu notions of purity and pollution. In 1903, for instance, a Parsi judge expressed his opposition to the idea that Parsi priests could admit lower-caste Hindus into the Parsi community without first "making them give up their unclean professions" (Fischer 1973:94).

    Among some groups of Indian Jews, castelike patterns were also present (I use the past tense here, because most Indian Jews have now emigrated to Israel and other countries). The Cochin Jews of the South Indian state of Kerala, for instance, were internally divided into castelike divisions with prohibitions on intermarriage (Mandelbaum 1939:424) and on entering each other's temples (Strizower 1962:112-13). And the Bene Israel, a Jewish community centered in Bombay, had endogamous subdivisions, one of which was considered particularly polluted in the sense that both commensality and intermarriage with them was forbidden (ibid.:30).

11. The differences between the Calcutta Chinese view and the stance held by those who accept the premises of the caste system was made clear to me in an interview I conducted at the Leather Research Institute in Calcutta. One of the officers of the organization pointed out that although a certain percentage of seats at the leather technology institute are reserved for *chamars*, few members of this caste apply, despite the fact that admission to a leather technology institute would mean a good-paying job, after completion of coursework, with a large leather manufacturer.

    Since the basis for the stigma *chamars* suffer is the polluting occupation they traditionally followed, those who are in a position to apply to an institute of higher education are unlikely to choose such a field. Chinese have not become involved in tanning as the result of training by institutes. These practices make evident the difference between evaluating tanning from within the caste system, as a polluting and stigmatizing occupation, and from without, as a potentially lucrative one.

12. The use of such four-character phrases is pervasive in everyday Chinese speech as well as in written texts. They are used for many purposes, including greeting, congratulating, enjoining, and describing recognizable traits or situations. Their compactness and economy of expression are usually lost in translation.

13. For a more detailed discussion of the sexual division of labor among the Calcutta Hakka, see Basu (1991).

Chapter 3
೫ುಂ

The Chinese in Northern Thailand: A Preliminary Perspective on Kinship and Ethnicity

Ann Maxwell Hill

Kinship has long been recognized as the source of some structural principles for the organization of Chinese communities overseas. The existence of social groups based wholly or partially on kinship principles — for example, Chinese surname associations, businesses and households — are important corporate manifestations of Chinese ethnicity in plural societies. The persistence and visibility of these groups in overseas Chinese communities, particularly in Thailand, tend to obscure the facts of individual, situational ethnicity and, consequently, some critical aspects of the relationship of Chinese kinship to Chinese ethnicity. We must ask not only how kinship organizes ethnic Chinese communities, but also how it affects individual choices of ethnic identity.

The latter question directs our attention, in the first place, to the relevance of kinship to the acquisition of the social skills and cultural knowledge which make such choices possible. It also compels us to look at kin relations, not as biological "givens," but as cultural resources which can be selectively utilized. To ally with or to deny one's Chinese kinsmen is an individual choice. From this perspective, perhaps it is possible to justify, anthropologically, our intuitive notion that kinship has much to do with the persistence of Chinese ethnicity in communities overseas.

Our perspective is brought into focus by considering two Chinese groups in Thailand — the Yunnanese Chinese living in Northern Thailand and the overseas Chinese, who have been studied in Central Thailand's urban centers. The Yunnanese are known to me from two years' fieldwork in Thailand's Chiang Mai province (1977-1979).[1] My observations on the overseas Chinese are based on others' writings about them and on limited personal experience with them in Thailand. A comparison of the two groups reveals some major demographic and other variables that have differentially affected each. Within the larger framework provided by these variables, we can look more closely at aspects of family and kinship among the Yunnanese that have had an impact on choices of ethnic identity. The Yunnanese case raises some questions that we ought to be asking in our research on the overseas group in view of the persistence of their identity as Chinese.

Comparison of Overseas Chinese and Yunnanese Chinese

Of the estimated 3.5 million ethnic Chinese in Thailand, most are overseas Chinese from China's southeastern coastal provinces, Guangdong and Fujian.[2] They are speakers of five dialects of Chinese — Teochiu, Hokkienese, Hainanese, Hakka and Cantonese; these speech divisions traditionally have been invoked as another criterion (in addition to kinship) for structuring relationships within the Chinese community. Although the history of Chinese political and commercial contacts with the early Thai kingdoms goes back to the thirteenth century, large-scale immigration of Chinese to Thailand did not begin until the 1800s. By the turn of the century, more than 30,000 Chinese, most of whom were poor and illiterate peasants, were arriving in Thailand annually. The number of Chinese sojourners to Thailand continued to increase, with only minor downward fluctuations, into this century, reaching a peak in the decade following

World War I (Skinner 1957:172). Then, in 1949, immigration quotas for the Chinese of two hundred per year virtually ended the legal entry of Chinese into Thailand.

While the modern Thai kingdom apparently has been successful in regulating immigration through its seaports, its northern borders with Laos and Burma, stretching across hundreds of miles of mountainous terrain, have remained intractable to government surveillance. The most recent, large-scale migration of Chinese into Thailand has been across the northern borders into the provinces of Chiang Rai and Chiang Mai. These Chinese have come, via Laos and Burma, from Yunnan province. Most arrived in Thailand in the 1950s and 1960s, some in the aftermath of the expulsion of remnant Nationalist (Guomindang) troops from Yunnan, Burma and Laos. Like the overseas Chinese, the Yunnanese have a long history of contact with Tai-speaking kingdoms. In the last several centuries, at least since the 1600s, they have come to Northern Thailand as long-distance traders, making the trek south from Yunnan and back again during the dry winter season.

The current population of Yunnanese in Chiang Mai and Chiang Rai provinces probably exceeds 30,000.[3] A small portion of this number are Muslim Chinese who traditionally have been active in the region's caravan trade and who now comprise small Muslim congregations throughout the north. The majority of Yunnanese, however, are Han Chinese. All of them, Han and Muslim, speak one of several dialects of southwestern Mandarin.

Demographic differences between the overseas and "overland" Chinese are considerable. In Thailand, the former group are a conspicuous and numerically significant minority. For the Thai, the overseas Chinese define what it means to be Chinese, a definition derived primarily from Thai interactions with Chinese shopkeepers or wholesalers of agricultural produce. There are few market towns in the countryside without their rows of Chinese shophouses and warehouses. Bangkok, the nation's administrative and commercial center, is home to approximately 50% of the overseas Chinese, who seem to predominate in the city's thronged streets and shops. One sees here, and in other urban areas, the source for the Thai stereotype of the Chinese as aggressive merchants and for the Thai belief that the Chinese have a strangle hold on the nation's economy.

If the overseas Chinese seem to be conspicuously Chinese to some, others point to the *luuk ciin*, or children of marriages between Thai women and Chinese men, as evidence of the assimilation of Chinese to Thai society. According to Skinner (1957), Chinese immigrants to Thailand before 1905 were predominantly male, and those who stayed and married took Thai wives. However, by the mid-1920s, significant numbers of Chinese women, as wives, were coming to Thailand. At the time of Skinner's study in the early 1950s sex ratios within the Chinese community were such that intermarriage with Thai was rare. The *luuk ciin* of the nineteenth and early twentieth century marriages tended to identify with the Chinese, but among their offspring, this tendency was diminished.

The post-World War II generation of overseas Chinese born in Thailand, those who are now in their late twenties and thirties, were likely to be raised in families where both parents were culturally and linguistically Chinese. However, they were educated in the Thai language, even if they attended Chinese schools, and are conversant with Thai culture. Most are Thai citizens. Only a minority, children of the approximately 310,000 Chinese who maintain Taiwan citizenship, are affected by legal restrictions because of their alien parentage (Wang 1981:253,257).

While travel between Thailand and the People's Republic of China has increased since the opening of diplomatic relations between the two countries in 1975, it is inaccurate to view the overseas Chinese today as having deep personal or political commitments to the PRC. The majority, who have benefited from the capitalist economy and relative political stability of Thailand, are rooted in the Thai milieu and no longer think of themselves as sojourners. Certainly most do not want to return to South China to live. Furthermore the immediate ancestors of the Chinese born in Thailand since World War II are buried in cemeteries on Thai soil, if their remains have not been cremated. The practice of sending the corpse back to China for burial near the ancestral village was available only to the wealthy in earlier days (Skinner 1957:131) and was virtually discontinued after the war (Coughlin 1960:46). To the extent that ancestral graves are a focus of family rites and sentiments for the Chinese, the numerous Chinese cemeteries throughout Thailand are a visible index of Chinese identification with Thailand and the demise of the sojourning mentality.

The overseas Chinese are regarded as having made a successful accommodation to Thai society, especially when compared to Chinese in other Southeast Asian countries (FitzGerald 1973:61-63). While there remain questions about the precise nature and depth of this accommodation, conventional wisdom tells us that with each successive generation born and raised in Thailand, the overseas Chinese become progressively more assimilated to Thai society, a process often phrased in terms of choice of ethnic identity (Skinner 1957:381; Coughlin 1960:190-191). That is, with each successive generation, there are proportionately more individuals in this group who choose to identify themselves as Thai more often. As a portent of the future, this model of generational assimilation points toward the eventual extinction of a recognizably Chinese community in Thailand, barring drastic changes in such variables as the rate of immigration, Thai government restrictions on Chinese education and other government policies aimed at the Chinese, and finally, the influence of both the PRC and Taiwan with Thailand.

Yet many observers would not subscribe to this position. The total effacement of the Chinese communities in Thailand seems unlikely in the foreseeable future. Recently, one writer has noted the expansion of expressly Chinese activities in the town of Ayutthaya and, while hesitant to extend his generalizations to all Chinese communities in Thailand, has suggested that ethnic traditions may be of particular personal significance to the post-war generation of overseas Chinese (Tobias 1977:305). His study of the Ayutthaya Chinese corroborates my own, admittedly more impressionistic, observations on the apparently flourishing overseas Chinese communities in Northern Thailand — the number and evident prosperity of Chinese voluntary associations, the packed soundrooms of theaters where Chinese film soundtracks play in the original Mandarin or Cantonese, the numerous Chinese bookstores, the restaurants and hotel banquet rooms filled with overseas Chinese celebrating family events and so on. It is difficult to dismiss these phenomena as the activities of only the older, immigrant generation of overseas Chinese. Perhaps there is reason, in the 1980s, to question the conventional wisdom on the relatively rapid assimilation of Chinese to Thai society, or at least to re-examine the model of generational assimilation. While the above issue is not the central concern of this paper, the following discussion of the Yunnanese may help us to understand this seeming paradox.

The Yunnanese Chinese, most of whom have come to Thailand during the last thirty years, may follow a different course of adaptation to Thai society than that attributed to the overseas Chinese.[4] They came to Thailand in much smaller numbers than the overseas Chinese, and their total population concentration in any one place has never exceeded several thousand. For this reason, as well as because of the relatively remote locations of rural Yunnanese villages, the Yunnanese have never been conspicuous as a distinct Chinese group in Northern Thailand. They tend to blend in with the heterogeneous population of Northern Thailand's market towns, most often indistinguishable in appearance from the overseas Chinese shopkeepers. To local Northern Thai, the Yunnanese are known as *haw*, a rather ambiguous ethnic label traditionally applied to long distance traders from Yunnan. However, Northern Thai seldom interact with the Yunnanese and know them mostly by reputation rather than from personal experience. While a few predominantly Yunnanese neighborhoods have grown up around mosques serving the Muslim minority, most Yunnanese live in compounds scattered throughout the towns of the North.

Unlike the overseas Chinese, the Yunnanese by and large have been able to find spouses within their own community.[5] During the two years' fieldwork in 1977-79, I was aware of only one Yunnanese-Thai marriage and only a few between Yunnanese and overseas Chinese or between Yunnanese and other ethnic minorities in Northern Thailand. While there was a period in the early 1950s when Guomindang soldiers married Shan women, who come from a group with whom the Yunnanese historically have had very close relations, the Shan women today are indistinguishable from Yunnanese women in dress and speech. In short, the *luuk cinn* phenomenon which has been related to the on-going assimilation of overseas Chinese in Thailand has failed to appear among the Yunnanese.

Another noteworthy aspect of Yunnanese demography is the high degree of mobility and communications maintained among Yunnanese living in Northern Thailand, Burma and even in their native province. Yunnanese identity as Chinese is continually reinforced by contacts with older and larger Chinese communities in Burma and Yunnan. A small but steady trickle of Yunnanese migrants from China enters Thailand via Burma each year. Yunnanese traffic between Thailand and Burma, on the other hand, is heavy; people move back and forth to do business, to attend life crisis events or just for fun. Burmese Chinese often come to Thailand for no other reason than its nightlife.

The most significant difference between overseas Chinese and the Yunnanese can be attributed to native place differences, specifically the skills and institutions which are particular to Chinese from the political and cultural periphery of southwestern China. Although there is not space here to review the history of Yunnan and the southwestern frontier, it is important to note that the Han Chinese have never predominated in the population of that area and that the area consisted for centuries of relatively autonomous political domains, some part of the Chinese administration, others not. Market exchange and communications within the area were functions of a caravan network which on the long hauls, connected Yunnan's market centers with those in Southeast Asia and with the water transport systems of the Yangtze River. As a consequence of these conditions, Yunnanese economic and political activities often entailed relationships with non-Chinese: political and military alliances, market relationships, marriages, etc. These are well-documented in Chinese dynastic and local histories and in biographies of Yunnanese informants.

Many of the conditions typical of the southwestern frontier can be said to characterize northern Burma, Thailand and Laos today. It is hardly surprising, then, that the Yunnanese have maintained many of these relationships with non-Chinese in the Thai context, where their historically institutionalized entrepreneurial and political roles with upland minority groups serve to maintain their identity as Chinese. The modern Thai polity and Thai culture provide few attractions for most Yunnanese when their livelihood is dependent upon their relationship with non-Thai and with other Yunnanese.

With the exception of periodic harassment of some Yunnanese for illicit activities, the Thai government has shown no consistent policy towards them that could be described as either pro-assimilationist or containment. The Yunnanese enjoy the same relative autonomy and not-so-benign neglect as the so-called "hill tribes." Some Yunnanese villages are nominally incorporated into the Thai administrative structure through a headman; others are not. Most Yunnanese have neither citizenship nor legal alien status. As a result, individuals and villages have worked with their own *ad hoc* arrangements with local Thai officials and sometimes with officials higher up to secure some measure of security.

Although I have merely summarized a very complex situation, it is clear that at present there are few reasons for expecting the Yunnanese to follow the same pattern of response to Thai society that conventional wisdom has attributed to the overseas Chinese. Differences having to do primarily with demography — size and distribution of the Yunnanese population in Thailand, marriage patterns, native place — indicate that the Yunnanese will not necessarily assimilate at the rapid rate attributed to the overseas Chinese.

Yunnanese Families, Women and Kinsmen

Now that we have a general picture of the place of the two groups of Chinese in Thai society, let us look more closely at how kinship has affected the persistence of a Chinese identity in Thailand. We have noted that both groups, historically, have intermarried with non-Chinese people, overseas Chinese men with Thai women in the late nineteenth and early twentieth centuries, and a proportionately smaller group of Yunnanese men with Shan or with other minority women. There is general agreement that these mixed marriages, in the case of the overseas Chinese, aided the process of assimilation, whereby *luuk ciin*, conversant with both Chinese and Thai cultures, could opt to identify with one or the other. Early on, as long as the queue and more traditional dress were fashionable, these choices were more fixed for the lifetime of an individual than they were to become later, when in the 1920s the popularity of Westernized dress and coiffures eliminated the marked differences in appearance between Chinese and Thai (Skinner 1957: 128). The Yunnanese, as noted, with the exception of some Muslim marriages to Thai women early in this century, have not intermarried with the Thai. The relative absence of such marriages has been interpreted as one factor inhibiting the assimilation of the Yunnanese, or conversely, it has been one factor promoting the continuity and vitality of Chinese culture among the Yunnanese.

The correlation between the persistence of a group's cultural identity and the frequency of group exogamy has long been accepted as self-evident in studies of Chinese in Southeast Asia (see Skinner 1960: 97-98 or Wu and Wu 1980: 120-122 for two versions of this generalization). It is based on the assumption that children of two Chinese parents are more likely to be inculcated with Chinese mores and language and less likely to be exposed to the indigenous culture than children in homes where only one parent, usually the father, is Chinese. A related, or underlying, assumption is that the presence or absence of Chinese wives in the household affects the cultural identity of the child.

This assumption, as an unexamined truism, invites further consideration of the contribution of Chinese women to the maintenance of Chinese ethnicity in overseas communities. What aspects of their familial roles — as mothers, wives, mothers-in-law, etc. — help to insure the continuity of Chinese culture from one generation to the next? Certainly for Yunnanese women, who seldom hold formal positions in associations or have major formalized roles in ritual, the family is where they are most effective as upholders of Chinese tradition. Not only do they provide their children with skills and knowledge appropriate to the Chinese world, they also are the most active family members taking part in the commemoration of ancestors, possibly the principle concern of the Chinese belief system. As mothers, they also initiate and supervise matchmaking, a process which tends to select in favor of young women deemed suitable to fulfill the traditional duties required of daughters-in-law.

Yunnanese women, whether born in Thailand or in their native province, are on the whole poorly educated and seldom have marketable skills that would qualify them for the kinds of jobs in government and business that exist in Northern Thailand. And, unlike Northern Thai women, they are unwilling to work as unskilled laborers in construction, food-processing, food service, hairdressing or other fields where wages are the lowest in the country. Nor do many of them have the language skills, let alone the connections, to get even this kind of work. If they are compelled to work outside the home, they prefer to work for other Yunnanese as domestics or shop clerks, where their ethnic and familial connections give some assurance of good treatment and higher wages than those paid to Northern Thai women. Some have learned dressmaking, in the hopes of opening a shop, but few are actually employed in the business.

The practical barriers to finding wage-earning work in Northern Thailand complement the Yunnanese conviction, prevalent at all socio-economic levels, that women belong in the home. This belief was articulated with consistency in daily interaction with Yunnanese. Implicit in informants' remarks about women who, of necessity, had work or business that took them frequently outside the home was the idea that women who went about freely were immoral.[6] Their freedom suggested that they were out of control, not properly subordinated to fathers or husbands. The fact of the number of scandals and calamities that befell these women lent credence to this view. Morality, too, seemed to be the issue in the education of women above the primary school level. Unlike some Chinese elsewhere, the Yunnanese did not seem concerned that education was wasted on daughters who would soon marry into another household (Wolf 1972:92-93). Rather, it was that education, beyond the acquisition of basic literacy in Chinese, would lead to immorality because it would inevitably involve the girl in the complexities and dangers of life outside the safe, controlled domestic sphere. As we shall see, literacy in women was desirable, even expected, to the extent that it was valuable in keeping accounts of family enterprises, facilitating a woman's role as household manager and inculcating her with Chinese notions of propriety. However, one still heard the old adage, *"wu cai you de"* — "(a woman) without talents is virtuous."

The admonition to stay at home was most stringently applied to married women. The fact that married women in their twenties and thirties were usually pregnant or nursing an infant reduced the possibility and the inclination to leave the family compound. Men, on the other hand, were seldom at home during the day. In the villages, they worked in the fields or were gone for long periods serving time with one of the irregular Guomindang units still in Thailand. Many men with families in town were traders, traveling back and forth between Thailand and Burma. As a consequence, Yunnanese children, when not in school, spent most of their time at home supervised by adult women. In small households consisting of a married couple and their children, with no servants, this supervision was minimal, since domestic chores, mainly food preparation, took up so much time. However, most Yunnanese households were not of this type, and there were usually several adult women to help with housework and the care of children.

The apparent surfeit of adult women among the Yunnanese was attributable in part to a higher mortality rate among men in a refugee population with a recent history of miliary activities. It also reflected the Yunnanese practice of leaving women and children with relatives while away on a trading venture or other business.

Although it is the case that in most cultures women play the major role in the socialization of young children, Yunnanese women were especially instrumental in teaching skills in two areas critical to the maintenance of Chinese culture — literacy and ritual. Since many of them were only barely literate and generally unread in either the classics of the Confucian canon or the ritual texts of Buddhism, how did they accomplish the inculcation of literacy and ritual?

Yunnanese women, especially mothers, promoted the learning of Chinese language in several direct ways. On a day-to-day basis, they were the ones who enforced attendance at Chinese schools and tutorial sessions. The Chinese are well-known for the high value they place on education. In Thailand, the children of Chinese immigrants and *luuk ciin*, strictly speaking, have made good use of the Thai education system as an avenue of upward mobility. Yunnanese children, too, attend Thai schools, but they also study Chinese. In the villages, Chinese schools seem to be exempt from the Thai legal restrictions on Chinese education, in 1978 limited to six hours per week. Still, the Chinese schools in the villages have not replaced Thai schools as the main source of education and remain, in most villages, auxiliary institutions requiring students to attend before or after their regular instruction in Thai.

In one household with which I was familiar, the woman sent her three children to Chinese classes at 6:00 a.m. They came home for breakfast at eight, then went to a Thai school outside the village. After Thai school they returned home for lunch and then went for two more hours of Chinese instruction. At night their mother made them sit down and practice characters in their copybooks. This regimen of instruction and study, which American college students might find daunting, was supervised by a woman educated only in village schools and whose husband was seldom in residence. With the help of a hired man, she also managed an active farm, raising pigs and poultry and working an acre of land which furnished pig feed and vegetables. But these enterprises and all household activities were subordinated to the schedule of her children's classes.

If this woman seems too good to be true, she was typical of other Yunnanese mothers at least in one respect: her insistence on the study of Chinese and her willingness to sacrifice time and household funds to this end. In town, where Chinese-run schools were more strictly regulated by Thai law, Yunnanese mothers also arranged tutorial sessions for their children. From other female kin and friends, they learned about study groups their children could join or tutors whom they could contact and hire. Again, these tutorial sessions were scheduled around attendance at Thai schools.[7]

One could dismiss the efforts of Chinese women to insure the literacy of their offspring as merely the fulfillment of their roles as mothers, but this is precisely the point. In interviews, I was told repeatedly by men and women that parents were obligated to educate their children; implicitly, however, women were expected to concern themselves with the day-to-day responsibilities entailed by this parental obligation. And they were especially attentive to instruction in Chinese. While I sensed some ambivalence among them in regard to Thai education, in spite of its obvious utility under the circumstances, they were adamant about the importance of Chinese literacy for their children.

Comments from interviews indicated that women, like men, saw a direct link between education and a good job. Literacy in Chinese, then, was desirable because it enabled some Yunnanese, mostly boys, to go on to high school or university in Taiwan, training which could lead to employment in Taiwan. But more importantly, education was expected to teach morality. In fact, Chinese language study *per se* was inseparable from instruction in Chinese values. The *San Zi Jing*, or the *Three Character Classic*, a simplified text for children summarizing in pithy, three-character expressions the whole of Confucian thought, was still used in Yunnanese village schools to teach language. Modern primers, published in Taiwan, consisted of stories of filial sons, diligent students, just emperors and other exemplars of good behavior. Women expected education to "lay the foundation of one's life," to shape the course of one's future; with little exposure to Thai society and values, their children's future was envisioned as a Chinese one.

There is another reason why Chinese women were concerned that their children were literate in Chinese. Many of them, denied education as girls or just barely literate, now viewed their own lives as hampered by lack of education. Older women, born and raised in the "feudal society" of Yunnan before World War II, described with some bitterness their childhood experiences. One eighty-year old woman had this to say about her brush with education:

> In my entire life, I went to school for only seven days. When I started school, I was thirteen years old. Because I had small feet, I was bashful so I didn't dare go to school again. Now, I can't read a word. I regret this very much.

As we have seen, Yunnanese women did not extend their enthusiasm for Chinese education to include high school or college for their daughters; quite the contrary. However, there is no doubt that they were convinced of the inherent goodness of basic Chinese literacy for all their children.

The matter of ritual, and women's participation in it, is analogous to how they contribute to the promotion of Chinese literacy. The responsibility for domestic rituals, in particular, was perceived to be the duty of women (cf. Freedman 1970:80-85). Most of these rituals were for ancestors of the *jia*, or family, into which the woman had married. Women lit the incense at dawn and twilight for the ancestors and placed sacrificial food on the altar, usually located in the main room of the house or in a more private room upstairs. Above the altar in most homes were three posters, one for all ancestors with the family surname, one for earth god (*tu di shen*) and the largest one, in the middle, for heaven and earth. Alternatively, some wealthier families had portraits of the most recently deceased male lineal ancestor.

A striking feature of Yunnanese women's observance of domestic rituals was the extent to which they involved their children in these activities. Children were often delegated to light the incense or renew the food offerings. Especially if there were older women in the household, children were instructed in the proper way to perform the modified *ke tou* appropriate to the domestic context. On special holidays celebrated at home, such as Zhong Qiu Jie, the Mid-Autumn Festival, older women told the children stories about the events and folk heroes connected with the holiday.

In most rituals that celebrated life crisis events or took place in temples, women played subordinate roles to ritual specialists or adult males, but they were conspicuous as participants and organizers. For example, women comprised the majority of supplicants to Guan Yin, the *bodhisattva* who is the most popular figure among the Yunnanese in the Buddhist pantheon and in Chinese mythology. On the birthday of Guan Yin and during observances of the Buddhist ritual cycle, the crowds in the temples were mainly women, some of whom would bring their children. They organized the vegetarian meals and the making of paper objects for sacrifice, and they sewed robes for themselves and for the men who were ritual specialists.

At life crisis events, women were more often in the kitchen than in front of the guests directing or participating in ritual performances. At mortuary celebrations, such as the 100th-day-after-death observance and Qing Ming, women functioned primarily as cooks and seamstresses (for making funeral clothes), only momentarily leaving their chores to perform the *ke tou* or other ritual obligations entailed by their relationship to the deceased. Their primary responsibility, on these occasions, was to feed and serve the relatives and guests who had gathered for the commemoration. This work was essential for the success of the rituals which were validated in the larger context of public acclamation and displays of largesse.

In short, women contributed substantially to the ritual life of the Yunnanese, thereby helping to reiterate and enrich Chinese cultural themes. Prominent among these themes, both at home and in temples, was the duty of the living toward their ancestors. Women, almost exclusively, undertook the domestic obligations to recently decreased family members and, in the process, introduced the young to the concepts of reverence for ancestors and the importance of family continuity. Buddhist rites, too, were occasions for fulfilling one's duty to ancestors; women did not make merit for themselves but did so for the sake of family ancestors. Life crisis events also were to celebrate the ancestors. Rituals relating to birth, marriage and death were personal rites only in the sense that they created and reinforced ties between the individual and the succession of generations. They were, in fact, public affirmations of the family's filiality and could not be staged without the organizational and culinary talents of women.

Women, though, contributed something more to one life crisis event than their labor at the feast. Yunnanese marriages were not, as both the English and Chinese clichés maintain, "made in heaven." Rather, they were arranged by mothers whose greatest wish was to see their children successfully matched. Some mothers interested themselves in matching their children long before they were of marriageable age, an age that varied tremendously, depending upon family circumstances. While child betrothal *per se* was no longer practiced, marriages sometimes resulted from long-standing agreements between families. More typically, a mother would begin to make discreet inquires about potential spouses, once she had decided the time had come for her child to be married. Sons could marry women younger, poorer and less educated than themselves. Daughters, on the other hand, were considered a poor match for men younger or less educated. And if the boy lacked a steady income, as was the case for so many Yunnanese men in their twenties dependent upon the vicissitudes of the Burma trade, marriage was out of the question. These customary exceptions regarding proper matches generally acted to reduce the number of suitable husbands relative to the number of suitable wives. Mothers of sons, therefore, had a wider field to search and, more often than mothers of daughters, initiated inquires. Mothers of daughters assumed a more passive role, accepting or rejecting offers.

Young people in their twenties talked of modern marriages as love matches, but most of the marriages that I knew about were arranged. Even in those matches initiated by couples, pragmatic considerations were decisive factors, in particular the question of compatibility between bride and her mother-in-law. Young women did not want to marry into a family where, because of different expectations, conflict with the husband's mother was inevitable. Young men, for their part, would rule out, or terminate relationships with, women whom their mothers would consider objectionable. In other words, young people were as aware as their senior generation that marriages were family, not personal, affairs.

In almost all marriages, selection favored girls who could meet the conservative standards of older women in their forties and fifties, women who had endured their own initiation into the adult world as daughters-in-law in the "feudal society" of provincial Yunnan. This circumstance means that Yunnanese children today continue to be reared in conservative traditional households, in spite of the existence of some so-called love matches and of some instances of liaisons not legitimated by proper rituals.

Many of the foregoing observations on Yunnanese women support what is already known about Chinese women elsewhere (e.g. M. Wolf's work, 1972, on women and the family in Taiwan). But women's activities, subsumed under familial roles, took on added importance in the context of a Chinese community in Thailand. In large measure, women, more than men, provided their children with the knowledge and skills appropriate to the Chinese milieu. Literacy, as we have seen, was encouraged by Yunnanese women, and there seems little doubt that literacy in Chinese, even of the most basic sort, teaches morality and, for males, may lead to greater opportunity. Certainly it enhanced one's ability to function as Chinese. Women's participation in ritual activities was important too. They carried on the domestic ancestral sacrifices and, generally, maintained the saliency of ancestral veneration within the Yunnanese community. Finally, they were instrumental in insuring the continuity of Chinese culture because of their major role in the selection of daughters-in-law, who had to measure up to the conservative standards set by the senior female generation. This, in turn, directly affected the family environment in which Yunnanese children are now being raised in Thailand. Traditional households, one may say, beget traditional households.

Coming from homes where both parents were Chinese, with the implications described above, most Yunnanese of all generations thought of themselves as Chinese and were rather proud of their distinctiveness from the Thai. With the exception of the generation now being educated in Thai schools, whom I shall comment on below, Yunnanese did not have the social skills to function comfortably in Thai society. That is, a Thai identity was neither a viable nor desirable option. Adult males invariably spoke enough Central Thai or Northern Thai for negotiating the marketplace and for interacting with Thai officials, but few of my Yunnanese informants had ever been in Thai homes, and their social contacts with the Thai were almost nil. Adult women had even less fluency with the language and culture of Thailand. Although encapsulation of the Yunnanese community with Thai society was ameliorated in part by business relations with overseas Chinese who often helped them navigate the uncertain waters of the Thai world, the Yunnanese remained relatively isolated.

Yunnanese in the Thai school system, certainly those who had completed high school and the handful who were university students, were much more at ease in Thai society than their parents. These people came closest to having the option of "double identity" ascribed by Coughlin (1960) to the overseas Chinese. In speech and manners, they were indistinguishable from their classmates. Their behavior, in some cases, amounted to almost an infatuation with Thai culture and a concomitant denigration of their Chinese background. For example, one young university student refused to speak the Yunnanese dialect even at home where everyone was Yunnanese and few were proficient in any dialect of Thai. Her linguistic behavior was a very clear statement to her family of her cultural preference. But if, as students, Yunnanese were eager to become part of the Thai world, at graduation they had to face the fact that job prospects were to be found primarily within the Yunnanese community. For most, their passion for Thai culture was necessarily short-lived.

Jobs in private enterprise in Thai society most often depended upon personal contacts. Thai students and children of overseas Chinese had the help of parents and relatives in finding positions in small industry, banking, food-processing, wholesaling, hostelry or whatever. Not a few in the overseas Chinese group went directly from high school or university to work for fathers already established in these fields. Yunnanese students did not usually have such contacts in spite of the fact that they may have had Thai friends their own age. Government employment was, in theory, another possibility for those with the proper citizenship credentials, but government salaries at the lower levels were not attractive to most Yunnanese.

Thus, the small minority of young adults in the Yunnanese community with the requisite education, language and social graces to move freely in Thai society were compelled to rely on their own community, especially their relatives, in seeking their fortunes. Finding a living was the major concern of these young people, a concern they shared with others their age holding degrees from Taiwan or American universities, or holding no degree at all. The most common livelihood among this group was the Burma-Thailand trade, particularly the gem trade, a variant on the established trading history of the Yunnanese which I have sketched earlier in this discussion. To get started in the business required extensive knowledge of ethnic politics in the Thai-Burma border area and long periods of waiting while negotiating. Patrilineal kin and sometimes affines provided the necessary expertise and contacts, as well as daily sustenance, for young entrepreneurs. Most Yunnanese could count on the help of a network of kin extending from Northern Thailand's towns and villages into the Shan States in Burma. Fictive kin, those to whom one had ritual ties of adoption or brotherhood, were also useful.

Livelihood was only the most obvious reason for dependence on kinsmen. In the northern city where I lived, there were few mutual aid associations of the type characteristic of the overseas Chinese communities. *Jai-li ren*, generally speaking, those people in your father's household, and the wider category of *qinqi*, those people with whom one acknowledged ties of blood (*xue tong xue xiang*) or marriage, were sources of aid when an individual was impoverished or ill and elderly. While even the most indigent Yunnanese received a proper burial through donations from the community, in life one had to rely on the help of family and kin.

The Relevance of the Yunnanese Response to Thailand

Some aspects of the Yunnanese experience in Thailand which we have just reviewed may have relevance for our understanding of the persistence of ethnicity among the overseas Chinese there. At least the Yunnanese case may help us identify some questions that ought to be explored in the context of our present knowledge of the overseas Chinese and in future research. To take the most obvious questions first, what do we know about overseas Chinese women, specifically those who were post-World War II brides and mothers of the generation of overseas Chinese now in their late twenties and thirties? What part have they played in fostering a strong sense of Chinese identity among their children? Were they, like Yunnanese women, actively involved in maintaining

Chinese literacy, mores and ritual as a part of their familial duties? And were they matchmakers, in the sense that Yunnanese women were? If there is any validity at all to an analogy between Yunnanese women and this particular group of overseas Chinese women, then it would not be surprising to find, as did Tobias, that children of overseas Chinese immigrants, now adults, contribute to the expansion of "expressively Chinese activities" (1977:305).

Our lack of information on women in the overseas Chinese community is symptomatic of the general neglect by researchers of family life. We do not know, for example, much about the critical relationship of fathers to sons in overseas Chinese families, and the extent to which filiality and ancestor veneration are still central familial concerns. Surely this relationship and related beliefs linking the present generation to ones past affect the persistence of Chinese ethnicity, since ethnicity entails reference to the past and the presumption of common origins.

Another issue raised by a consideration of the Yunnanese is the question of ethnicity and the life-cycle, namely the changes in the significance of family and kin throughout an individual's life. We have seen that Yunnanese schooled in Thai institutions through high school or university are more likely than others to have the necessary skills and inclination to identify as Thai. But most are returned to the Chinese fold, so to speak, when it comes time to generate a livelihood. Although most of the students and ex-students I knew were just embarking on their careers, I believe their relations with Thai acquaintances and their accessibility to Thai society will wane over the long term as business and family concerns necessitate attention to relationships within the Yunnanese community and reliance upon kinsmen. We must also keep in mind that most of these young Yunnanese will marry other Yunnanese, in deference to their mothers who could never tolerate a Thai spouse.

Several studies have indicated the importance of education, both Thai and Chinese, as a factor in the differential assimilation of overseas Chinese to Thai society (Skinner 1957:381-382; Boonsanong 1971: 7-8, 32). Observations made to me by Thai teachers support my own impression that students of Chinese descent in the upper levels of the Thai education system appear to be the most highly assimilated groups among the Chinese (cf. Tobias 1977: 305). If we assume that this group will retain their attachments to and contacts with Thai society throughout their lives, then indeed the generational model of assimilation may be applicable to them. We can expect each successive generation of overseas Chinese to identify as Thai more often than previous ones, especially in light of the trend which indicates that the number of students of Chinese descent in Thai educational institutions is increasing (Skinner 1957: 371; Coughlin 1960;: 191 Wu and Wu 1980: 31).

However, the overseas Chinese community is also susceptible to the vicissitudes of earning a living that manifest themselves among the Yunnanese students. Competition for the limited number of good jobs commensurate with one's high school certificate or college degree is keen, and Chinese relatives in banking and other businesses remain instrumental in finding a position. The overseas Chinese, like the Yunnanese, have an obvious interest in maintaining and exploiting their own ethnic networks. Whether or not for some portion of the overseas Chinese community, there is a period in the life cycle when participation in Thai society and adherence to Thai values becomes critical is an important question. So, too, is the question of the periodic influence of kinsmen and family on individuals as they embrace careers and marriage. An examination of these questions bears on the apparent paradox of flourishing Chinese activities and organizations in Thailand today coincident with the historically documented trend of assimilation.

Many of the issues brought to light by a comparison of the Yunnanese Chinese and overseas Chinese in Thailand point to the need for more anthropological attention to a subject that has been our traditional preserve: kinship, including familial roles, socialization within the family, kin networks and rituals related to kinship. Now that we have a general picture of some of the factors affecting assimilation of Chinese in Thailand, thanks to the pioneering work of Skinner and others cited in this essay, we need to refine this larger vision with reference to the day-to-day activities and concerns of individuals. The Yunnanese response to Thailand suggests, for example, that studies of the mundane affairs of domestic life may enhance our appreciation of the current practice of group endogamy among the overseas Chinese, or that we might better understand the effects of education on ethnic identity if we relate it to instrumental ties among kinsmen. If the Yunnanese case, which we have only begun to explore, is any indication, studies of family and kinship among the overseas Chinese in Thailand may yield new perspectives on individual choices of ethnicity and on the larger questions of the persistence of Chinese ethnicity.

Notes

1 Research for this essay was funded in part by Grant No. 77-2265 from the National Science Foundation, Grants for Improving Dissertation Research, 1978. Almost twenty years have passed since the fieldwork on which the essay is based was carried out. During this time, much has changed for the Yunnanese Chinese in Thailand, as well as for the overseas Chinese. In fact, today I would no longer use the term "overseas Chinese" to describe the highly assimilated descendants of Chinese immigrants from China's southeastern coastal provinces, but in the context of this essay, the rubric was useful for distinguishing them from the Yunnanese Chinese. For developments among the Yunnanese Chinese in Northern Thailand since the 1970s, see my book, *Familiar Strangers: Ethnicity and Trade Among Yunnanese Chinese in Southeast Asia*, forthcoming from Yale University Southeast Asia Studies, Yale Center for International Area Studies.

2 This estimate is from Wu and Wu 1980:67. Their figure is derived from projections based on Skinner (1957) and agrees with the ROC (Taiwan) estimate for 1974.

3 The figure is based on rough estimates of Yunnanese village populations and of urban Yunnanese in the market towns of Chiang Mai and Chiang Rai. It does not include Guomindang troops.

4 Han Chinese predominate in this group, and my subsequent observations on family life are based on experience with the Han. Although much of what I have to say about family life also applies to the Muslim minority among the Yunnanese, and the two groups live together as neighbors and occasionally intermarry, the Muslims set themselves apart from the Han on two points: they say they do not eat pork and do not sacrifice to ancestors. While these distinctions raise important questions of likenesses and differences between the two groups, such issues are not explored in this essay. See below.

5 See Suthep's study (1977) of the Muslim community in Chiang Mai town, the Yunnanese among them numbering several thousand. Some in the latter group are married to local Northern Thai women or to Pakistani Muslim women (1977:33-34,I24).

6 This value judgement was not applicable to elderly women who attained a sort of asexual status after child-bearing years. Especially if they had passed on household responsibilities to daughters-in-law, they were allowed more freedom of movement than the younger generation of women.

7 Only a minority of Yunnanese possessed government I.D. cards certifying their Thai citizenship. However, in the countryside regulations restricting Thai education to Thai citizens were more lax than in town. This is one of the reasons why urban Yunnanese sometimes sent their children to the rural villages to study. Not only did they have access to better Chinese instruction, but they could also attend Thai schools.

Chapter 4

ഇ൫

The Chinese in the Philippines: From Aliens to Cultural Minority

George H. Weightman

I. Prologue

The Philippine Chinese community has been characterized by patterns that are often contradictory. While much smaller than similar communities of compatriots in Indonesia, Thailand and Malaysia, the Philippine Chinese have occupied a crucial economic position since the early Spanish colonial period. With the possible exception of the Chinese in Singapore, they are the most educated Chinese in Southeast Asia. In many ways they are the most "modern" and most "Chinese" of all the overseas Chinese in Southeast Asia.

Though a Chinese community has existed in the Philippines since Ming times, the present Chinese population is of comparatively recent origin. Indeed, most are descended from those who entered the Philippines during the American colonial period of Chinese exclusion. In a society featuring considerable historic antipathy toward the Chinese, a large proportion of the Chinese community is of mixed Sino-Filipino descent (the Sinicized Chinese mestizos). In addition many Filipinos — even some hostile to the Chinese and their culture — boast of their Chinese ancestry (the Filipinized Chinese mestizos). See Weightman, 1967, for a discussion of these often competitive groups.

Historically the size and distribution of the Philippine Chinese community have always been the subject of political controversy and scholarly uncertainty. Both the size and distribution of the community have fluctuated and changed dramatically through the years of foreign rule (Spanish, American, and Japanese), after Philippine independence, and now the "New Society".

Always the Philippine Chinese community has demonstrated an amazing capacity "to role with the punches". Massacres, expulsions, forced assimilation, exclusion policies, communal riots, civil wars, nationalization (actually de-alienization) laws, and even favorable climates of accommodation have molded and shaped the community. Yet over time, the community with its basic institutional structure has so far always been able to perpetuate itself,

II. Demographic and Historic Context

A. Size and Distribution

No where else in southeast Asia has the term "Chinese" been so narrowly defined as in the Philippines (Purcell, 1968). All political and economic statistics refer only to "aliens" — or more specifically and correctly, those who annually register as alien Chinese with the Philippine Bureau of Immigration.

During the American colonial period the number of alien Chinese grew rapidly by immigration (despite the exclusion policy) and by natural increase since Chinese born in the Philippines could not easily become citizens in the American Philippines. This pattern continued in the early years of Philippine independence. However, the development of restrictive policies both legislative and judicial (Weightman, 1960; Agpalo, 1962) against the Chinese soon produced a dramatic reversal and decline in those registering as "aliens". By 1982, less than 30,000 Chinese were registering as aliens. (Weightman, 1982).

Social scientists and historians have always been more interested in the number of ethnic Chinese (i.e., those who think of themselves as Chinese or are so regarded by others) in the Philippines than in mere "alien" Chinese. In the early sixties, when alien registration numbered nearly 150,000, social scientists ranged in their estimates of ethnic Chinese in contradistinction to Chinese citizens from 400,000 (Weightman, 1960; I.H. Reynolds, 1965) to 650,000 (Amyot, 1960 and 1973). These projections were based upon provincial Chinese school registrations (Weightman and I.H. Reynolds) or formal clan membership in Manila (Amyot).

Significantly and unfortunately, Philippine politicians and journalists would subtract the alien registration figures from Amyot's highest ethnic estimates and, then, would lump the difference as "illegal aliens". Similarly apologists for the Chinese communal structure would argue that the official alien registration figures reflected the actual number of Chinese in the country. The "number game" became an endless source of confusion, producing more sound than light.

Until the last few decades of Spanish rule, the Chinese were confined to the area immediately surrounding Manila. For a long period they had been confined to a ghetto just outside the walls of the city proper. At the same time an older community continued to survive in Jolo, the capital of Muslim Sulu. By the middle of the nineteenth century, Chinese communities began to flourish in Iloilo and Cebu.

Although the American colonial rulers tried to apply exclusion policies and to make political assimilation of Chinese and Chinese mestizos more difficult, they removed restrictions on the internal movement of the resident Chinese. Quickly Chinese began to settle in all areas of provincial economic activity. (See Wicksberg, 1960; Larkin 1972; Hunt, 1954, for detailed discussion of the role of the Chinese and Chinese mestizos in economic development and change). This spread of the Chinese throughout the Philippines was speeded during the Japanese occupation when many Chinese and Chinese mestizos fled from urban centers to the relative safety of the rural areas (Tan, 1981).

By the beginning of Philippine independence, only half of the total Philippine Chinese community lived in the Manila area. There were sizable provincial communities in all areas of economic growth and development in the Philippines. Indeed, the size of the local Chinese community could be taken as a good indicator of the level of economic development of the area (I.H. Reynolds, 1965).

In the last two decades, however, there have been striking demographic changes in the distribution, size, and composition of the Chinese community. There has been a dramatic exodus of the most modernized, most assimilated Chinese and mestizos as part of the "Third World Brain Drain" to America, Canada, Australia, and elsewhere. In addition, a sharp decline in many of the old provincial Chinese communities has occurred. Chinese in centers like Solo, Marawi, and Cotabato were hard hit by the upheaval of civil war. Others moved out of areas of economic decline such as Iloilo (Omohundro, 1981) and the Bicol region. In the meantime, the Chinese population in Metro Manila has grown rapidly as the old Chinatown in Manila (Binondo, San Nicolas, and Santa Cruz) expanded north-ward into Kalookan City and Malabon. Enclaves of Chinese also developed in the more exclusive suburbs of Manila. By now, more than seventy per cent of the remaining Chinese in the Philippines now reside in the Greater Manila area. This new pattern is having profound repercussions on the processes of assimilation, economic development, and ethnic dynamics.

Formerly the acquisition of Philippine citizenship had been so difficult and costly (officially and unofficially) that few Chinese were able to afford it. By 1972, less than 200 Chinese a year received certificates of naturalization, and this low figure represented an increase over the past (see Weightman, 1982 :1013 for a detailed discussion of this issue). Under a martial law "Letter of Instruction" (No. 270, April 11, 1975), President Marcos set up provisions to facilitate a reduction in the size of the alien group which by then was 90,401. Though Hunt and Houston (1979) were enthusiastic about this procedure becoming the basis of a quick assimilation, it seems primarily an ingenious way of preventing the new embassy of the Peoples' Republic of China (henceforth PRC) from having too large an "alien" base for concern. However, only 38,841 applicants including wives and dependent children had applied by the end of the twice extended deadline. Only 19,327 applicants and family members had been approved with nearly 10,000 applicants still pending by mid 1982 (Weightman, 1982). Apparently less than half of all registered "aliens" in 1975 applied. And of these, less than half received citizenship by 1982. Yet, less than thirty thousand (28,348) were still registering as aliens in 1982. Costs and political difficulties have caused most "aliens" to simply stop their annual registration. Thus, alien figures, which never were too reliable, have become thoroughly meaningless as a guide to the number of ethnic Chinese.

Weightman (1960) and L.H. Reynolds (1965) had not only estimated the number of ethnic Chinese to be less than Amyot (1960 and 1978) had, they were not optimistic that the group would continue to grow at its previous rate. Their conservatism and pessimism, based upon a provincial orientation (Sulu and the Ilokos) have proven more accurate than Amyot's. The community never approached the 600,000 estimate of Amyot, and now it is estimated (Weightman, 1982 : 2) to range from 250,000 to 350,000.

Most of the issues of citizenship and of racial "mixture" seem so vague, uncertain, and legalistic, that one might wonder what might cause a person to identify or be identified as "Philippine Chinese". Operationally, anyone, regardless of citizenship, of at least partial Chinese ancestry through the patrilineal branch in the Philippines whose first language (i.e., "native" but not necessarily "mother's" tongue) is one of the southern Chinese languages — usually Hokkien — is considered to be Philippine Chinese. (Omohundro's attempt, 1981, to identify Chinese ethnicity with a certain mercantile role is rejected by most other social scientists (Szanton, 1982). There is a smaller sub-community of Cantonese speakers, and still smaller groupings of Hakkas and other southern Chinese groups. Interestingly, both the Philippine Spanish and Tagalog term "Chino" means a Hokkien (Amoy). Cantonese are usually referred to by Filipinos as "Macaos". Hokkiens tend to refer to Cantonese in a somewhat patronizing term, "country (rural) cousins". However, both Hokkien and Cantonese perceive themselves and are perceived by others as being "Chinese".

The marked imbalance in the Chinese sex ratio historically in the Philippines has long led to unions of *Chinese men* with Philippine *women*. Marriage of ethnic Chinese *women* with Philippine *men* has been historically rare and almost taboo amongst the Philippine Chinese since the offspring of such a union would not belong to a Chinese clan. The rare offspring of such present day marriages are not seen by the Chinese as even being Chinese mestizos.

This whole question of how Chinese mestizos are identified as Filipino or Chinese brings us to the issue or past colonial and present Philippine policies toward assimilation of Chinese and the status of their "mixed-blood" offspring.

B. Assimilation Processes in the Colonial Period

Nowhere else in Southeast Asia did the Chinese face more restrictions and cope with a more precarious existence (especially in the early centuries of colonial rule) than in the Spanish Philippines. During the Spanish era there were systematic government sponsored massacres in 1603, 1639, 1662, 1686, and 1762. A non-governmental inspired massacre took place in 1819. Filipino rebel leaders planned another during the Filipino War of Independence at the end of Spanish colonial rule (Purcell, 1968). Even during the American period, severe communal riots occurred in Manila, 1924, and San Pablo, 1931. Periodically during the Spanish period, the Chinese would be expelled (1686 and 1747) or severely limited (1615, 1755, and 1804).

Yet, probably nowhere else in Southeast Asia — except in traditional Siam — was it more easy for the Chinese and their mestizo descendants to escape such restrictions and merge often as a new elite with the local society (Wickberg, 1960; Larkin, 1972). Wherever possible there were separate communities and separate governments for the mestizos. They paid only half the head tax of foreign born Chinese. In addition, they, unlike the Peranakan Chinese of Indonesia, never constituted a continuous separate community. Their children were Filipinos — legally, socially, and culturally. Wickberg described them as "not a special kind of local Chinese" but a "special kind of Filipino" (Wickberg, 1960: 24). Only in Muslim Sulu did the Indonesian pattern seem to be developing before Sulu's independence ended at the end of the nineteenth century.

It has been estimated that it took on the average three generations for the Chinese migrants and their descendants to merge into the native communities of Southeast Asia. However, in the Spanish Philippines, the process was often more rapid. Chinese mestizos or even locally born Chinese could become citizens upon declaration at the age of twenty-one. Naturalization was even possible for foreign born Chinese. Catholic Chinese had the Dominican friars as their political champions. The fees for Christian Chinese were usually less than those for non-Christian Chinese. In addition, Christian Chinese were not subject to expulsion decrees. Indeed, they were not even permitted to return to China. (Not too surprisingly, the Philippine Chinese were the first Chinese in Southeast Asia to establish local cemeteries. The maintenance of such cemeteries was an early concern or formal Chinese organizations).

Technically, Chinese mestizos and Catholic Chinese had fewer privileges and paid higher taxes than the native Filipinos in the Spanish era. Socially and economically, they appear to have occupied a superior position. The Spaniards seemed to have preferred them on a personal basis to the native population. Their patterns of preference became more marked as the Spanish era drew to its end. The economic development in the Philippines which followed the opening of the Suez Canal in 1869 brought new waves of Chinese to the Philippines. The newly emergent native elite which was largely of Sino-Hispanic racial extraction became increasingly hostile to the political dominance of the *Peninsulares* (Spaniards born in Spain) and of the economic dominance of the Chinese.

Dr. Jose Rizal, the national hero of Chinese mestizo ancestry, in his polemic novel, *El Filibusterismo*, bitterly assailed the alliance of the friars (especially the Dominicans) and the Chinese mercantile elements. The revolutionary plans of the novel's protagonists, which were markedly paralleled by the Katipunan insurrectionists almost ten years later in 1896, called for the massacre of most of *the peninsulares* and of the Chinese.

Filipinos are aware that some of their greatest heroes and political leaders were of part Chinese ancestry — Rizal, Osmena, Sandico, Yalu, Osorio, Palanca, Aquinaldo, Paterno, Cuenco, Teehankee, and Marcos, to name only a few,. Out of this interracial blending has emerged a vigorous group of Filipinos who still dominate politics, business, finance, the arts, science, education and literature. Most of the higher officials of the civil service are Filipinos with a pronounced proportion of Chinese and/or Spanish racial traits. The elite mestizos of both cultural traditions have extensively intermarried. The Hispanicized Chinese mestizo landlord class of the Central Plain of Luzon almost constitute a group apart (Larkin, 1972). Chinese mestizos are represented to an extent far out of proportion to their number in the student, professional and mercantile classes. A large proportion of the Filipino Catholic clergy are also of this background. These Filipinized mestizos have always been the great political and economic rivals of the Chinese and the Sinicized mestizo allies. (For a discussion of the complex dynamics of racial animosity in a personalistic society see Weightman, 1964, 1967 and 1968).

In summary, the Spanish colonial pattern was to make it as difficult as possible for the Chinese to remain Chinese while at the same time the Spaniards made it very easy (almost mandatory) to assimilate as quickly as possible. It was no wonder that Chinese mestizos at that time moved so rapidly into Filipino society. The coming of the Americans was to change dramatically this pattern. In fact, the American colonial rulers totally reversed the pattern.

"Probably no other element in the Islands has profited more directly from the changes that have been wrought since 1898" wrote Hayden about the impact of American colonial policy on the Chinese in the Philippines. (Hayden, 1950: 695).

The Chinese prospered as legal restrictions were removed and as efficient government reduced extralegal or "indirect" taxation. Even more important to rapid economic development was the removal of uncertainties in the police powers of the colonial authority. At least during the early decades of American rule, administrative extortion and corruption seemed to be diminished or at least were better concealed. The American officials were not necessarily more honest than the previous officials. The removal of many of the previous restraints eliminated many opportunities for bribery or extortion. However, bribery and other irregularities characterized the immigration procedures from the earliest days of American administration.

The influx of American capital in turn acted as a stimulus to the Chinese capital already in the Philippines. With the peace and order problem solved after the Fil-American War, the Chinese were able to commence on a renewed scale the economic penetration of the Philippines, particularly in the opening fields of Mindanao and the mountain province of Luzon.

The institutional structure of the community, which had operated under considerable restraint and concealment in the Spanish period, developed openly. Chinese religious practices with respect to Buddhism, Taoism, and *Shen* (spirit) worship became more overt. Chinese observances of the New Year and Ching Ming were openly held. Secret societies operated more openly as musical associations or "masonic lodges". The Chinese school system began a rapid development. Political struggles from the homeland spread to the Philippines though often in a concealed and attenuated fashion. The Philippine Chinese became outspoken champions of the new wave of nationalism sweeping China in the decades leading to the long struggle against the Japanese.

While the American colonial government removed most of the restrictions which had previously pushed the Chinese toward political and social assimilation, it, at the same time, made it virtually impossible for Chinese or their mestizo descendants to become citizens of the Philippines. Coupled with the application of Chinese exclusion laws to the Philippines, the composition of the community became set.

The present Chinese community provides a picture of anything but an "old community" long cut off from Chinese mainland cultural patterns. The vast majority of the present day Chinese are descended from those who migrated to the Philippines in the post 1900 period *despite or because* of practices connected with the application of "exclusion".

Harriet Reynolds (1965 : 92) reported that eighty-three per cent of the adults she studied in the "old" community (1956) in the Ilokos were China born. Weightman (1960) found that the Jolo community, which traces its origin to the coming of the Ming fleet in the early fifteenth century, still had at least one third of its total population born in China in 1957. As late as 1972, Omohundro (1981) reported more than twenty per cent of the "old" community of Iloilo to have been born in China.

Although the exclusion practices failed to prevent the growth of the Chinese community in the Philippines, they undoubtedly kept the rate of growth under control. "Exclusion" prevented the great waves which characterized migration to Malaysia, Thailand, and Indonesia in the first half of this century. The other Southeast Asian Chinese communities are now numbered in the millions; the Philippine Chinese are numbered in the hundreds of thousands.

Of great significance was the tendency of exclusion to "fix" permanently the composition of the community. Former residents, their dependents, and the dependents of residents clearly had priority and contacts. New migrants had to be drawn from the same limited areas that had contributed to the migrant population in the Spanish period. Even when the immigrants fell into categories designated by Chinese informants as "illegally legal" (use of false documents and/or bribes) or "illegally illegal" (smuggled entry), those with contacts with resident Chinese obviously had better opportunities than those who were migrating from areas not previously represented in large numbers.

Those from the Amoy area and the Macao area were not so vulnerable to exposure nor were opportunities so limited as for other Chinese speech groups. The illegal dependents, while not actual relatives of residents, tended to be from the same clans, the same multiple surname associations, the same villages, or at least the same speech groups of the resident "relatives".

In considerable part, the operations of the American Exclusion Act explain why the Philippine Chinese are *not* marked by the wide range of speech groups which is the pattern of other overseas Chinese communities in Southeast Asia. Speech group rivalries and diversities elsewhere in Southeast Asia facilitated the use of the national language ("mandarin" or *kuo yu)* as a common language. In the Philippines, Hokkien has persisted as the language of community.

Ironically, so many Chinese entered during this period of exclusion, that, when the new Commonwealth Government in early 1941 abandoned the policy of exclusion in favor of a quota system of 500 for all nationalities, there were vehement protests from the local Chinese community and the Chinese consulate.

Practices associated with accommodation to exclusion evasion contributed to the widespread phenomenon of aliases among the Philippine Chinese. Informants repeatedly speak of "real" or "stone names" (i. e., the name used on tomb stones) and "false" or "paper names" used on official forms and registrations. Many Chinese appear to have several Chinese and Filipino names. This writer knows of a large family where none of the sons has the same "paper name" of the father. Only one uses a Chinese surname; the other sons use different Filipino surnames. And the father's surname is not the "stone name" ! However, the father's paper name at least affiliates him to the multiple surname association of his and his sons' stone name. Often this writer only learned the stone name of close friends by accompanying them to cemeteries on Ching Ming or All Saints ceremonies. Although paper names are crucial in dealing with Filipino officialdom, the stone names determine family and clan obligations. Often Chinese are unaware of the paper names of their Chinese associates. Within the community, it is the stone name which guides social behavior.

Of profound importance for the issue of legal assimilation was the American reversal of the previous Spanish policy. Throughout the American colonial rule (until the Commonwealth Constitution of 1935) Chinese could *not* become Philippine citizens. In the Philippines, the citizenship bar was even more severe than in America. Not even locally born Chinese could become citizens. Mestizos, that is children of Philippine mothers could elect Philippine citizenship at twenty-one. There was considerable legal confusion with respect to this provision since any Philippine women married to a Chinese became a Chinese! (After Philippine independence this optional election of citizenship by mestizos was revoked. Under martial law it was later restored).

Thus, the American colonial policies reversed significantly the policies of the Spaniards. No longer was political assimilation possible or social assimilation encouraged. At the same time, the Americans removed the political and economic restrictions that might have encouraged assimilation. Culturally and economically the Chinese flourished as the resentful Filipinos sought to restrict this alien community while the Philippines moved toward greater self-determination. These developments in the American colony coincided and reflected the political upheaval and nationalistic surges of pre-World War II China. Various Chinese factions, sometimes not in a very concealed manner, contended for dominance in this overseas community.

The Japanese invasion in late 1941 and the resultant occupation brought great hardships to both the Chinese *and* Filipino communities. Repression was particularly swift to the Philippine Chinese leaders who had actively led the anti-Japanese boycott movement of the thirties. Very shortly after their arrival in Manila, the Japanese arrested many and executed several Chinese. Other Chinese active in the boycott movement went underground throughout the occupation.

Both the Chinese and Filipinos suffered heavily during the occupation and the destructive liberation that followed. Each community developed guerilla movements with communist and anti-communist factions. Many urban dwellers of both communities were forced to flee to the relative safety of the rural provinces. The war experiences inflamed the nationalistic sentiments of both groups. In addition, the Japanese used every means to encourage anti-Chinese hostility in the Philippine government which they imposed. Each community had to confront the emotionally traumatic experience of a collaborationist issue during and immediately after the Japanese occupation. (See Jensen, 1956; Tan, 1981 for detailed treatment of this short, tumultuous period).

C. *Changing ways-in an Independent Philippines*

A new and fateful era began for the Philippine Chinese when the Philippines became an independent republic early in the postwar period. The new nation adopted a policy toward the Chinese which combined the *most* severe patterns of the Americans and of the Spaniards. The acquisition of Philippine citizenship was made even more difficult and legal migration ever more curtailed than during the last years of American rule. At the same time, supervision of the growing Chinese school system was given by treaty provision to the Nationalist (Kuomintang, or KMT) Chinese embassy. The community was perceived and treated as an alien enclave under seige. Through a series of laws and judicial precedents, the Chinese aliens were barred from owning residential urban land, from engaging in rice milling or the retail trade, and from all professions other than medicine. (See Agpalo, 1962, for a Nationalist justification of these processes, and Weightman, 1960, for a consideration of the ethnic dynamics of these processes),

Philippine nationalism was fanned by many who sought to whip up anti-Communist hysteria against both Filipino and Chinese progressive elements. By the late sixties, all Chinese shop signs in Manila had been banned — allegedly to encourage assimilation and to suppress potential communist propaganda. Increasingly, the Chinese schools were criticized and restricted but no one seriously argued or desired that the Chinese students be absorbed into the overburdened Philippine educational system. As the naturalization process was made more difficult and expensive, there was renewed agitation against "insincere" naturalized citizens and the use of "dummies" to avoid economic restrictions. Edicts after the imposition of martial law in September of 1972 would soon reverse many of these trends.

By the early seventies, it was obvious to President Ferdinand Marcos that some "solution" had to be achieved before the inevitable recognition of the Peoples' Republic of China (PRC) would complicate the presence of a large alien community. Martial law permitted President Marcos to begin many economic and political reforms that would have been blocked or been politically unwise in "the old society".

Under Presidential Decree No. 176, all foreign schools were required to filipinize their curricula, ownership, board members, administrators, teachers, and school population. Thus the old Chinese curriculum was to be totally scrapped, and the Philippine curriculum was to be substituted. However, a form of Chinese curriculum still survives in many of these schools unofficially. Indeed, many schools have merely adapted rather than been changed. (See Weightman, 1982, for the complications of filipinization).

While the Chinese school system may have been reduced, the flowering of Chinese culture has been officially encouraged by a government which seeks cordial relations with the PRC. Chinese store signs have not only returned to Manila, Chinese is also used on street signs in Manila's Chinatown. First Lady Imelda Marcos has with her Chinatown Beautification Project fostered development projects in Chinatown to promote tourism. Chinese ceremonies connected with the

Chinese New Year and Ching Ming have again gone public. Chinese dragon dances and firecrackers mark not only traditional Chinese rituals but Catholic festivals associated with Christmas, Easter and the Pentecost. (In early republic days, Chinese had felt it prudent to avoid overt displays of their culture). At present, Philippine Airlines is the only airline that flies to both Taiwan and the PRC. Many Chinese and Filipinos frequently include both on their travels abroad.

Under martial law, President Marcos was able to establish relations with the PRC without having to cope with anti-Chinese and anti-Communist hysteria which would have occurred at an earlier time. As mentioned earlier, Marcos also made easier the process of naturalization. So far, the result of this move has been a condition of statistical and research confusion to match that of the special status of the former Chinese schools. Tension and resentments especially among those hostile to both Marcos and the Chinese remain. Given time the Philippine Chinese may successfully manage the transition from alien group to local cultural minority, but there are many uncertainties in the future Philippine political process.

III. Major Institutional Structures of the Philippine Chinese

A. Family and Clan

The Philippine Chinese brought with them a family pattern in many respects independent of other political and economic forms. Among the Hokkien and Cantonese, family migration had for many decades prior to World War II been a marked pattern and preference. As noted earlier, the immigration policies of the American colonial government in the Philippines encouraged such tendencies.

The family system that the Philippine Chinese brought with them may anthropologically be described as a patronymic, patrilocal, patriarchal and patrilineal system. The nuclear family has tended to be overshadowed by the stem family and often by the extended or economic family *(chia)*. Ideally in the traditional literature, the *chia* consisted of five generations living together "under one roof". This rarely occurred; two or three generations were more common.

Some social scientists have attacked the concept of the *chia* as the typical rather than the idealized form of Chinese family life. Large extended families have been a feature of only the highest socioeconomic groups in China and among Philippine Chinese. However, much of this criticism is too concerned with the physical aspect of "under one roof". The crucial characteristic of the *chia* is that the property and other forms of wealth of the group are held in common and administered by the *chia-chang,* who is the oldest effective male member of the group,

Such an emphasis on the economic unity of the *chia* is particularly relevant for understanding it in the Philippines. The attainment of the *chia* under one roof in the Philippines has been made difficult by (1) the ban on the sale of residential land to aliens, (2) the congested urban concentration of most Chinese residential areas, and (3) the adoption of an Hispanic-Malay style of architecture often ill-suited to an extended family system. Not only many members of the family unit of the Philippine Chinese live in entirely separate establishments, they often live in separate towns, other provinces, or even other countries.

It is probably only among the poorest Chinese families in the provinces and in Manila that the household (*hu*) and the economic family (*chia*) are identical. Even the household may at least be larger than the nuclear family. Although it is not necessary for the *chia* to be under one roof, much prestige is attached to such an achievement. This is clearly in recognition of the obvious economic physical, and social obstacles that only the wealthy, powerful, and prestigeful can overcome. Weightman (1965: 11-12) described the characteristics of such *chia* in Jolo. At present social scientists are studying such families in the Manila area.

In general, households of higher income status tend to hold together longer than households lower in the economic scale because of the flexibility and strength provided by their economic positions. Chinese traditional customs exalted the maintenance of these economic arrangements. Precisely because of these strong sanctions for such a pattern, an almost eventual division of the property is usually accompanied by great bitterness and considerable animosity. These bitter legal and extra-legal controversies waged by branches of powerful Chinese families tend to be concealed from Filipinos.

The Chinese in the Philippines come from areas of south China which are characterized by villages of only one or two clans. Hence, lineage and village clan associations are quite common in the Philippines. While other Chinese institutions were often banned in Spanish times, these clan village associations were already important in settling economic disputes, aiding migrants, and serving as agents for recruiting a work force.

The Philippine Chinese not only adapted commercial property to the old functions of common land ownership for the *chia,* they also adapted the old clan structures to a different political and economic environment.

In the Chinese clan, which is patrilineal, relatives who belong to the same clan possess the same clan name *(hsing).* It must be reemphasized that one is referring to the true, stone name, *not* the false, paper name. The clan lays great value on the stability, continuity, and perpetuation of those *chia* it contains. In turn, these *chia* may resort to the clan as a protective and supporting device.

If the surname distribution in the Philippines be any indication, the concentration of certain surnames in South China must be quite marked. Weightman (1965) reported the five most common Chinese surnames in the Philippines to be Tan (Ch'en), Lim (Lin), Chua (Ts'ai), Di (Li), and Ong (Wang). Together they totaled nearly forty per cent of the entire Chinese community. Tan (Ch'en) is by far the largest. Among the Jolo Chinese, Weightman found that these names represented more than fifty per cent of the entire ethnic Chinese community. The Jolo Tans were nearly twenty-five per cent of the total. Because of the long history of intermarriage in Jolo, Tan was found to be the most common name among both the Muslim and Christian Filipino groups. Since the destruction of Jolo in February, 1974, the local Chinese have not yet established any formal institutional structure. However, with the aid of a rich Manila benefactor, they did build a Tan clan lodge.

There is a tendency for occupational and commercial specialization along clan lines, e.g., the Dis in lumber, Yus in hardware, and the Mas in the hotel restaurant trade. Formerly a Go owned the largest premartial law Chinese newspaper, the *Fookien Times.* While it operated, a large part of the staff was also of that clan. Even the old KMT embassy reflected this concern with clan ties. Most of the staff were of the Ch'en clan. Although not Hokkien Tans, the first two KMT ambassadors were of the Ch'en clan. Their pictures used to be displayed in the clan halls of the Tans. However, clans in the Philippines have tended to divide along linguistic lines. The Hokkien and Cantonese maintain separate clan and multiple surname association lodges, but the rules of clan and multiple surname exogamy still hold for the two speech groups.

Despite the inroads of modernism, clan and multiple surname association exogamy still hold. Even in the large, modern Manila community, clan endogamy is quite rare and disapproved. Exogamy is maintained by example, persuasion, and group pressure. In addition, certain clans are inclined to promote affinal ties in order to promote alliances. (Omohundro, 1981: 127).

Multiple surname associations, which have already been mentioned, are exogamous alliances of two or more clans which claim some fictive or historic bond. While many social scientists have ignored or minimized the multiple surname associations, they are important in the Philippines. These exogamous, mutual aid groupings add to the social, economic, and political power of certain clans. Some anthropologists regard these groupings as mere alliances, but since they are exogamous and maintain ancestral lodges in Manila, it is more accurate to refer to them as multiple surname associations. The most prominent numerically, economically and politically are (1) the Tan-Oh-Yao-Chan-Ghu; (2) the Cua-Chua; and (3) the Lu-Co-Kho-Dhu-Kee. Cua and Lu multiple surname associations have been historic rivals. In addition, the Chan-Cu and the Yu multiple surname associations, while not too large, wield considerable economic power. Another multiple surname association traces its origin to a blood pact made in the time of the Three Kingdoms. The "Northern Names" multiple surname association groups its members in one Manila lodge. (A "Northern Name" implies Chinese who arrived in the Hokkien area of China later than most others). For decades, Muslim Chinese (not local converts) concealed their religious practices from others in a Manila multiple surname association lodge.

In any commercial endeavor, preference is given in order to members of one's *chia*, one's village clan, one's speech group's clan, one's speech group's multiple surname association, one's speech group, one's clan or multiple surname, relatives from another speech group, and finally to any Chinese of another speech group. A point of structural strain is the recognition to be given a clan relative of another speech group. As noted earlier, the clans divide along speech group lines, but the rule of clan exogamy still holds. As the Cantonese speech group declines in numbers, its members who remain in the Philippines strive to minimize previous differences. Virtually all Cantonese in the Philippines speak Hokkien anyway for social and economic reasons.

As most Chinese regardless of class now claim Filipino citizenship or at least no longer register as Chinese aliens, it has become more difficult for the Chinese to operate through the political and cultural forms which developed during the American period and the early years of Philippine independence Consequently there has been a revival of interest in clan and multiple surname association membership. It is no mere accident that the Jolo Chinese established its first formal clan lodge before rebuilding the school, the Shen Temple, or the chamber of commerce. The family, the clan and multiple surname association, and religious institutions have once again become the keys to preserving Chinese identity and economic ascendancy in the Philippines.

B. Religious Institutions

"Honor the gods, but keep distant from them" was Confucius's advice to his followers. Certainly ambivalence had characterized the Philippine Chinese response to the fanaticism of the Spanish friars and Muslim *Juramentados*. Yet, despite the cynicism and disdain of many Chinese, some Chinese even practiced Buddhism, Taoism, spirit *(Shen)* worship, and Islam during the most repressive periods of Spanish rule.

Even today, most Chinese — including the Christian elements — still practice some forms of ancestor veneration. These patterns are particularly pronounced during the Filipino holiday, All Saints Day (November 1st) and the Chinese Ching Ming (fifteenth day of the fourth lunar month). Particularly in the Chinese cemeteries, which every provincial community boasts, is the religious eclecticism of the Philippine Chinese pronounced. Buddhist, Christian, and Islamic patterns are mixed. Nothing in the behavior of the crowds at the Manila Chinese cemetery can readily distinguish Catholics, Protestants, Buddhists, or ancestor venerators. (Ironically, the Manila Chinese cemetery has become a major tourist attraction).

Shen or spirit cults have invested the Virgin Mary with attributes of the Goddess of Mercy (Kuan Yin). Saint James or Santiago has become the city god of the Manila Chinese. *El Santo Niño de Cebu* is treated by Manila Chinese as the traditional god of good fortune.

McBeath (1973) has observed that even though Philippine Chinese are now far more likely to identify with Christianity than with Buddhism, they still do not merge into the Filipino religious scene. Most Chinese Protestants attend all-Chinese churches, which in the Manila area may still divide along speech group lines (e.g., the Anglican parishes for Hokkien and Cantonese). In some areas, the Chinese Catholics have their own Chinese parishes. But even in racially and culturally mixed Catholic churches, differences in ritual behavior easily distinguish Chinese and Sinicized mestizos from Filipinos and Filipinized mestizos. Our Lady of Grace Church in Kalookan City provides candles for Filipinos and joss sticks for Chinese. Filipinos kneel before some statues, while Chinese ceremonially bow before others.

Despite the pressures and advantages of Christian affiliation, more than 60,000 Chinese still identify themselves as Buddhists. They and some Christian Chinese have generously contributed to a rapid development and expansion of Buddhist and Taoist religious facilities. The Buddhist schools and to a lesser extent the Chinese Protestant schools have been most resilient with regard to preserving Chinese language training and Chinese traditional practices despite new changes in official policies. The elite Chinese Catholic schools, which are *not* headed by ethnic Chinese, have experienced some deterioration in Chinese language skills. Increasingly, their students must resort to out of school tutoring.

This paper is most directly concerned with the processes of assimilation and their relation to the Chinese family system, However, it is germane to point out how religious institutions may interlink with family institutions and be used as a means for the preservation of Chinese cultural patterns. Kuan Yin, the happy Buddha with children, and *el Santo Niño* share many shelves in Chinese shops and homes.

C. *Other Institutions — in Eclipse*

Probably no other institutional agency so directly and effectively strove to keep the Chinese "Chinese" and to make the mestizos Chinese than did the Chinese language school system which was sanctioned by the Treaty of Amity (Article 6) between the Republic of China (KMT) and the Republic of the Philippines.

By 1961-62, there were 168 Chinese schools (42 in Manila and neighboring provinces) with an enrollment of 65,000. Writers, especially Americans, have often been unnecessarily critical and naive in their evaluation of this system at its height in the late fifties and early sixties. For all its many faults and limitations, this system was superior to any other overseas Chinese language system.

More crucially for the Philippine Chinese and many provincial Filipinos, these schools tended to be academically superior to provincial public and non-elite private schools. A few of the more exclusive Chinese sectarian schools in the Manila area offered a dual system of Chinese and Filipino schooling equal to the most expensive elite schools. Their main function, often misunderstood by critics, was not to teach the Chinese national language, but to keep the Chinese — especially the mestizos — ethnically Chinese (e.g., Hokkien). When financially able, the Cantonese used to maintain separate Cantonese schools in Manila and Cebu. This primary attempt to keep Chinese "Chinese" was reflected in the larger numbers of girls in the Chinese schools than boys,

By 1956 the Philippine government was attempting to gain control of these schools. In a process long, complicated, and often devious, the Philippine government came eventually by the early sixties to control the Philippine (English and Tagalog) sections of these schools through the Philippine Bureau of Private Schools. This supervision tended to obscure rather than to clarify the status of these schools, their numbers, and their enrollments,

The Philippine Constitution of 1972, whose full implementation has not been achieved, required the full Filipinization of all schools in the Philippines. As mentioned earlier, President Marcos, apparently worried about ramifications of future recognition of the PRC, decreed Filippinization of all schools. Thus, the old Chinese curriculum was to be totally scrapped, and the Philippine curriculum was to be substituted. This was to happen several years ago. However, a form of Chinese curriculum still survives in many schools.

The situation is becoming increasingly confused. But, despite decrees and the lack of accurate statistics, the system still operates although not as well as before. Yet, it operates better than most Philippine public and non-sectarian private schools. In many provincial towns, the "Chinese" school is still the best school. In a place like Cotabato, the "Chinese" school now enrolls more Filipinos than ethnic Chinese. Certainly, however, except in the Buddhist and perhaps Chinese Protestant schools, It has become far more difficult to maintain high literacy in Chinese.

Formerly a local Chinese school, a Chinese (Hokkien) Chamber of Commerce and where appropriate, a Cantonese Association seemed the minimal formal structures required for a Chinese provincial community. Now the schools are in decline. The Cantonese Associations have often ceased to exist as the Cantonese seem more prone to emigrate. Indeed, their Cantonese family and clan connections undoubtedly facilitated their movement to the United States, Canada, and Australia where the Chinese communities have been historically Cantonese.

Since most of the prominent Chinese businessmen are now officially Filipino, there is a tendency for the most important Chinese to avoid formal affiliation with Chinese Chambers of Commerce. They now participate indirectly through representatives or resort to their leadership in family or religious institutional agencies. Both the Federation of Chinese Chambers of Commerce and its old rival, the Manila General Chamber of Commerce, have tended to go into eclipse. New patterns of formal leadership are emerging, but it will not be as easy as in the past to identify the "real chiefs" rather than the mere "talking chiefs".

The semi-legal or criminal associations continue to lurk on the edge of the community. They can no longer be easily recognized as the allies and rivals of the now disestablished KMT embassy or the KMT party, but they still exist. The Triads (Hong Men or Ang Men) have been naively described as good samaritan Masons (McBeath, 1972) and the music associations as being mere musical enthusiasts (Lui Chi Tien, 1969, and Omohundro, 1981), but they are still as sinister as ever. Few Philippine Chinese will even acknowledge their awareness of the dreaded music associations. Their power and secrecy will probably long ensure their survival.

IV. Change and Continuity, Implications for the Future

A Filipina friend of this writer returned from a visit to the "New Society" in the Philippines, with the observation, "It never looked better, and it never was worse". This general observation cannot be so neatly applied to the status of the present day Chinese community. This in part because of so much uncertainty about what is said is being done and what actually is being done.

The movement of the Chinese out of the provinces back into the expanding ghetto of Manila had begun by the early sixties. Coller (1960) early warned how this pattern would reduce cordial ethnic interpersonal dynamics and would promote ethnic conflicts. By the late sixties, large portions of both Sinicized and Filipinized mestizos contributed heavily to the "brain drain" or "brain exchange" of professional and middle class elements. Political unrest in the seventies combined with provincial economic stagnation to empty many of the smaller Chinese communities. Cantonese, perhaps because of their clan contacts, were particularly prone to migrate. And in general, it was the Cantonese who historically had been able to maintain better relations with the local population (Wickberg,

1960; Weightman, 1960). All these recent demographic changes intensify class differences within the community and raise serious questions about the assumptions that some social scientists have made about the complex process of assimilation.

In general, the Philippine Chinese appear relieved to see the end of the near chaos of the early seventies. Government extortion is now more stable and predictable. At least during the first years of martial law, it was perceived as much less than formerly. It now seems to be growing rapidly, but the Chinese had fearfully been prepared for this development. As a group, the Chinese have little sympathy for the Marcos regime, but they have much less for his "liberal" critics who tend to be drawn from elements in the society who have appeared almost pathologically anti-Chinese. There is always the danger that elements opposed to Marcos or forces opposed to the PRC might again attempt to whip up the ugly aspects of anti-Sinicism (Coller, 1960) which lie still too close to the surface.

If the Marcos regime lasts harmoniously for a long time and if contradictions within the Chinese community are resolved, then a solution to a perennial problem may be achieved. But these are big "ifs". The most westernized and, hence, Filipinized Chinese are leaving the country. Other Chinese are withdrawing from the smaller enclaves into a few large ghettos. The new naturalization process still penalizes the poorest Chinese. The school system of the Chinese has not so much been transformed as it has been made chaotic. Sinophobia is being whipped up by groups opposed to Marcos and the PRC. (See Lande, 1978; Poa, 1979, to see how even scholars can fuel ethnic animosities).

Chapter 5
ೞಌ

The Chinese in Brisbane: Segmentation and Integration

Lawrence W. Crissman
George Beattie
James Selby

Brisbane is the capital and major metropolis for the northeastern Australian State of Queensland. Because of the city's location in the extreme southeast corner of the state at one end of an agriculturally productive and well populated coastal strip that extends for thousands of kilometers to its north, the Brisbane metropolitan area contrasts with the other Australian state capitals in having somewhat less than half of the total population of its state, which was just over 2.25 million as determined by the Census of June 30,1981. Estimates based on that enumeration indicate that there were from 7,400 to 8,500 Chinese resident in the metropolitan area, with perhaps a quarter of those numbers to be found elsewhere in the state, principally in smaller cities. The Chinese therefore comprise less than 0.5 per cent of the population of Queensland, whereas they constitute about 0.75 per cent of the people living in Brisbane. There would appear to have been nearly 90,000 Chinese in all Australia in mid-1981, 0.6 per cent of the total of 14.9 million enumerated in the Census, but they are disproportionately concentrated in Sydney and, to a lesser extent, Melbourne, each of which has a distinct "Chinatown" in its central business district.

Large numbers of Chinese first came to Australia in the 1850's, attracted by the discovery of gold in the southeastern Colonies. Despite discriminatory head-taxes and sometimes violent prejudice, they numbered over 25,000[1] in Victoria by 1857 and almost 13,000 in New South Wales by 1861, fewer than a dozen of whom were females. By 1871, over 25,000 had left those two Colonies, but another 12,000 had arrived in Australia including some 3,000 in Queensland, only one of whom was female. Some of those Queensland Chinese worked on goldfields near Brisbane but the others, some of whom had been imported from Amoy, were employed as labourers on plantations along the northern coast, there being less than fifty in Brisbane itself. Gold was discovered in northern Queensland in the early 1870's, and large numbers of Cantonese joined the rush, bringing the total number of Chinese in the state in 1881 to 11,229 (twenty-three of them female, only 115 of them in Brisbane). Total numbers in Australia that year were again over 38,000, with nearly 4,000 in the Northern Territories (a large area extending generally east and then south of Darwin in the sparsely settled center-north of the continent), where they then constituted over one-half of the non-aboriginal population. Restrictive laws introduced in Queensland in 1877 and other states in 1881 were effective in reducing the numbers of arriving Chinese, and the continued high level of departures, plus increasing mortality rates in Victoria's by then aging Chinese population, contributed to the beginning of a long decline in the Chinese population of Australia.

In 1901 there were just under 30,000 full Chinese in Australia (less than 500 of whom were female), with a disproportionate 7,672 or 26 per cent in Queensland (but only thirty-five were female). 408 were counted in Brisbane, only a small fraction of the numbers in Sydney (3,474) or Melbourne (2,431) which each had over one-third of the Chinese in their States. Only 6 per cent of all Chinese males over the age of fifteen in Australia at that time had, or had had, wives in the Commonwealth, although many had families back in China. If it is assumed that all the Chinese females enumerated were married to Chinese males, even that low percentage indicates that perhaps as many as 1,000 Chinese males had managed to obtain non-Chinese wives. The additional 3,090 persons enumerated in 1901 as "Half-Caste Chinese" (as they were designated at the time) were presumably their children[2].

As the gold fields petered out, the Chinese drifted into other occupations. Less than 8 per cent of the 8,428[3] employed Chinese returned in the Queensland Census of 1901 were miners, and some of them were working alluvial tin deposits. Over half were market gardeners, fruit growers, or were otherwise employed in agriculture, while just over 15 per cent were labourers, servants, or hotel/boarding house workers. Over 14 per cent had gone into some kind of retail business, a third of whom were hawkers. Very few Queensland Chinese (fifty-eight) were cabinet makers, unlike their cohorts in New South Wales (662 or 6.6 per cent) and Victoria (620 of 10 per cent), and none operated laundries, whereas a total of 338 Chinese did in the other two States (1901 Census figures, again reported in Choi, 1975).

One of the first acts of the new Federal Government of Australia was the Commonwealth Immigration Restriction Act of 1901. Unlike the contemporary Oriental exclusion legislation in the United States, its aim was not to preclude Chinese entry totally, because of trade and diplomatic considerations, but merely to make it uniformly difficult throughout the new nation. The net result of the law and its amendments was to disallow the entry of any non-Europeans who might possibly offer competition to white labor, and even those Chinese who were employed by other Chinese were in general only allowed into the Commonwealth of Australia on a replacement basis: for every returning gardener, clerk, or cook, another could come in.

It was virtually impossible for any Chinese to bring a wife into Australia on a permanent basis, and one had to be a wealthy man even to get one in temporarily. From 1914 to 1940, 5,231 Chinese women entered Australia, while 4,962 departed, for a net gain of only 269. That increase only occurred after 1937-38, and it more than doubled the number of foreign born Chinese females in Australia at the time. During the same period, there were 6,800 more male departures than the 66,000 arrivals (figures from Choi, 1975). Some of the departures and subsequent arrivals represent Chinese visiting their wives and families in China, while other arrivals and then departures involve students, peripatetic merchants, and transient seamen. The majority of the excess of departures over arrivals represent those in the over-sixty age categories who went back to China in retirement. Altogether, those leaving Australia and not returning contributed over 50% to the decline in the numbers of Chinese prior to World War Two. The remainder resulted from mortality among those too young or too poor to return to China.

Of the estimated 10,000 full Chinese residents in Australia in 1940[4] approximately one-fifth were female, two-thirds of whom were Australian born. Perhaps up to a third of those were not yet of marriageable age or were unmarried, so the number of married Australian-born Chinese women would have been in the neighborhood of 1,000, far less than the number of married Chinese men, indicating that many of the latter had wives outside Australia, presumably resident in China. Some 500 or so wives were in the Commonwealth for temporary visits at that time. Statistics for intermarriage are difficult to generate and interpret, as information was only recorded in terms of birthplace, not "race". However, from 1907 until 1940, when Chinese-born Russians had began to arrive in Australia as refugees from the war in China there were 70 recorded marriages in all Australia in which both bride and groom were born in China, 202 in which the bride was China-born and the groom was born elsewhere (the percentage increases during the time), and 870 marriages in which the groom was born in China and the bride elsewhere (the percentage decreases with time). Marriages of Australian-born Chinese did not appear in such statistics unless they married China-born persons. The ready conclusion to such figures is that most if not all of the Chinese-born brides would, during those years, have married Australian-born Chinese men. It seems reasonable, as a conservative estimate, to assume that an equivalent number of Australian born Chinese women would have married China-born men. The conclusion to this suppositional exercise is that a minimum of nearly 700 China-born males would have married non-Chinese during that 33 year period.

The number of part-Chinese enumerated in the censuses does not increase appreciably over 3,090 from 1901 to 1911, climbs to 3,669 in 1921, and then falls off slightly in 1933, when 300 fewer females were counted than males. In the next census, taken in 1947, only 2,950 were counted, this time with a deficiency of 250 females. Choi (1975:51) attributes the declining numbers of part Chinese between 1933 and 1947 (when they held a steady one-fourth proportion of all "Chinese") to under-enumeration. As he points out, Australian censuses have always been completed by heads of households, and it was up to them to return their children by non-Chinese spouses, or themselves if only one parent had been Chinese, as "H-C", for Half-Caste, rather than simply and unprejudicially as "Chinese" or "European" or whatever. Because Australian census figures represent such voluntary declarations, there is no way of ascertaining where the "missing" part-Chinese do appear, although some have certainly been counted as full Chinese just as some have been included as Europeans or Aboriginals. In any event, the significant aspect of "Chineseness" for this study, or any other one that is behaviorally oriented, is clearly not actual ancestry, but identity. Therefore, those persons who do not identify as Chinese, or who are not so identified by their head-of-household, can be presumed not to be culturally or socially Chinese in that context, whereas those who do identify as, or are proclaimed to be Chinese have to be regarded as such, notwithstanding any non-Chinese progenitors. That is the policy that will be followed in the remainder of this paper, in so far as the readily available information allows.

During World War Two, over 1000 Chinese were evacuated to Australia from New Guinea and the Pacific under official auspices. There are reports that many more arrived unofficially in small boats in a preview of the recent arrival of "boat-people" from Southeast Asia. They are said to have been absorbed into the existing Chinese communities and to have escaped any official enumeration down to the present. There may be an element of truth in such stories, but the numbers involved could not have been large, as the total number of full and part-Chinese in Australia was only slightly over 12,000 according to the 1947 Census. The largest concentration was in Sydney which may have had as many as 6,000 at the time. Queensland's share had fallen to 19 per cent of full Chinese, but it had one-third of the approximately 3,000 part-Chinese who were enumerated, for a total of just over 2,700. Brisbane had only one-quarter of the Chinese in Queensland, for a total of less then 700. If there had been considerable numbers of illegal immigrants they would have been apparent in a community of that size.

The Census figures are greatly at variance with those given in a short account of the history of the Chinese in Brisbane by Conrad Young. He claims, on the basis of an informant's account, that "at the beginning of the 20th century, having the Triad Holy Temple (actually built in 1885) as the center of worship, the number of Chinese residents in Brisbane reached about 4,000" (Young, 1975 : 129). He goes on to state that "the Chinese community dwindled in the 1930's to about 3,000," and that their numbers eventually declined at some unspecified time to "the fringes of less than 2,000 people." These figures are clearly far too large.

Whereas it is likely that a fair number of Chinese working remote tin deposits or employed in agriculture could have escaped enumeration in any of the censuses until well into the post-War period, it would have been far more difficult for urban Chinese, especially those with visible businesses, to escape detection. 1933 census figures published in the 1983 *Queensland Yearbook, Number Two* show 256 male and 62 female Chinese in Brisbane and a total of 2,164 males and 417 females in all Queensland. Such early census figures do, however, refer to a much smaller city, and may not include as part of the Brisbane Chinese population various market gardeners and fruit growers whose erstwhile fields are now part of Brisbane's sprawling suburbs.

Young's catalogue of Chinese businesses in Brisbane during the first quarter of the 20th century, the heyday of its "Chinatown," includes the following: numerous Chinese stores (including three he names plus two small tea shops serving a Chinese clientele) and several gambling rooms patronized by Chinese in the lower Albert Street area that he identifies as "Chinatown"; several Chinese stores in the Fortitude Valley area, none of which were situated near one another (four are identified); several Chinese furniture makers "at the end of the city" (three mentioned directly); and several Chinese businesses near City Hall (one named). The total of one 'numerous' and four 'severals' is of course indeterminate, but in this case would probably be somewhere between twenty and thirty, a range that fits a Chinese population of 300-400 much better than one of 2,000-4,000, so there is every reason to accept the census figures as being generally correct.

The visible community structure of the Chinese in the first half of the twentieth century in the various Australian state capitals and other concentrations of Chinese (Cronin, 1973) appears to have been in accordance with the "segmentary model" propounded by Crissman (1967) to describe the way in which Overseas Chinese Communities are divided internally into "speech groups" in the first instance, and then on the basis of native places and/or surnames. There is no evidence in the literature on the Australian Chinese for surname associations, but there is abundant mention of associations based on localities in China (Huck, 1967; Choi, 1975; Cronin, 1973). As the overwhelming majority of Chinese who came to Australia in the Nineteenth century as well as those who replaced some of them in the chain migration during the first half of the Twentieth century were Cantonese speakers,[5] there was no major basis for the division among speakers of the different distinct languages that are such a marked feature of some overseas Chinese communities, particularly in Southeast Asia. However, geographical and dialectical divisions among Cantonese speakers have been significant in Australia. Melbourne was basically a Szeyap community, with Toisanese predominating, while Sydney and Brisbane, the only other sizable centers of Chinese agglomeration, both had a majority of Chungshanese (Choi, 1973; Huck, 1967). Young (1975 : 131) names for voluntary associations in Brisbane that "were identified by the name of the dialect spoken by its members," and implies that there were more. (He also mentions that some Brisbane Chinese were from Fukien province.) Although there have been some revivals of certain such associations in Melbourne and Sydney, primarily because of the rising value of real estate that they happen to own, the Brisbane associations faded away long ago, and the "Triad Temple" was derelict until restored during the early 1970's after its premises had been successfully taken over by members of the Chinese Club, the only identifiable Chinese organization of the time.

Except for wealthy Chinese who often made use of such associations to further their political aims, Chinese "benevolent organizations" in overseas communities usually provided important social and other functions primarily for single mate "sojourners" who congregated in the premises they maintained in order to eat familiar food, speak their own language, talk about home, and gamble with their compatriots. The gradual decline and eventual disappearance of most such associations in Australia reflects mortality among the aged remnants of the Nineteenth century influx of immigrant Chinese, as well as the increasing proportion of assimilated, or at least integrated, Australian-born Chinese for whom they held little attraction.

In 1947, when total Chinese numbers were at their lowest since 1855, there were only 8,365[6] full Chinese resident in Australia. Slightly fewer than half were Australian-born, as were an additional 3,000-4,000 (or even more) part-Chinese. Some Chinese immigrants were still market gardeners at that time, while other Chinese, including some of the Australian-born, had moved into the wholesale or, especially, the retail fruit and vegetable business. Few, if any, cabinet makers or laundrymen were left due to difficulties in finding enough workers produced by restrictive immigration laws or as a result of prejudicial legislation governing the status of establishments employing Chinese (Choi, 1974 : 53). A major expanding area of employment and entrepreneurship was in Chinese restaurants and, especially, take-out cafes, which were beginning to become popular with white Australians. However, there were increasing numbers of relatively well-educated Australian-born Chinese who were able to find employment or business opportunities in the growing Australian economy in areas that had not been open to Chinese before the war. These trends, which have accelerated since the 1950's, were augmented greatly by the changed nature of Chinese immigration during the post-War period,

There were no major changes to the Immigration Restriction Act until 1958, but efforts to deport the war-time refugees who did not want to leave ended in 1949 with changed governments in both Australia and China, thereby creating some additional 800 Chinese with rights of residence. A large scale influx of Asian students, including large numbers of Chinese from Hong Kong, Malaysia and Singapore, began after 1959 and has grown steadily since, at least until the imposition of special fees for foreign students in tertiary institutions which began in the early 1980's. Some of the earlier Chinese students were able to stay in Australia because of employment or marriage, while others, up to the present, have been able to return to Australia after spending some time abroad.

In 1956 a more "liberal" attitude was adopted towards foreign-born Chinese already in Australia — they could change employment freely, could become permanent residents with full entitlements to social services, and could even become naturalized citizens with the right to introduce dependents after 15 years residence. At the same time, restrictions on the entry of replacements for returning Chinese were tightened. In 1958 the infamous "dictation test" in any European language chosen at the whim of immigration officials (which had been instituted in 1903 on a South African model) was abandoned and the entry of "distinguished and highly qualified" persons was allowed, nominally without regard to their "race." In 1966, the "White Australia" policy was finally officially set aside, although preference was still given to European migrants. However, since that time non-Europeans can become naturalized citizens in five years, the same as Europeans, and can then bring in their dependents. At the same time, immigration was opened to persons with high attainments, professions, and skills that were in demand without respect to their origins, and such persons could also bring their dependents with them (Choi, 1975). The effects of these changes in immigration policies on the Chinese in Brisbane, Queensland, and Australia are displayed in Table 1.

Table 1
Number of Chinese in Brisbane, Queensland, and Australia, 1947-1981

Figures in brackets are full-Chinese, A.=Australia and F.=Foreign Born

	Brisbane[1]	% of	Q'land	% of	Australia	Transient [% of Foreign Born]	Students [% of Foreign Born]	Refugees [% of Foreign Born]
1947								
A. Born	427	24.4	1,754	26.3	6,678			
	(188)	24.4	(772)	20.7	(3,728)			
F. Born	235	24.4	965	17.8	5,416	776 [14.3]		800 [14.8]
Total	662	24.4	2,719	22.5	12,094			
	(423)	24.4	(1,737)	19.0	(9,144)			
1961								
A. Born	766	36.6	2,096	25.0	8,393			
	(420)	36.6	(1,150)	21	(5,550)			
F. Born	552	36.6	1,508	10.1	15,175	1,597 [10.5]	7,824 [61.6]	
Total	1,318	36.6	3,604	15.3	23,568			
	(972)	36.6	(2,658)	13.0	(20,725)			
1966								
A. Born	896	40.2	2,216	22.9	9,658			
	(583)	49.4	(1,181)	19.8	(5,976)			
F. Born	601$_e$	50.0$_e$	1,211	7.1	17,065	1,570 [9.2]	8,502 [49.8]	
Total[2]	1,497	43.7	3,427	12.8	26,723			
	(1,184)	49.5	(2,392)	11.0	(23,041)			
1976								
A. Born	643	46.7	1,376	13.9	9,892			
F. Born	1,753	70.4	2,490	9.3	26,746	2000$_e$ [7.5]	9000$_e$ [33.6]	100 [.04]
Total	2,396	63.6	3,866	10.3	36,638			
1981								
A. Born	700$_c$	46.7	1,500$_c$	12.5	12,000$_e$			
F. Born	7,300$_p$	81.1	9,000$_p$	12.0	75,000$_p$	2,500$_e$ [3.2]	10,000$_e$ [13.3]	30,000$_p$ [40.0]
Total	8,000$_e$	76.2	10,500$_e$	12.1	87,000$_e$			

1 Brisbane figures for 1947 and 1961 were all calculated proportionally to the known percentage of the total Queensland Chinese in the city.
2 These 1976 Figures were supplied by Charles A. Price, A.N.U.
e Estimates
c Calculations based on natural increase since 1976 at the Australian average.
p Projections based on 1976 proportions of Chinese in various immigrant groups, adjusted for known or presumed changes.

After discounting transients and students, Choi (1975 : 65) calculated that the average annual growth of Australia's resident Chinese population from 1947 to 1966 was only about 150 per year, with about equal numbers of males and females. That figure is likely to be low, as he assumed that there were no Chinese foreign students in Australia in 1947 whereas there must have been some. However, there does not appear to have been any Australian equivalent to the large numbers of Mandarin-speaking Chinese professionals and students who were sent to the United States by the Nationalists after World War Two (Choi, 1975 : 106). When the Chinese Communists gained control of China, a number of wealthy and well connected Chinese were allowed into the United States, and many of those already there for training elected not to return to China or to join the Nationalist remnants in exile on Taiwan. Such people formed an intellectual and financial elite for the Chinese in the United States that was lacking in Australia. Nonetheless, in 1966 there were more Australian Chinese professionals (17 per cent) than blue collar workers (14 per cent, compared to 35 per cent in the total Australian workforce), while 18 per cent of Chinese were in white collar positions, another 18 per cent were in the service sector, and 15 per cent were in transport and communications. Only 4 per cent were employed in agriculture (Inglis, 1972).

In the 1960's the Chinese in both Sydney (Lee, 1963; Teo, [nee Lee], 1971) and Melbourne (Huck, 1967; Choi, 1972 and 1975) were no longer concentrated around the old "Chinatowns" in the central business districts. They had declined considerably with the death or departure of the remnants of the old sojourners, and were principally just collections of groceries and speciality shops serving the widespread Chinese population, and restaurants which drew non-Chinese clientele from all over. The great majority of Australian Chinese were by then dispersed throughout the suburbs in accordance with their occupations. All of the authors who have written about Chinese in that time period have emphasized the high degree of integration or outright assimilation of the Chinese who, unlike their early Twentieth century precursors, did not experience any great amount of prejudice or overt discrimination and were able to take their place as individual members of Australian society according to their wealth, education, and employment,

A similar situation existed among the much smaller numbers of Chinese in Brisbane, which saw its share of Queensland's Chinese climb from under 25% in 1947 to nearly 50% by 1966, simultaneous with the decline in Queensland's share of Australia's Chinese from 19% to 11%. As the state total went from 2,719 in 1947 to 3,604 in 1961, and then declined to 3,427 in 1966 presumably because of a loss of aged foreign born, the city's Chinese numbers grew steadily, though slowly, to nearly 1,500. Queensland appears to have had a much higher than average proportion of Australian-born Chinese and part-Chinese from the end of the 19th century onwards. As late as 1966, only a third of the state's Chinese were foreign born, and Brisbane is estimated to have had half of them. Even so, the Australian born were a 60 percent majority of the city's Chinese population, whereas they were only slightly over a third of the Australian total.

That situation had reversed dramatically by 1976, when only 643 Australian-born Chinese were enumerated in Brisbane due to the disappearance of a number of part-Chinese from the Census category.[7] Foreign born Chinese approximately trebled their numbers during the decade to 1,753 (out of 2,490 in all Queensland). Most of the new Chinese, who came into Australia at an average rate of 866 per year from 1966-1976, settled in the capital cities. Due to the new immigration policy, there were, in addition to the continuing high numbers of students, many family groups headed by professionals or other well-educated and well-employed men. They did not, of course, congregate around the old Chinatowns (Brisbane, after all, lacked even the semblance of one at the time), but added to the suburban dispersal of the Chinese that was evident in the mid-1960's. Prince (1975:51) reports concentrations of Chinese in Brisbane's old affluent western suburbs near the University of Queensland, with others scattered throughout the sprawl that constitutes the city.

The origins of the newcomers also changed, as just under 30 per cent of the 1976 total of 26,748 foreign-born were from China, and many of them had been in Australia for a long time. Some of the newcomers born in China would have been raised in Hong Kong and educated in English, while the Hong Kong-born contributed 4,556 to the total in their own right, and Singapore and Malaysia together accounted for 9,265. The estimated 9,000 foreign Chinese students were largely from those places. Other significant numbers of Australian Chinese were born in Indonesia (898), Papua New Guinea (1301), Fiji (243), and Timor (603). Another 1,927 came from all over the world.[8] The estimates for the major components of the Brisbane and Queensland Chinese in 1976 are displayed on Table 2. Brisbane had less than its proportional share of

Table 2
Composition of the Brisbane, Queensland and Australian Chinese, 1976 Census

	Brisbane	% of	Q'land	% of	Australia
Born in:					
Australia	643	46.7	1,376	13.9	9,892
China (and Taiwan)	450*	60.0*	750*	9.7*	7,749
	(25*)	(50.0*)	(50*)	(24.3*)	(206)
Hong Kong	200*	72.7*	275*	6.0*	4,556
Singapore	100*	80.0*	125*	6.2*	2,007
Malaysia	350*	77.8*	450*	6.2*	7,258
Indo-China	25*	83.3*	30*	18.2*	165
Papua New Guinea	500*	76.9*	650*	50.0*	1,301
Other	100*	66.7*	150*	4.3*	3,504
Total	2,393	62.0	38	10.6	36,638

*Estimates, derived from census tabulations made by Charles A. Price, A.N.U., which show for all Australia the proportions of declared Chinese among people born in the specified countries. He has also provided total figures for Australian and foreign born Chinese in both Brisbane and Queensland. None of his figures include proportional distributions of respondents who did not state their race. These estimates are educated guesses based on total numbers from the countries resident in Brisbane and Queensland, plus knowledge of the Brisbane Chinese.

foreign-born from China, Hong Kong, Malaysia and in the residual "other" category, largely because the Chinese overseas students were (and are) concentrated in Sydney and Melbourne, and there are few if any people in Queensland from Timor and some of the other places like Christmas Island that have contributed significant numbers of Chinese elsewhere. However, nearly one-half of the Chinese from Papua New Guinea have come to Queensland, and most of them are in Brisbane. There are also proportionally more Australian-born Chinese in Queensland's northern coastal cities than in Brisbane.

A Chinese Club of Queensland was founded in Brisbane in 1956, ostensibly to focus ethnic celebrations and to prepare the children of members for Australian citizenship, which at that time may have looked like becoming remotely possible. The original membership was drawn from the established merchants and professionals, some of whom were Australian-born. However, the club was, and has remained, essentially a Cantonese organization. Chinese language classes were conducted for a time, and a variety of Australian sporting activities were promoted, along with judo (Chinese martial arts had not yet been popularized). The Chinese Club was active in creating a Chinese Temple Society which gained title to the potentially very valuable premises of the abandoned "Triad Temple" in an Act of State Parliament in 1963. The temple was subsequently renovated with materials imported from China, and has had as its caretaker for many years the English widow of a Chinese man (Prince, 1975), while the members of its governing Committee have been Christian members and officers of the Chinese Club.

As time passed, the Chinese Club in Brisbane became active in fund raising for charitable organizations including the Lady Mayoress' Charitable Fund, and has evolved into the sort of Chinese community front-organization that is found in Hawaii and other American cities. It is basically the same as other "ethnic" clubs in Australia, such as the German Club and the Greek Club. Typically it is now most active in promoting the celebration of events in the Chinese calendar and other affairs at the Club itself, at which prominent figures in non-Chinese business, professional, and especially political circles are ostentatiously included. The main message they are putting across seems to be that, "We Chinese in Australia might have our quaint traditions and strange festivals, and we do know how to prepare deliciously different food, but we are really just regular guys like you other Australians and it is quite safe to do business with us." Despite rumours of a pro-communist circle among some members, the club is largely regarded by non-member Chinese as a kind of established men's group that is limited to those with wealth and standing in the larger Australian community. It presently claims to have about 400 members, a quarter of whom are non-Chinese associates, while only 20% are Australian-born Chinese. According to its brochure, some members live in other states and even overseas. Despite some apparent degree of internal factionalism and hints of financial difficulties, the club has ambitious plans for the construction of new premises and a block of flats on land it owns.[9]

The influx of Chinese from Papua New Guinea began in the mid-seventies, around the time that the country was granted its independence from Australia. Those Chinese who had or were qualified for Australian citizenship had the option of staying, but many, especially those with the substantial capital required to start new businesses, decided to take up residence in Australia. The New Guinea Chinese are an interesting group of people in their own right who were studied by David Wu (1970 and 1977) prior to the independence of the former Trust Territory.

> Prior to 1958 the Australians largely restricted the Chinese to New Ireland. After that date, they were allowed to become naturalized Australian citizens, and were thereby free to move throughout the territory, where they could exploit the virtually unoccupied niche of retail trade. It offered such opportunities that many left government positions in order to go into business. (Crissman, 1977 : 100-101)

Approximately one sixth of the New Guinea Chinese have some degree or other of Melanesian ancestry, and their first language was predominantly Melanesian pidgin (Wu, 1977), although many were educated in English. Such was their emphasis on success in business that wealth and achievement in commercial activities became the sole indicator of their social standing. In addition, that same criterion was even used to attribute full Chinese identity to some "mixed blood" persons and to deny it to others who were not successful.

When the New Guinea Chinese first began arriving in Brisbane they were welcomed by the established Cantonese in the Chinese Club, presumably because of the considerable wealth and business energy they brought with them. However, it soon became apparent that the newcomers wanted to change the nature of the Club and its activities to suit their drinking and gambling proclivities. According to hearsay, such were the animosities that were generated by this cultural conflict that on one occasion the police had to be called in to restore order and prevent more overt violence. After that fracas, the local New Guinea Chinese went their own way and formed their own social club, called the Cathay Club, located in a southern suburb near where their residences are concentrated.

In 1979, some of the increasing number of professional Chinese from the region of the Straights of Malacca founded the Australian Asian Family Association, which has subsequently expanded its geographical focus to include all Malaysia plus Singapore, but it has no plans to include any others with different origins. Membership fees are very modest, but the group is quite selective about who is admitted. Current membership is about 250, including a few non-Chinese, but all appear to be professional people. The association is involved with celebrating Malaysian versions of ethnic Chinese festivals in order to keep their children in touch with their cultural heritage, but the identification that they wish to retain is with the Chinese from the Southeast Asian region they themselves were born in, not with China *per se,* or with the province of Fukien that many of their ancestors originally came from.

Some members of the Australian Asian Family Association also belong to the Brisbane Chinese Christian Church, which is multi-denominational but has some Baptist connections. It was begun about 1981, and has a current congregation of around 100 persons including a good number of expatriot students. It conducts the normal sort of Church related social events in addition to religious observances, which are held at their premises in a southern suburb. There is another Chinese church that meets on the other side of the river that divides the city, near the concentration of well-placed Chinese that Prince mentioned.

The local overseas Chinese students[10] maintain two separate clubs centered on the University of Queensland, The Hong Kong Student's Association and the Singapore Society. The latter one apparently includes Malaysian students as well. They hold dances, go on outings, and organize athletic contests with each other. The Hong Kong organization puts out a publication with the curious title of *Zealots,* now in its 15th year, which contains articles and features in both Chinese and English. The whole orientation is to student life and to keeping in touch with events of interest back home. There would appear to be little contact between the Chinese students and the permanent Chinese residents from their respective places, as the former have their studies and special interests and will eventually have to go back home, whereas the latter have their families, friends and professions in Australia. However, some ex-students who have gained residence rights in Australia do retain membership in the relevant student organization.

Prince, writing in 1975, mentions that in addition to the Chinese Temple and the Chinese Club there had been two other Chinese institutions in Brisbane "in the recent past". One was the Chinese Citizen's Association and the other was the China Society. However, she gives no indication of what their constituencies might have been. She goes on to discuss the Australia-China Society, which as she points out was devoted "to the establishment of good relations with communist China". It is still in existence, having been founded in the mid 1950's by trade unionists and other white Australians. According to Prince it held little appeal for members of the Chinese community. However, this seems to have changed somewhat since the Whitlam Government established diplomatic relations with the peoples Republic of China, and the controlling force in the organization is now Chinese although a number of non-Chinese, including some prominent academics, are also members. It is affiliated with a similar national organization and runs a bookshop selling literature from the PRC, through which tours of China are available. There is no question as to where the sentiments of its 200 or so members lie, or what its connections are. There appear not to be enough people associated with the KMT Government on Taiwan, or enough outside support from it, to create an organization with opposing political allegiances. Most Brisbane Chinese are not very politicized, except perhaps the newcomers from Indo-China.

The most visible "Chinese" organizations in Brisbane are the various martial arts academies, some of which appear to be quite prosperous. One of them has sponsored an organization called the Australian Chinese Association that has as its ostensible purpose the promotion of Chinese culture, presumably meaning things like T'ai-chi Ch'uan and festival performances like the "Dragon Dance", although Mandarin language classes are said to have been offered. The membership, like the clientele of the academies, is primarily non-Chinese, although the leadership has been described as a splinter group of the Chinese Club.

As a matter of fact, participation by the Brisbane Chinese in any of the various associations that have been described is not particularly high. George Beattie, who conducted an extensive survey of a representative sample of Chinese in the city (excluding those from Indo-China) in 1981, found that only fifty-nine of his 196 interviewees said that they were members of any club whatever (including one who was a member of the Old Irish Association). Only thirteen belonged to one of the Chinese organizations, including one who belonged to two. The ones mentioned were the Chinese Club (12), the Australian Asian Family Association (6), the Cathay Club (4), the Hong Kong Students Association (5), the Australia-Chinese Society (2), and various martial arts and related organizations (3). However, a much higher 37 per cent had visited some club in the previous six months. Given the dispersed and occupationally integrated nature of the local Chinese population that was sampled, it is perhaps not surprising that the Chinese associations do not appear to play any great role in the lives of the large majority of Brisbane Chinese. They are however, indicative of the major components of the local Chinese population, and in the absence of any others, such as a Chinese Chamber of Commerce, for instance, they say quite a lot about the Brisbane Chinese. Significantly, club membership was considerably higher among Australian-born Chinese who on the whole tended not to belong to specifically Chinese associations.

Only 66 per cent of the Brisbane Chinese sampled by Beattie agreed with the statement that "Most Australians are friendly towards the Chinese," but only eight totally disagreed, the remainder being somewhat ambivalent indicating that they thought that there were many Australians who were not disposed to be friendly towards them, even though most (84 per cent of the total), did have some close non-Chinese friends. When asked whether they had been visited recently by a non-Chinese friend, 120 out of 196 respondents replied in the affirmative, with percentages ranging in the eighties for Australian and Malaysian born, in the sixties for Hong Kong and New Guinea Chinese, and in the forties for those born in China and other countries. The lower proportion of China-born who were visited by non-Chinese friends is explainable by the fact that they include more elderly people, some of whom speak little or no English. There are a number of older people from New Guinea as well, as they often came in large family groups, but language is not a particular problem for them, or for the Hong Kong born either, except for a few elderly women. The relatively high degree of interaction with non-Chinese displayed by the Malaysian Chinese, which was equivalent to that of the Australian born, is not surprising, as they are the most highly educated, professional, and dispersed of all the Brisbane Chinese.

Foreign born interviewees were graded according to their English proficiency. 89 per cent of those from Malaysia and Singapore were rated as fluent, with the New Guineans close behind with 85 per cent, although that could be the result of a sample bias as older, presumably non-English speaking family members are underrepresented. The remainder, with the exception of one individual from each group who was regarded as having only a fair command of English, were all rated as good speakers. In contrast, only 60 per cent of the Hong Kong born Chinese were judged to be fluent, while an additional 21 per cent had good proficiency and only three females were merely fair. However, the China-born present a very different picture. Only a third were fluent in English, while an equal proportion were unable to speak any at all, the other third being about equally split between the good and the fair. There were twice as many females as males among the non-English speakers, who together with those with only fair ability had a mean age on arrival in Australia of nearly forty and had on the average been in Australia for nearly fifteen years.

Despite the high proportion of the Brisbane Chinese sample who can speak good or fluent English, a majority (56 per cent) claimed that some variety of Chinese was the language usually used at home, while an additional 8 per cent said that both Chinese and English were used to approximately the same degree. If the Australian born are excluded, only 17 per cent of whom use any Chinese at home, the percentages rise to 61 per cent and 9 per cent respectively. Table 3 shows the differences among the foreign born according to their origins. Unsurprisingly, the China born overwhelmingly speak Chinese at home, while the only group in which English predominates are the Malaysians. A good number of them were educated at the tertiary level in Australia, while others had an English education in Malaysia or Singapore. The New Guinea Chinese, who among those sampled are nearly as fluent in English as the Malaysian / Singaporean group, contained far fewer persons with tertiary, or even secondary educations, and their families contain more elderly people in Australia. There is an association generally between level of education attained and the use of English in the home, but some of the reasons for it are complex while others are apparently simple.

Table 3
Language Used at Home in Per Cent

Born in	Chinese	English	Both
Australia	17%	83%	0
China	81%	19%	0
Hong Kong	62%	19%	19%
Malaysia	29%	61%	10%
New Guinea	63%	28%	9%
Other countries	44%	37%	19%

Beattie's Brisbane sample contains many more men than women who had intermarried with non-Chinese, but that is an artifact of the sample selection as it was drawn from people on the electoral rolls or in the telephone book with Chinese names. The discrepancy largely disappears in a tabulation of respondents' relatives who had intermarried. 60 per cent of the male Australian-born Chinese had married non-Chinese, while 87 per cent of them had relatives who had. Among males in the sample, the Hong Kong born (6 per cent) and the China born (12.5 per cent) had the lowest frequency of intermarriage, with those born in other foreign countries being only slightly higher: Malaysia 19 per cent, New Guinea 18 per cent, and others 16 per cent. However, and except for the residual "Others" (31 per cent), around 50 per cent of the rest of the Chinese from China, Hong Kong, and Malaysia all had relatives who had married non-Chinese. Australian Bureau of Statistics information on interracial marriages continues to be of little use for reasons mentioned, but they do indicate an increasing degree of intermarriage by people born in China, who by now are again mostly Chinese, as the white Russians and other World War II refugees would in general have married some time ago.

Attitudes expressed by respondents in the Brisbane sample were quite neutral with respect to marriages with non-Chinese, with only 17 per cent ranking "must be Chinese" first in a list of characteristics held to be most important in choosing a marriage partner, but even they also mentioned that they felt that love and compatibility were also very important. Actually, over one half of the interviewees declined to rank the characteristics included in the questionnaire because love and compatibility were not on the list. Of those who did consent to rank the choices offered, 38 per cent put "family background" first. "Work position" was the second or third preference of the majority, while "must be Chinese" was regarded as least important by most. There would appear to be few impediments to marriages with non-Chinese among any of the Australian Chinese in the categories already discussed.

All the numbers of foreign-born Chinese from traditional sources increase substantially from 1976 to 1981, as a comparison of Tables 2 and 4 show, but the arrival in Australia of Indo-Chinese refugees has changed the composition of the Australian Chinese quite fundamentally. Refugee intakes began with small numbers in 1975 and 1976, then increased dramatically from 1978 and have remained at high levels since. Only a few Vietnamese, Kampuchean and Laotian refugees in the first intakes were ethnic Chinese, but the majority of "boat people" refugees from Vietnam who flooded into the camps in Southeast Asia in the later periods were in fact Chinese.[11] Nancy Viviani (1983) has put the overall proportion of Chinese in the camps before 1980 at at least 60 per cent, and maintains that the process of selecting those who were sent to Australia was essentially random,[12] so that the same proportion of ethnic Chinese came to Australia. The manager of the Wacol Migrant Centre in Brisbane has said that as high as 80 per cent of the refugees settled in Brisbane were Chinese. Unfortunately, the immigration department appears to be uninterested in the ethnic composition of its refugee intakes as it has made no attempt to distinguish ethnic Chinese from ethnic Vietnamese, etc., and no official figures will ever be available.

Our estimates for the increase in Chinese numbers by June 1981, based on 50-60 per cent of all Indo-Chinese refugees being ethnic Chinese, are shown on Table 4. Although they were only about one third of all Chinese in Australia at that time, they comprised approximately one-half of the total number of Chinese in Brisbane as they were distributed among the states in rough proportion to their populations, but only about 1,000

Table 4

Estimated Composition of the Brisbane, Queensland, and Australian Chinese, 1981

Born in	Brisbane	% of	Q'land	% of	Australia	Assumed % of Chinese among newcomers
Australia	700	46.7	1,500	12.5	12,000	100
China including Taiwan	1,100	68.8	1,600	11.6	13,750	90
Hong Kong	500	62.5	800	7.9	10,100	75
Singapore	150	75.0	200	6.7	3000	66.7
Malaysia	650	72.2	900	8.1	11,150	33.3
Indo-China	3,000-4,000	83.3-88.9	3,600-4500	14.4-15.0	25000-30,000	50-60
Papua New Guinea	1,000	80.0	1,250	50.0	2,500	25
Other	300	85.7	350	4.1	8,500	.17
Totals	7,400-8,500	72.5-77.3	10.200-11,000	11.9-12.1	86,000-91,000	

*Increase in 1981 census figures over 1976 figures for numbers born in the specified countries were apportioned to the Chinese according to the percentages in the last column, The .17 per cent for "other" is an aggregate figure-the increase *of e5.000* was actually calculated on a country by country basis.

refugees settled outside the state capital. Their numbers have continued to grow since the 1981 Census, but perhaps less rapidly as they probably were not quite so highly represented in the new arrivals to the refugee camps after 1980, although the picture is confused. Most of those who came under the "orderly departures" scheme were Chinese, but their numbers have not been great.

The Chinese who came to Australia from Vietnam were almost all from Cholon, Saigon's Chinatown. They all speak Vietnamese in addition to a Chinese language, usually Cantonese. Despite this basis for ethnic affinity, the established Cantonese-oriented leadership of Brisbane's Chinese Club, whether Australian-born or from China or Hong Kong, is on record as opposing the entry of refugee Chinese. After all, the last thing they want are large numbers of new, unacculturated, poor Chinese to come and undo all their hard work in establishing an identity for local Chinese as affluent participants in the Australian business and professional worlds. As well, they potentially threaten the established club leadership.

Unlike the ethnic Vietnamese, many of whom are Catholics who were associated with the government of South Vietnam and who have lost both a war and a country, the ethnic Chinese were basically an apolitical minority in Vietnam, and are able to cope with their status in Australia much better. In fact, the two groups have little in common, however indistinguishable they may appear to be to other Australians (including the Immigration Department), and in Brisbane, as in Sydney and Melbourne, they have segregated themselves residentially after leaving the migrant centers.[13] In Brisbane, few of the ethnic Vietnamese have moved far from the Wacol Migrant Centre, while the ethnic Chinese have tended to congregate in the West End, an old suburb across the river from the Central Business District which has been a low rent migrant area since World War II.

About the same percentage of ethnic Vietnamese and ethnic Chinese refugees in Brisbane were unemployed when Viviani conducted her survey of Indo-Chinese refugees in Brisbane in 1979 and 1980, and both had suffered the same "deskilling" due to non-acceptance of professional and educational qualifications. However, in contrast to the ethnic Vietnamese, the new Chinese are not particularly highly educated, and what education they have had is in Chinese. They are essentially business oriented, but unlike the New Guinea Chinese who have a similar business background, most of the refugees were unable to bring any capital into Australia and have had to start from scratch. However, there are some who have been able to acquire money by mobilizing Cholon Chinese connections with other Southeast Asian communities, and even Hong Kong and Taiwan. Some small businesses providing Chinese goods and services, such as noodle sellers and groceries, are beginning to appear. Interestingly, some Vietnamese Chinese have resumed their old relationship with the ethnic Vietnamese by supplying their needs for such things as duck embryos for their Tet celebrations, and by acting as labour brokers or the organizers of piece work for them. However there have not been any great inroads by the refugee Chinese into the established Chinese businesses, such as restaurants and stores in Brisbane's new "China town" that began to form in The Valley just to the north of the Central Business District in the late 1970's.

Some of the new Chinese have found employment with old Chinese, and familiar stories of low wages, long hours, and other exploitation are heard. However, most of those who are employed have obtained factory work or are otherwise working for non-Chinese. Reports of discrimination and prejudice in the workplace are not uncommon, but seem to be much more prevalent when a number of refugees are employed by the same firm. Most of the ethnic Chinese, again in contrast with the ethnic Vietnamese, live in corporate domestic units in which most adults contribute to a common budget. Some of these are surrogate families formed by groups of young single males, who make up a significant portion of the new Chinese. (All of the above information is from Viviani, 1983).

It is interesting that the Vietnamese Chinese have begun patronizing the old Chinese Temple, where they actually engage in traditional types of supplication of the deities, much to the consternation of the Chinese Christians who maintain it as a Chinese curio and the Englishwoman they installed to explain it to the curious. The Vietnamese Chinese have also been the preponderant subscribers to the new Saturday Mandarin language schools that have been organized, first in the West End but now in outlying suburbs as well, by established Chinese, some of whom have Nationalist connections. The hundreds of refugee children sent to such schools to learn Mandarin is perhaps indicative of their parents' ambivalent feelings about being in Australia. In any event, it is clear that they do not want their children to lose their identities as Chinese, and consider weekend Mandarin language instruction to be more important for their children than more practice in English.

There is yet another category of new Chinese who have recently been entering Australia. These are wealthy capitalists from Malaysia and Singapore and, especially quite recently because of fears of the impending Communist takeover, from Hong Kong. Some are merely foreign investors seeking profitable places for their spare millions, whereas others are immigrating and establishing businesses or factories in what they regard as a safe haven for their wealth. Overall, the numbers of people may not be large, especially in comparison with the tens of thousands of poor Vietnamese Chinese, but the amount of money involved is significant. According to press reports, Asian investment in Australia, most of it in property, amounted to $1000 million in the March quarter of 1983, $417 million of it from Hong Kong alone.

In a recent article, Richard H. Thompson has proposed what he terms a "class model" to replace Crissman's "segmentary model", which he claims "no longer describes a contemporary social organisation of North America's urban Chinese communities" (1980:265). His alternative is applicable only to major Chinatowns with a population over 50,000, and in which the majority consists of recently immigrated Chinese. Although none of the Australian capital city Chinese populations are that large, Sydney's is getting there, and a large and increasing percentage of Australia's Chinese are very recent immigrants. Thompson's essential thesis is that the old Chinese community organizations began to decline when they were unable to recruit new sojourners, and the old Chinatown merchant elite was replaced by a new, suburbanized, largely professional or capitalist Chinese elite. Then, when immigration restrictions were relaxed in the 1960's, both Canada and the United States began receiving large numbers of new Chinese, primarily through and from Hong Kong. Although they came as family groups, they congregated in the inner areas of large cities which had had declining Chinatowns, thereby reviving them in terms of population if not prosperity. Although many of the newcomers, the family heads anyway, were relatively well educated, they were confined to lower-level proletarian positions in large scale capitalist enterprises, often ones owned and operated by well connected, bicultural American-born Chinese.

Advantages of the "class model" are said to be: 1) it highlights the complex internal stratification in the Chinese community; 2) it emphasizes economic and political aspects of community organization; 3) it ties events occurring in the Chinese community to larger processes occurring in the national and world economics, 4) it best describes the composition and goals of new organizations and associations; 5) the Chinese in North America themselves perceive their social organization as class based, and 6) it offers a structural basis for community organization as opposed to a model that emphasizes differing cultural or psychological orientations (such as Weiss, 1974, proposes). The structure of large Chinese communities is described in terms of four classes: the Chinese bourgeoisie, the Chinese petty bourgeoisie, a Chinese "new middle class", and a Chinese proletariat. Thompson admits that his "class model" describes relatively less about contemporary large Chinatowns than Crissman's "segmentary model" did for traditional urban overseas Chinese communities, primarily because class is not as exclusive an organizing principle as ethnic segmentation used to be.

Are Australia's capital city Chinese communities headed towards a class system such as Thompson describes? All the elements are certainly there, especially now that the Vietnamese Chinese proletariat has been added and overseas Chinese capital is pouring in. However, there are still profound ethnic cleavages among the Australian Chinese, perhaps more so than among the North American Chinese, who have always been preponderantly Cantonese, except for the post-war Mandarin speaking capitalist and professional elite. Most of the Australian Chinese may have originally been Cantonese, but the major divisions based on birthplace as shown in Tables 2 and 4 have replaced the old ethnic distinctions derived from origins in China with a new set of ethnic distinctions based on cultural and other differences derived from the very different situations in the countries where they were born and/or raised. Australian Chinese are in fundamental ways more like other Australians than foreign born Chinese. Malaysian and Singaporian Chinese are highly Westernized and the ones who came to Australia were highly educated professionals. Hong Kong people have their own identity and cosmopolitanism, whereas the China-born Chinese are perhaps more traditional. The New Guinea Chinese have their own distinct characteristics, while the Vietnamese Chinese are first and foremost Vietnamese, even as the other Chinese in Australia view them. Therefore, for the time being anyway, the "segmentary model," modified to incorporate intermediate origins, is still relevant to Australia's Chinese communities. Analyses in terms of a "class model" may become increasingly relevant, however.

Notes

1. All of the figures in this paragraph and the next are official Census totals as reported in Choi (1975). There have been claims that the Chinese were seriously under-enumerated in these early tallies, and that there may have been as many as twice the recorded numbers of Chinese. Even if that was the case, the patterns would be about the same.
2. Many Chinese (and some Japanese) took aboriginal women as wives, especially in northern Queensland and the Northern Territory. Unlike whites, who also cohabited with aboriginals, Chinese fathers took an interest in their children and stayed to be cared for in their old age. However, the children of Chinese fathers and aboriginal mothers are unlikely to have been counted as part-Chinese because anyone with any aboriginal ancestry was legally classified as aboriginal and denied civil liberties, As a result, such children were raised as members of aboriginal communities, not as Chinese. They and their descendants, who constitute 5-10 per cent of the northern aboriginals, are called "yella fellas" because of their known ancestry and rather distinct physiognomy. There are also "white fellas," who have some noticeable degree of European ancestry, and "black fellas," who are not noticeably mixed. The fact that the yella fellas are a category of aboriginal and have not maintained any Chinese connections is neatly illustrated by the way they employ their fathers' first names or nicknames (Achee or Parted, for instance) as their own last names in aboriginal fashion, rather than retaining their Chinese surnames. Some of the most prominent aboriginal political and economic entrepreneurs have known Chinese forbears and obvious Asian features.
3. Cronin (1973: 3) gives a similar figure of 8,587 for Chinese in Queensland at the end of the 19th century. These numbers are significantly larger than the one given in the last paragraph for the total number of Chinese in Queensland, an anomaly not present in comparable figures for other states. If the numbers of employed "Chinese" include part-Chinese, which could explain the difference, then a disproportional percentage of them were in Queensland at the time.
4. These estimates for 1940 are derived from figures for other years presented in Choi (1975)
5. Some Hokkiens are known to have settled in Sydney, but their numbers were never significant (Teo 1971). Sydney's Chinese community is far larger and more diverse than any other in Australia, and is said to have included Teochiu from Swatow, Hailams, and people from various Northern localities (Choi, 1973; Huck, 1967; and Teo, 1971).
6. The total census figure for 1947 of 9,144 included 779 transients, mainly seamen.

7   The 1976 Census form did not specifically include Chinese as one of its racial categories, but "Chinese" was one of the two classifications that were extracted from the "other origin" category. Respondents were instructed to state one origin only, and if mixed to indicate the one to which the person considered himself/herself to belong. Considerable numbers of Australian-born part-Chinese appear not to have claimed to be Chinese, as the number of ABC's nationwide only increases by 2.4 per cent over 1966, while the numbers in Queensland fall by a precipitous 40 per cent and Brisbane loses 29 per cent.

8   These figures were supplied by Charles A. Price, B.N.U.

9   Information on Chinese associations in Brisbane was gathered by James Selby, who approached the Chinese Club for help in establishing a representative sample of elderly Chinese for inclusion in his M.Phil research on the availability and use of public services by elderly people in Brisbane (Selby, 1983a; 1983b). They eventually produced a list of nice little old ladies and gentlemen who made less use of public programmes than other categories of the aged because they were so well cared for by sons or daughters. However he also came across some other aged Chinese who were less fortunate, including one sorry old man who had been victimized by other Chinese since his arrival before World War Two.

10 In 1983 the University of Queensland had 79 students from Hong Kong (15 female), 154 from Malaysia (48 female), and 42 (12 female) from Singapore. Other Chinese in small numbers from other places such as Papua New Guinea and Oceania were no doubt there as well, but cannot be readily identified. Griffith University had only a handful of Chinese students from overseas. There were perhaps as many as 100-200 overseas Chinese students in private secondary schools in Brisbane.

11 According to some reports, Kampuchean Chinese are heavily represented in the Thai-Kampuchean border camps from which increasing numbers of refugees have been taken by Australia since 1980. These Chinese, who are mainly Teochiu, seem to be given preference by Australian immigration selectors because their urban background has provided them with skills that will make it easier for them to adapt to Australian conditions, and because they are thought to be less able to return to Kampuchea under any future circumstances. Approximately eighty per cent of Kampuchean refugees in Adelaide, where many have gone, are in fact Chinese (Roger Fordham, personal communication). About half of the East Timorese refugees who have made it to Australia are Hakkas. There are around 3,000 of them in Darwin, where they comprise 5 per cent of the total population, while a similar number are in Melbourne (Suzi Hutchings, personal communication.)

12 Another view is that selection in the Malaysian camps was based on an assessment of a person's potential for making the boat journey to Darwin. As the arrival of "boat people" in Australia itself was a potentially explosive internal political issue, it was defused by accepting those people who might have been able to come on their own (Roger Fordham, personal communication),

13 This has not been the pattern in Adelaide, where Vietnamese Chinese and ethnic Vietnamese have generally settled in the same low-rent, unskilled-job area in the northwest of the city. Kampuchean Chinese, on the other hand, have not moved too far from the southern location of the Catholic-run center which processes them. The situation in Perth is not clear, although it is known that large numbers of Indochinese refugees who were originally settled there have moved to Melbourne or Sydney, sometimes in convoys of chartered busses.

Chapter 6

The Chinese in New Zealand: Persistence, Change and Innovation

Charles P. Sedgwick

A Chinese community has lived in New Zealand, initially as sojourners and later as residents, for over 100 years. In this time the population has grown from a group of twelve miners brought from the inhospitable Australian gold fields to a population of 14,860 in 1976, dispersed all over New Zealand with substantial communities in the larger urban centres. While the current Chinese community, even as a minority, lives relatively peacefully, the history of their predecessors was markedly different, perhaps best described as survival in a complex environment.

This article attempts to trace the strategies used by the Chinese community to ensure their survival while at the same time offering sufficient ethnographic material to dilute the astringency of analysis.[1]

The development of the Chinese community can best be viewed as derived from the influence of sets of relationships originating from three interrelated spheres of activity. The more obvious of these are those relationships that link the Chinese community to New Zealand society and to China.

The reaction to these two spheres gives rise to a third, the social relations within the Chinese community, which suffers the unintended consequences of action taken in regard to the other spheres of activity. The very nature of collective action to confront pressures from other contexts has led to new alignments of power, dissensions, arguments over legitimate authority, and fragmentation within the Chinese community.

Two further assumptions emerge from the above. First, the Chinese community has survived in New Zealand through the ability to respond to external influences and internal conflict resulting from the sets of relationships specified above. Second, these responses are identifiable in the organisational history of the community. This view essentially attempts to merge the central concerns of Crissman (1967) and Wickberg (1979).

Crissman refers to the nature of the organisational structure in the overseas Chinese community as 'segmentary structure'.[2] His basic assumption is that all overseas Chinese communities have a similar segmentary organisation which uses, as the basis of its divisions, certain ascribed criteria that have to do with the way overseas Chinese make distinctions among themselves (see Crissman 1967 : 185-189). These distinctions constitute, for Crissman, 'relevant ethnicity', and their use is defined by the situation in which Chinese find themselves (Crissman, 1967 : 189). Crissman sees the segmentary structure in the overseas Chinese community, therefore, as a set of alternative ways by which the community can divide and organise for particular interests, but the pattern of segmentation, he maintains, is unique in each case.

The usual criteria by which Chinese make distinctions between themselves include speech group, surname and locality. In the New Zealand context, locality has provided the fundamental identity out of which organisation has been developed. Above these locality associations, in the segmentary system, are what Crissman calls 'community organisations'. They in effect have a dual purpose. Their internal role is as administrative organs of the communities from which their membership is drawn, and their external role is reflected in the fact that they have "names and stated purposes which are sometimes chosen more with an eye toward official government regulations" than a reflection of their real interest (Crissman, 1967 : 194). They are the informal, unofficial government of the Chinese community and the supposed mediator between the community and the dominant host society. The executive of these particular associations, according to Crissman, is usually wealthy and bilingual, capabilities which provide the opportunity to seek power and prestige through community organisations.

The segmentary structure, including the above types of associations, according to Crissman, provides a means whereby a Chinese community can govern itself without having "noticeable governmental institutions achieving a representative political system and hierarchical administrative system" (Crissman, 1967 : 200).

This segmentary system, therefore, becomes the key to the structure of the Chinese community and the strategies devised to articulate needs and concerns. However, it is clear from a cursory look at the history of most overseas Chinese communities that the organisational structure and the needs of the community change through time. Wickberg (1979) has, by treating the organisational structure of the community as a variable, suggested that complexity or simplicity within structure is a function of a Chinese community's contextual needs and not necessarily merely a function of size and composition.[3] Further, he asserts that to understand the absence of certain organisations in a Chinese community one must understand the external relations of that community including, in his particular study, the influence of cultural links with China, Canadian government policy and social discrimination.

This point is particularly germaine to the New Zealand case, for it is those variables, together with the influence on and of the internal dynamics of the community, that provide the impetus for change and persistence within the segmentary structure.

Crissman notes that the evidence of the segmentary structure, closely allied to Chinese culture and the basis of innovation in the overseas community, is a manifestation of ethnicity. However, considering the role these organisations perform in responding to both external and internal influences on the community, it would seem legitimate to infer that they also have an explicit political role.

Merging the notion of ethnicity with the political, I would argue that in the New Zealand context the persistence and innovation within the Chinese community as manifested through their organisational structure constitutes an example of political ethnicity.[4]

Chinese came to New Zealand at an important time in the development of the colony, as it experienced a gold rush.[5] A small number of Chinese arrived in 1866 at the invitation of local businessmen who assured them of protection by the law. The initial migrants came to the province of Otago, formerly a booming centre of gold mining but by 1866 already in decline. The presence of Chinese, it was hoped, would rescue the ailing business community. However, the Chinese who moved into the gold fields quickly organised on the basis of kinship or locality (in China), not only to mine claims efficiently, but also to provide a network of communities complete with sufficient businesses including supply shops, gambling and opium halls to provide all the necessities of a dispersed mining clientele.

The European reaction to the early Chinese presence in the gold fields was mixed. A Select Committee had been assigned the task of examining the Chinese immigration issue in 1871 following a considerable outcry against their presence, but after interviewing thirty-six Europeans and one Chinese man, it decided to take no action. The report did, however, collect a sizeable list of negative value judgments about the Chinese which would in future years be part of a justification for all manner of legislation, but in 1871 they were not sufficient to stop the government hiring Chinese labour for its railroad construction, The one Chinese man interviewed by the Select Committee was assigned the task of negotiating with his fellow countrymen. However, his methods of recruitment and pay were challenged by the labourers, and he was taken to court by his fellow countrymen. The court case made it abundantly clear that neither the court, railroad contractors nor the government knew anything about Chinese business arrangements, and the scheme was quickly terminated.

From the 1870's through the late 1880's the profitability of mining had declined sufficiently to force Chinese out of the goldfields to seek work elsewhere. This meant a gradual northward movement through New Zealand and the settlement of individuals and groups in many boroughs which had never before seen Chinese people. The change of residence meant a number of things. Primarily, occupations changed as evidenced by a steady growth in laundries, fruit and vegetable shops, and market gardens. Secondly, the dispersed, virtually anonymous Chinese, as far as the rest of New Zealand was concerned, moved into larger urban centres, particularly the capital, Wellington, which became the headquarters of the Chinese community. Thirdly, change in residence and occupation had forced the Chinese to become almost entirely dependent on European clientele without the necessary language skills. The situation unfortunately led to animosity and hence to increasing government opposition to the continued immigration of Chinese to New Zealand.

In 1881 the New Zealand government began what was to become thirty-nine years of relentless attempts to restrain Chinese immigration to New Zealand. Twenty-one separate bills went before parliament and while only a small proportion passed, their presence occasioned hundreds of pages of parliamentary debate. The provisions imposed included a £10 poll tax in 1881, increased to £ 100 in 1896 along with restrictions on the number of Chinese who could travel per boat. In 1896 they were specifically excluded from old age pension provisions; from 1900 onwards every Chinese was finger-printed before entry; and in 1907 they were subjected to a language test in addition to the poll tax and also lost their right to naturalisation after having it for fifty-five years. According to one author the sustained debate over Chinese immigration both in parliament and in the press created a 'racial consciousness' in New Zealand (Hall, 1927 : 231), a phenomenon that would give rise to anti-Chinese organisations in 1895, 1907 and 1926.[6]

The recipients of the effort failed to be daunted by the opposition and even when their number were declining[7] and events in China gave cause for concerns[8] continued to make concerted efforts to ameliorate the antagonism towards them.

Despite the difficulties inherent in organising a population that was dispersed and in the midst of adjustment to new occupations and increasing hardships from immigration restriction, concerned Chinese merchants and others from the larger urban Chinese centres organised and set about articulating their needs to the dominant society by means of petitions.

Between 1883 and 1907 the Chinese community submitted nineteen petitions to the New Zealand government. Those that involved more than private issues appealed on the basis of international treaties, humanitarian values and their own ability to fulfill the normative requirements in New Zealand including their contribution to the economy, to have immigration restrictions amended or canceled, to maintain the right to naturalisation and finally to get diplomatic representation. Their success was minimal, with the exception of the appointment of diplomatic representation, but they did succeed in maintaining a profile that prevented the government from ignoring its unaccepted Chinese minority while perhaps preventing any more excessive action than had already been taken. In terms of the internal politics of the Chinese community, it facilitated the emergence of a small group of leaders who became part of the first organisation that linked the politics of the New Zealand community to the politics of their homeland (T'ung Meng Hui, 1905). The petitions also drew Peking's attention to the problems of the overseas communities and although they had largely remained disinterested in the early 1880's, in 1887 and 1907 Chinese commissions were sent to New Zealand to investigate the situation. The details of the first visit are unknown but in

1891 the Chinese government made a request to the Foreign Office for representatives to be assigned to New Zealand, which the Prime Minister of New Zealand refused (see AJHR, A.1A : 4). The 1907 commission received more publicity, but it was hardly beneficial to the Chinese community. One of the Commissioners stated that ". . . they (New Zealand) must not judge the Chinese by representatives of their race mostly from the slums of Canton they saw here . . .' (New Zealand Times, 20 June, 1907). Despite this, diplomatic representation was accepted in New Zealand, and in 1909 a Chinese Consul arrived to represent approximately 2,515 Chinese men and fifty-five Chinese women.

The Consul's presence brought the cessation Chinese petitions, for they now had an advocate who presumably would protect their interests. However, it became clear relatively quickly that the Consul, from northern China and American-educated, was not in New Zealand to represent all Chinese. His sympathies were minimal for the plight of fellow countrymen and limited to merchants, students and visitors. His key interest was to develop trade between the two countries, but his attention was drawn to the internal politics of the New Zealand Chinese community, which, he discovered, was already divided, as evidenced by the existence of the T'ung Meng Hui (1905) and the Chee Kung Tong (1907). The Consul, unhappy with the political implications, was instrumental in organising the Chong Wah Wui Koon, a community organisation designed to cut across existing political factions. Its constitution stated:

> The Association endeavours to forge better friendly ties amongst our compatriots, foster the spirit of mutual help, and play a mediating role where divergent opinions arise among our people. This organisation promotes the progress of the society as a whole and is not involved in party politics or religious affairs.
>
> (Rules of the New Zealand Chinese Association 1909 : 1, translated from the Chinese).

Representatives of this organisation came from sixteen localities where Chinese resided in New Zealand, and their selection ignored the existing political groups. Membership included 61% of the New Zealand Chinese at the time.

The effectiveness and longevity of this organisation was interrupted, however, by the revolution of 1911 in China, which established a new government and its own political party, the KMT. The new political party spread to New Zealand from Australia and subsequently established newspapers in two New Zealand cities where Chinese were concentrated by the early 1900's. The presence of the KMT added yet another faction to a community already divided between the Chee Kung Tong and a group of monarchists who supported Yuan Hsi Kai. The tension created by this situation, in addition to European hostility generated by the Returned Serviceman's Association after World War 1, brought about the demise of the Chong Wah Wui Koon and a further fragmentation of the community into locality associations. The Poon Fa Association, formerly present in the gold fields, was reorganised in 1916, followed by the Kwong Chew Association in 1920, and the Tung Jung Association in 1924.[9] All these locality associations were concerned with avoiding both the counterproductive aspects of internal political factions in the community as well as conflict with European society. Their most active role, however, was seen in the organisation of various social occasions in the community including the celebration of traditional events like Ching Ming. They also arranged for passages to and from China and provided hostel facilities and business houses in Hong Kong to benefit travellers delayed in transit and merchants wishing to import Chinese goods to New Zealand.

The 1920's were uncomfortable times for the New Zealand Chinese. Chinese merchants came under scrutiny over customs duty, and a developing Chinese market garden activity in which 41% of the population was involved drew attention from a number of organisations. Under the initiative of a White New Zealand League, a major campaign was launched against the Chinese over the issue of land use and intermarriage with Maori women who worked for Chinese gardeners. These issues, together with a small rise in the total population and a doubling of the number of Chinese women in the community, were sufficient to instigate a renewed call for more stringent anti-Chinese legislation.[10] The result was a provision instituted in 1920 which required every prospective immigrant not of British or Irish birth to apply to the Minister of Customs for a permit before entry into New Zealand. Curiously despite the intent of this legislation to effect a total exclusion of the Chinese, a quota system was initiated in 1921, allowing 100 Chinese to enter each year with payment of the poll tax. They did not, however, have to face fingerprinting or the language test, but the British government and the Chinese Consul were nevertheless indignant. The former resented the loss of instrumental control over New Zealand's immigration policy, and the latter opposed the general restrictions and the remaining poll-tax provision. Neither protest changed the legislation.

For the Chinese in New Zealand the situation looked grim. Their home land seemed destined to continual internal dispute with two governments competing for power; their home districts were embroiled in civil strife; and New Zealand, increasingly attractive as a place of residence, was much harder to enter as a Chinese immigrant. By 1927 China's internal political problems led to open hostility between the Chee Kung Tong and the KMT in New Zealand over the appropriate flag to fly at the celebration of Double Tenth. Although the dispute at the time led to two celebrations, the victory of Chiang in 1928 left no uncertainty as to who controlled China and the New Zealand Chinese community.

Once the KMT was firmly established in its political role amongst New Zealand Chinese, there was again a move to unite the various associations under a community-wide organisation. A meeting was called by leading Chinese to bring together the Consul and representatives from all existing associations. The decision was made in 1928 to start another Chong Wah Wui Koon with its headquarters in Wellington and with representatives from each of the associations on the executive. The association, with four affiliated branches, was of vital importance during the depression and afterwards. In 1930, it was able to renegotiate the temporary permit provisions for Chinese students with the government.[11] In 1931 it welcomed the President of the Legislative Yuan, who had come to New Zealand to raise funds for the new capital buildings to be constructed in Nanking. And in 1932 the association along with its affiliated branches provided a unanimous response to a vindictive petition signed by 1,457 Europeans demanding that all Chinese be repatriated. Their published reply methodically contradicted the assertions made in the petition about excessive remittances, a lower class of Chinese in New Zealand and their unsanitary behaviour *(Evening Post,* 7 November, 1932). The petition and its demand died a quiet death, and rather than forcing pressure for repatriation, the Chinese gained increasing acceptance during the depression. For the first time their Double Tenth celebrations were publicly acknowledged and reported in the press, as was their ability to be a self-sustaining community without any government help in the form of social security, and their generosity to those who needed help.

While the Chinese profile in New Zealand improved with the hardship of the depression, the situation steadily deteriorated in China. The civil war and the activities of Russia and Japan towards China alarmed local Chinese and coincided with a fervent nationalism that went through the community after 1928. In 1935, with the arrival of a new Consul, the Chong Wah Wui Koon was reorganised along lines similar to the 1909 version, with regional representation from twenty-six branches including those formed in 1928. The New Zealand Chinese Association, as it was known, recognised other associations but had no delegates from them, only representatives from local communities who were expected to act on behalf of the whole community and not on behalf of sectional interests. The leadership that emerged during this period was a stable one with families plus considerable investment in business activity.

Within a year of organising, the new community association, with pressure from one of its branches, organised a collection to support China in their war with Japan. Despite the Consul's reticence about forcing local Chinese to donate, by the end of 1937 the national executive had achieved the task of organising a national campaign which was to include all New Zealand Chinese and collected, in the period from 1937 to 1944, £174,149.[12] The New Zealand Chinese donations were the highest in the South Pacific and ranked second per capita amongst overseas Chinese communities in the world (NZCGMJ, 10 October, 1954).

The organisation of the collection, including the powerful centralised executive, the mandatory weekly financial obligations placed on all New Zealand Chinese, and the right to impose sanctions on defaulters, led eventually to conflict. The conflict emerged in the form of dissent that focused on the issue of the association's assumed authority to appropriate the funds collected. Some local communities wanted to control their own collection, and others discontinued collecting as enthusiasm for the effort waned.

However, it was not these concerns alone that caused the tension. The temporary immigration provision which had allowed a number of families to be brought together in New Zealand prior to and during the war had given rise to a growing proportion of younger Chinese in the community.[13] While the economic activity of these young people was determined by their kin, their education was under the control of New Zealand society, a situation which had previously been compensated for by a mandatory educational sojourn in China for children who had been in New Zealand for some years. Now, with their home localities embroiled in war, repatriation for education was both risky and expensive, which forced the community to seek alternatives. The Consulate and the national association, realising the problem, encouraged each community to organise its young population through the medium of Double Tenth,[14] local schools and sports groups. Language and sport became during the war years the two idioms through which Chinese ethnicity and nationalism could be articulated, indirectly providing the impetus for local communities to be concerned about their local needs. Concern for their future in New Zealand had, together with any misgivings people might have had about the collection campaign, provided basis for fragmentation. However, the context in which it occurred demanded new organisational forms. None of the existing locality associations was capable of providing for the needs of younger community members.

Two responses emerged initially. First the Chinese Anglican Church in Wellington, marginal to the existing associations but supported by the Chinese community, proposed substantial building plans to provide for youth in 1945. Second, three years later, various Chinese sports organisations from local communities suggested to the national association that an annual sports tournament be held involving representatives from all Chinese communities where association branches were supposedly in existence. The first such meeting (1948) was a success but required considerable organisation, since leisure time was a relatively rare commodity before the 1960's and days with businesses closed, while demanded by the national association, met with opposition.

In an annual sports tournament the New Zealand Chinese had one event, partially free from political overtones, which demonstrated their unity and preserved the integrity of their ethnicity amongst the younger community members. However, there were other problems: the remaining collection funds and their use after the war divided the two major urban Chinese communities, and the 1949 victory of the CCP and the Korean War of the 1950's placed additional pressure on the local community. The notions of 'left' and 'right' entered community politics, partially exacerbated by cold-war polemics and a conservative KMT.

Where the KMT was strong in New Zealand, it claimed the right to remaining funds, but the national association maintained its use was their prerogative, and local communities asserted that it belonged to the individual Chinese communities. The solidarity and cohesion of the war years dissipated, and fragmentation of the Chinese community was inevitable. No publications could reach local Chinese as they had during the war, the Consulate was of an exiled government whose recognition as the legitimate government of China was debatable, and the PRC was considered part of the communist threat, making Chinese residents in New Zealand uneasy. In addition, New Zealand government policy was keen to discourage any sign of manifest ethnicity in the Chinese community, either as a result of continued immigration or exclusive organisation, so active steps were taken to make such developments difficult if not impossible.

The complexity of the situation required careful articulation and the organisations that eventuated in this period were understandably unique, straddling all three spheres of social relations; that is, with the PRC and the Republic of China, with New Zealand, and within their own community.

In the post-war years a whole new segmentary structure appeared in the Chinese community parallel to that which already existed. A number of organisations emphasised sport as a focus and as the particular medium through which the young Chinese could articulate and maintain their ethnicity. The Progressive Club, the Eastern Club and the Northern Soccer Club, as well as numerous other sports clubs around the country, were organised by young people supported by elders who approved of their intra-ethnic activity, and met annually at the Double Tenth sports tournament. While the use of sports was hardly unique as a medium of association, this development was partially free from the hegemony of other associations and ostensibly provided for the young in the absence of European influence. Of equal importance, however, was the fact that sport was an acceptable cultural idiom not only within the community but in Taiwan (and later the PRC) and particularly in New Zealand.

A counter-emphasis to sport, however, was Chinese culture, which was acclaimed as having primary importance by the Chinese Anglican and Baptist Churches as well as the Auckland Hui Sur (1950). Like the sports organisations, the churches were not new, but now under almost complete Chinese control they saw Chinese culture, the maintenance of ethnicity, and Christianity as complementary. Both churches provided community facilities financed through donations and fund-raising bazaars, dinners or cultural performances.

The Auckland Hui Sur similarly emphasized Chinese culture as a means to maintaining Chinese ethnicity through the medium of opera and Chinese films. The facilities, however, neglected provisions for a school and sports, which meant that culture for a period of years was the prerogative and foremost concern of older members in the community. It was not until a counter-organisation, partially related to a traditional locality association and partially made up of concerned parents, brought pressure to bear on the Hui Sor, threatening to take its young population or potential members away, that the latter relented and quickly provided facilities for a school and later a new complex almost entirely for sports.

Three other organisations became prominent along with the above, two reflecting specific views of the external relations of the Chinese community and the other coming closest to being a community association.

In the former category was the Anti-Communist League (1952) and the Chinese Cultural Society (1951). The Anti-Communist League was the inspiration of the Republic of China created in New Zealand, as elsewhere, to capitalise on the anti-PRC rumours moving amongst the overseas Chinese communities and to strengthen ties with Taiwan. These rumours were about the persecution of relatives in China who were being ransomed to draw overseas funds to the mainland instead of to Taiwan. The organisation in New Zealand was closely aligned with the Embassy until 1972, with the KMT where it still existed, and with the New Zealand Chinese Association. It was vocal about its anti-PRC feelings, created an image of a very pro-Republic of China, Chinese community and was later matched by a European version in the Free China Society.

The counter to this organisation was the Chinese Cultural Society formed by younger members of the community who had experienced China after liberation and were keen to maintain their knowledge of developments. The organisation itself was small, but there was sufficient interest, quietly expressed amongst local Chinese through willingness to receive the material and see films they distributed, to make it viable. Although of concern to the New Zealand government, and to some in their own community, they were allowed to persist but not without having the ideological label of 'left' attached to them. Like the Anti-Communist League, this organisation also had its European version in the New Zealand China Friendship Society, which was started at about the same time and was considered by many Chinese to be safer politically than being associated with their own organisation. Both of the groups had a commitment to seeing China recognised by the New Zealand government, which finally occurred in 1972, but only the European version has survived, with an extensive Chinese membership in some centres. The external links were maintained with both Taiwan and China after 1972 by individuals making their own choice. Diplomatic representation, however, was from the PRC, and while there are still links with the Republic of China government, they are adjunct to trade relationships and not purely diplomatic nor acknowledged formally by the New Zealand government,

The organisation in this period that came closest to the role of the New Zealand Chinese Association as a community-wide group was the Chinese Grower's Association, started during the war, and by 1949 publishing its own journal which was distributed all over New Zealand. The significance of the organisation and the journal was that, aside from providing for the sectional interest of Chinese growers, it also became the voice of the Chinese community. It carried overseas news, published announcements by the Chinese Embassy and commented on Chinese associations and community affairs. Market gardeners were both rural and urban, young and old and the membership of the grower's association cut across locality, political and community factions, remaining purposefully apart from intra-community conflict. What was particularly unique about the organisation, however, was the fact that it had been initiated on the suggestion of the Prime Minister during the war and together with the journal was subsidised by the European grower's organisation, which by definition formally represented all growers no matter what ethnic group they belonged to. The subsidy, of course, was a proportion of the levy collected from all growers including the Chinese, but the fact that some was returned acknowledged the autonomy, if not the ethnicity, of the Chinese growers. Increasingly this very fact became anathema to both the European growers and the New Zealand government. The former reacted by insisting on amalgamation, and when that failed they dropped the subsidy and gave the Chinese growers formal representation at annual meetings, with the government's approval. The government, aside from condoning the action of the European growers, also suggested forcefully that all foreign news be dropped from the journal and that it print material relevant only to its membership.

Neither move destroyed the growers' organisation, but the removal of the subsidy meant the journal could no longer be published after 1972, and at least three growing areas opted for joining the European organisation or organising their own co-operative. When foreign news was purged from the journal, however, it was replaced with a poignant analysis of Chinese associations and the conflict between them, focussing particularly on how certain people used the associations for private gain rather than public good. It was particularly germaine at the time, for it was partially the conflict between associations and the suspicions held by some against former leaders in the community that gave rise to the parallel segmentary structure outlined above. The realisation that the needs in the Chinese community had changed dramatically, that their relationship with the New Zealand government and society was qualitatively different after the war than it had been before, and that their relationship with a homeland was again a question of two governments as it had been in 1927, required new ways of articulation. The articulation, however, was one that needed to bridge the gaps between factions, localities, young and old and most importantly stem the dominant threat of assimilation and loss of ethnicity.

In the mid 1960's there were attempts to resolve some of the sources of past conflict, and this initiated a series of organisational changes which reasserted the position of some traditional associations.

In 1965 the New Zealand Chinese Association had come under scrutiny in Wellington, partly due to an argument over regional representation to the national body and partly over alleged misuse of the association headquarters' deed. The general situation resulted in an unclear role and tainted reputation for the national association later resolved through a reoganisation of its leadership under the scrutiny of the Chinese Grower's Association, which in the interim had assumed the status of a community organisation. Some maintained that an organisation which had been started to bring unity to the community had brought only disunity and given rise to autocratic control by the central executive. In an attempt to be responsible, the reformed association announced its recognition of young Chinese scholars in the community with awards for outstanding performance in exams, talked about building or extending the hall for recreational purposes, and proposed to write a history of the New Zealand Chinese.

Only the first of these proposals was carried out, but the idea of providing facilities had become the concern of a larger forum in the community. At the time the Seyip, Tung Jung and Poon Fa Associations had facilities but they were limited in size and adequate only for banquets or for school classes. In 1966, however, the Seyip Association announced plans to build a hall; the Chinese Anglican Church started a collection for a new building programme and the Eastern Sports Club decided it was going to build a hall. All three were to cater for an increasing young population but the emphasis was different. The church, as it had done in the past, wanted to provide the most comprehensive facilities including a youth hostel, chapel, missioners house and additional activities, while both the Eastern Club and the Seyip Association appeared more concerned with a sports facility. The following year the Christchurch Chinese community also planned to provide a cultural centre for the community, and in 1968 the Auckland Chinese Hui Sor, as noted previously, expanded its functions to include a school. Both of these groups placed their emphasis on culture as did the Chinese Anglican Church, although the Auckland Hui Sor, already established and having a larger population to draw on, was able to move considerably further to consider a sports facility, and in 1969 they started their own journal to plot their progress. In 1970 the Auckland Hui Sor and the Chinese Anglican Church both started to collect for their respective projects. The Auckland group set out purposefully to steer a course between existing groups in the community, and found itself having to justify this position, receiving criticism from those who thought the project ought to come under the New Zealand Chinese Association branch and from others who thought that a locality association was sufficient. Both the Chinese Anglican Church and the Auckland Hui Sur organised public meetings to state their position but the latter group met with more support from the community than did the Chinese Anglican Church.

The issues that formed the basis of the argument were essentially the same in both cases, having to do with distribution and use of power in the community. The Chinese community had a history, confirmed in both the *Chinese Grower's Monthly Journal* and the *Auckland Chinese Hall Journal,* of community leaders using the status of associations to place personal gain above community needs. The presence of this in the past had left doubt in the minds of many especially when community projects were undertaken on behalf of all in the community. The doubt turned into distrust, antagonism or apathy and a refusal to co-operate.

In 1970, both the Chinese Anglican Church in Wellington and the Hall in Auckland were established groups, aware of the kinds of factions that operated in the community, but whereas the Hui Sur group was able to pull the Auckland community behind them, the Chinese Anglican Church found themselves in a competitive situation. The other associations did not give them the mandate to act on behalf of the community but nevertheless they persisted.

The outcome of the Wellington situation was two major hall projects, the second generated by an alternative alliance between the Chinese Ambassador (prior to recognition of the PRC in 1972), the Eastern Sports Club, and the Wellington City Council. The result was ideally to be a community hall with all existing associations affiliated, but even in this case there was reticence, and any assumed affiliation on the part of what became the Wellington Chinese Sports and Cultural Centre was met with denial or criticism. The Chinese Anglican Church for their part had to rely on individual support, massive, well publicised fund raising, and the argument that they included sports and culture as part of their place whereas the other project was equipped largely to be a sports centre.

It took nearly seven years for the projects to be completed and the Chinese Anglican Church was able to complete only the first stage of their plan. Inflation, over the fund-raising period, increased the costs in all the projects, placing greater dependence on the local community's generosity. In Wellington the situation was worse, for in the end the Chinese community supported both projects.[15] The segmentary system in both Auckland and Wellington had survived, however, with individual units maintaining their autonomy yet supporting projects for community facilities. Curiously, the two projects in Wellington and the one in Auckland were all recipients of government money, and the Chinese Anglican Church is still nominally under the control of the New Zealand Anglican Church. So there is a sense in which they are a compromise in the area of ethnicity. In each centre there had also been a noticeable change in leadership in the early 1970's, which some argue accounted for the push to complete the projects. The new executive was made up of young professionals who were at last taking their position as a leaders in the community.

The situation outlined above was not unique to the two major Chinese centres in New Zealand. Other smaller communities with increasing population, young people and an energetic professional group have attempted to pull local people together, often with the focus of a community project. In each case the problems have been similar, albeit on a smaller scale, forcing any new community effort to articulate its needs usually within a set of historic factions or divisions that already exist in the community. In most cases they have chosen to try to avoid conflict.

The innovation derived from the experience of the post-war years had, therefore, not destroyed the segmentary system in the Chinese community but rather built on it appropriately to reflect the new context within which the community existed and the kinds of needs this situation generated, but there is a tension in the way this is articulated. The debate as to whether the Chinese community's ethnicity is articulated best by culture or sport is still ongoing. There is also some tension over who actually represents the Chinese community and despite the continual fluctuations that go on within the New Zealand Chinese Association it has maintained its integrity, still holding its annual meetings which are still sufficiently well attended to decide on policy, albeit heavily dominated by representatives from the two large urban communities. The right to actually implement policy, however, is the prerogative of local branches who guard their autonomy, for the hegemony of the centre is no longer accepted. The national association is still acknowledged both locally and nationally as the watch dog of the community which demands to be consulted but may not have sufficient power to impose any sanctions on non-compliance with policy.

Other associations also persist as part of the segmentary system including both the community centre groups (and the Chinese Anglican Centre), the locality associations and the Chinese Grower's Association. The Chinese Anglican Church while part of the European dominant society is still largely operating within the Chinese milieu so its inclusion as a community organisation in this context is considered legitimate. The sports organisations for the most part have been re-incorporated as part of currently existing organisations so whereas the autonomous unit may no longer persist its membership is still part of the organisational life in the community.

Discussion

The central concerns of this historic overview are to show, by using the analytical points made by Crissman (1967) and Wickberg (1979), how a Chinese community has been able to survive in an alien environment. As noted at the outset, their respective contributions provide the key to understanding the structure of the Chinese community and the possible influences that might alter this structure through time. In this case study of the New Zealand Chinese community, therefore, it has been necessary to alter Crissman's view of the segmentary system from synchronic to diachronic.

The segmentary system, therefore, rather than being entirely an innovation from the Chinese city exported to the overseas situation, becomes instead a means whereby the overseas community continues to adjust to the context in which it finds itself. Rather than the segmentary system being the end result of the analysis, it is the means (a variable) which is used to describe the changes and their causes which have affected the Chinese community through time (see Crissman 1967 : 185). The context which influences the configuration of this segmentary system, as noted before, included not only those factors referred to by Wickberg but also the internal machinations in the segmentary system which created new alliances and factions,

The segmentary system in the New Zealand Chinese community provides a map to the internal and external relations of the community, and as a system appears to develop through cycles. The cycles can generally be described as periods characterised either by relatively few associations and a tendency for collective action and cooperation between groups or, on the other hand, conflict and/or fragmentation.

The periods when collective action is either endorsed or voluntarily accepted by the Chinese community have invariably appeared at times when internal conflict, fragmentation and external pressure, together or singularly, forced changed. In 1909 the influence of the Consul in conjunction with the internal conflict between the T'ung Meng Hui and the Chee Kung Tong were sufficient, and in 1927 hostility in New Zealand and the dispute between the KMT and the CKT provided the necessary impetus. In each case, a Chong Wah Wui Koon was formed, in the former case with regional representation and in the latter with associational representation. The 1909 situation occurred when a demographic and occupational change was underway in the community and prior to the re-organisation of locality associations. The 1927 situation, however, post-dated the emergence of locality associations, themselves the result of dissension within the first community organisation and its inability to resolve political differences in the community, and was coincident with a period of concerted public anti-Chinese activity in 1907. After 1927 the Chong Wah Wui Koon survived, but underwent a change in identity as it became the New Zealand Chinese Association, which had on its executive representatives from sixteen areas within New Zealand. The geographic representation avoided the political hegemony of the KMT and other associations, but with the war collection this re-organised community association itself wielded hegemony over the community. In this situation, the intensive feelings of nationalism were superimposed for a time over intra-community conflict, which in effect allowed an organisational elite, largely made up of urban merchants (Chinese goods and fruit and vegetable shops) who had emerged, in the 1920's, to exercise power over the community from 1927 till 1965. However, neither the collective action from 1937 till 1944 nor the power of the New Zealand Chinese Association was sufficient in itself. In the course of the collection, fragmentation occurred in a diversity of forms, which were the intended and unintended consequences of the collection. One variation of the fragmentation was an encouraged flourishing of youth organisations in local centres which were intended to retain an impressionable youth within the Chinese community by providing activities to encourage morale and morality. This started during war time, when it was largely focused in the annual Double Tenth celebrations, but after 1947 a diversity of formally organised sports groups emerged, some attached to locality associations and Chinese Churches, while others were autonomous. This fragmentation was resolved when these groups moved to change the Double Tenth into an annual national sports tournament.

The unintended fragmentation resulted from a developing antipathy to the hegemony of the New Zealand Chinese Association headquarters in conjunction with a declining fervour for an increasingly costly nationalism when families were faced with an escalating cost of living in New Zealand. This tendency, again a result of internal and external influences, led to the development of associations representing local community autonomy (Tai Tung and Film Club Auckland), sectional economic interests (Chinese Commercial Growers), alternative political views (Chinese Cultural Society, Anti-Communist League), and other groups which cut across all allegiances (such as the Chinese Churches, which were concerned to provide *community* facilities as well as youth clubs).

At the same time as this proliferation of associations and organisations, obsolete immigration restrictions were being changed and separated families and spouses were being reunited. Consequently there was a consistent tendency for the community, now exempt from influential external influences, to turn inwards towards unresolved intra-community issues.

By the late 1960's and early 1970's the proliferation of associations and groups was replaced by a dual process of elimination and amalgamation in the segmentary structure. In the major cities, groups planning large community centres, including the Auckland Hui Sor, the Wellington Chinese Sports and Cultural Centre and the Anglican Chinese Centre (Wellington) which drew support from existing associations, absorbed some groups under their control and sometimes called on the entire community for support. In Auckland the Film Club and Tai Tung group joined the centre project, and in Wellington the Eastern Sports and Mui Shuit Club became part of the Sports and Culture Centre, while other associations, including the local branches of the national association and the locality associations, gave their support in some cases reluctantly. The Church Centre, on the other hand, avoided the associational affiliation and drew its support from across a whole community.

The groups that disappeared were largely predictable. With the recognition of the PRC by New Zealand in 1972, the Anti-Communist League and the KMT faded quietly from existence. Simultaneously the Chinese Cultural Society disappeared as renewed contact with the homeland became freed from the paranoia that had developed during the anti-Communist era preceding the Korean War.

The process outlined above was unique, for not only did it provide an example for other smaller communities to follow, but it also resolved, most importantly, a number of problems related to the internal and external relations of the Chinese community. Clearly it had built on the segmentary system that already existed, and even with the completion of the projects the fundamental units of the system, including a once nearly ineffectual national Association, had been preserved. What had happened was the provision of parallel community organisations that could allow at the same time an emerging leadership of young professionals to take its place in the community while elders retained their roles at the head of existing associations. Even though the departure of the Consul from Republic of China and the recognition of the PRC in 1972 had caused accusations of 'left' and 'right' politics in the community and the alteration of the Double Tenth Annual Sports to an Easter Tournament, the organisation structure could absorb the differences and allow for groups to acknowledge either China or Taiwan, depending on their allegiance. With the existence of alternative community centre organisations in a number of Chinese communities, parallel in many instances to the local branches of the national association, a basis had been posted for the resolution of local differences without excessive conflict and, as in the large urban centres, the provision of permanent facilities for future generations which would promote leadership positions for those that would follow.

The segmentary structure as it has developed in New Zealand, therefore, provided a means whereby the Chinese community has been able to respond not only to sets of external influences but also to the effect the above have had on the internal structure of the community. This process has tended to move through cycles from periods of corporate, collective activity under community organisations to varying degrees of fragmentation, finally resulting more recently in an innovation that has perhaps broken the cycle by providing parallel community organisations, decentralised and capable of generating future leaders, resolving internal conflicts and participating as a mediator between the Chinese community and the dominant host society.

Appendix I
Chinese in New Zealand: General Chronology of Events

Year	Males	Females	Total	Legislation and Government Activity	Associations and other Events
1862					First Chinese person arrives
1866					12 Chinese miners brought to NZ by Ho Ah Mei
1867	1,219		1,219		Murder of Chinese miner-petition from fellow countrymen follows
1869					First Chinese come direct from China Poon Fe Association- Lawrence
1870					Chinese missionary brought to gold fields by Presbyterian Church
1871	2,641		2,641	Select Committee convened no action	
1872				Government contract to employ Chinese labour on rail-road construction	Chinese petition against Judge Beetham
1873					Court case—John An Tong v Ah Foo
1874	4,814	2	4,816		
1878	4,424	9	4,433	First immigration Bill-fails	
1881	4,995	9	5,004	1881 Act 10, tonnage restriction	
1882					Ch'eung Shin Tong (first shipment in 1883)
1883					Chinese petition to Government (Wellington)
1886	4,527	15	4,542		
1888				1888 Amendment Act, tonnage restriction increased	Chinese petition to government (Auckland) Cherishing Virtue Union 1888-1889
1891	4,426	18	4,444		Chinese petition to government (Auckland)
1892					Chinese government appeals to Britain for appointment of Consuls in Dominions—NZ response—no Second shipment (Ch'eung Shin Tong)
1894					Anti-Chinese League (Wellington)
1895					Anti-Chinese League (Christ-church); Chinese petitions to government (Wellington)
1896	3,773	86	3,859	1896 Amendment Act, 100 poll tax	Two Chinese petitions to Governor (Wellington)
1898				Old Age Pension Act—Chinese	
1900					Chinese petition to government (Wellington)

136 The Overseas Chinese: Ethnicity in National Context

Appendix I (Contd.)
Chinese in New Zealand: General Chronology of Events

Year	Population Male	Female	Total	Legislation and Government Activity	Associations and other Events
					Chinese petition (re opium use) all over NZ
1901	2,885	78	2,963	Opium Prohibition Act 1901 Amendment Act	Six Chinese petitions (re opium use) all over NZ
1902					Ch'eung Shin Tong-third shipment of 'sin yan' but Ventnor sinks; Canton Village Mission established by NZ Presbyterians
1904				Seddon opposes Chinese labour for Transvaal	Two petitions to government-opium and gambling
1905					T'ung Meng Hui (Wellington)
					Lionel Terry shoots Joe Yung in Wellington
1906	2,515	55	2,570		
1907				1907 Amendment Act-reading test	Chee Kung Tong (Wellington) Hwang Hou Cheng's visit to investigate NZ Chinese
1907					Anti-Asiatic League (Masterton and Palmerston North); White Race League (Wellington) Chinese petition to government (Wellington)
1908				Discontinuation of Chinese naturalisation - Cabinet decision	
1909					Chinese Consul arrives Chong Wah Wui Koon
1910				Opium Amendment Act-1910 Amendment Act Temporary permit for Chinese Students, merchants and tourists	
1911	2,542	88	2,630		Revolution in China, Republic established
1912					Anti-Chinese League (Christ-church); Double Tenth celebrated; KMT organized (Wellington)
1916	2,017	130	2,147		Poon Fa Association (Wellington)
1918					KMT (Auckland)
1919					RSA opposed to Chinese after WWI
1920				Amendment Act-entry permit required reading test and fingerprinting dropped-poll tax retained	
1921	2,993	273	3,266		
1924					Tung Jung Association (Wellington)

Appendix I (Contd.)
Chinese in New Zealand: General Chronology of Events

Year	Population			Legislation and Government Activity	Associations and other Events
	Males	Females	Total		
1925					White New Zealand League (Pukekohe)
1926	2,927	447	3,374		White New Zealand League (Auckland)
1927					Northern Expedition under Chiang Kai Shek; White New Zealand League (Wellington)
					Double Tenth dispute (CKT vs KMT) in Wellington; Chong Wah Wui Koon organised
1929				Government Select Committee on Employment of Maoris on Market Gardens	
1930				Temporary Permit scheme for Chinese students reinstituted at request of Chinese	
1931					Money collected in NZ to build Nanking KMT government buildings — Lin Sen from Legislative Yuan visits NZ; Auckland Chinese Young Men's Club organised
					Lloyd's petition for repatriation of all Chinese confronted by Chong Wah Wui Koon
1935				Temporary permit system extended for wives and children of NZ residents at request of Chinese—10 permits per year	New Zealand Chinese Association (Wellington)
1936	2,432	511	2,943		Seyip Association (Wellington)
1937				Pension Amendment Act Chinese eligible provided they are naturalized	Double Seventh Commemorated-Japan attacks China
					First All Representatives Conference Collection campaign commences
1938					New Zealand Chinese Weekly (Wellington) starts; New Zealand Chinese Association as national organization—regional branches organized
					Q Sing Times—(Auckland) starts
1939				Foreign exchange provisions extended for Chinese Temporary permit provision for wives and children of residents allowed	

Appendix I (Contd.)
Chinese in New Zealand: General Chronology of Events

Year	Population Males	Population Females	Population Total	Legislation and Government Activity	Association and other Events
1940				Above permit provisions withdrawn	Fifth All-Representatives Congress proposes Youth organisations for all communities; New Zealand Chinese Association proposes to build headquarters in Wellington
1942					Chinese growers encouraged to organise by Labour government
1943					Chinese Commercial Growers Association started
1944				Finance Bill No. 3 poll tax removed	
1945	3,414	1,526	4,940		War ends with Germany and Japan-civil war in China continues
1946					Chinese Anglican Missioner reorganises church; Chinese appeal to Governor General over refugees in NZ
1947				Government gives permanent residence status to 2,731 Chinese Entry Permit provisions of 1920 re-instituted—50 permits for 1948	Public Questions Committee of Presbyterian Church takes up refugee situation with government; Auckland Chinese Sports Club; Chinese Progressive Club (Wellington)
1948				Naturalisation for Chinese resumed (1952) after appeal by Inter Church Commission representations	Double Tenth becomes an annual national sports tournament
1949				National party succeeds Labour Permit system extended to those married before March 1951-300 issued 1951-52	Chinese growers apply for labour assistance—immigration; Chinese Growers Journal started
1950					Korean war—KMT and CCP influence? Visit from Dr Ma (PRC); Seyip Youth Club (Wellington)
1951	3,184	1,648	5,723		Rumours of intimidation of overseas Chinese; Chinese Cultural Society; Chinese Baptist Church organised; Eastern Sports Club (Wellington)
1952					Anti-Communist League (national); Chinese growers request agricultural news in Chinese; Chinese Anglican church proceeds with new hall
1954				All resident Chinese can apply to bring wives to NZ provided they have been naturalised	Tai Tung (Auckland) Opera Club started; Canterbury Chinese Cultural society (Christchurch); Film Club (Auckland)

Appendix I (Contd.)
Chinese in New Zealand: General Chronology of Events

Year	Population			Legislation and Government Activity	Associations and other Events
	Males	Females	Total		
1956	5,700	4,583	10,283	NZ born Chinese allowed to bring wives to NZ	Chinese Anglican church plans new hall; President of Chinese Building Workers Union (PRC) visits NZ
1957					Delta Club (Wellington Chinese Youth Club) started; Chinese Baptist church opens new hall; Subsidy for Chinese grower's organisation discontinued
1958				Naturalisation	
1959					Auckland Chinese Hui Sor started Economic Council of Republic of China vists NZ
1960				Debate over recognition of PRC	NZ Chinese Commercial Growers Journal told to discontinue political news; Rewi Alley visits NZ
1961	4,919	3,611	8,524		Auckland Chinese Hall opened NZ Chinese Association branch reformed in Christ Church
1965					NZ Chinese Association election and finance dispute; Poon Fa Association buys a hotel (Wellington); Income tax investigation for growers
1966	5,700	4,583	10,283	Import quota for rice extended	NZ Chinese Association branch in Christchurch attempts to build a hall
1968					Auckland Chinese Club formed; Auckland Chinese Hui Sor provides free school; Pukekohe community sets up a school
1969					Wellington Chinese school started; Auckland Chinese Hui Sur starts Journal and plans a new community centre; Auckland Chinese Hui Sor Youth Club; Chinese Anglican Church starts opera group and plans Chinese centre
1970					Auckland Chinese Sports Club and Tai Tung join Auckland Hui Sor; Seyip Association arranges national tour for a Chinese cook; Seyip Association and Eastern Sports contemplate building of community centres; Free China Society

Appendix I (Contd.)
Chinese in New Zealand: General Chronology of Events

Year	Population			Legislation and Government Activity	Associations and other Events
	Males	Females	Total		
1971	7,025	5,793	12,818	Naturalised NZ Chinese not given right of entry to Australia-approved 1972	Chinese Anglican Church holds Orient Evening (Wellington); Chinese Sports and Culture Centre organisation (Wellington)
1972				Chinese visitors' visas for NZ subject of publicity	First television documentary on NZ Chinese; PRC table tennis team visits NZ; Argument—Anti-Communist league, Free China Society, KMT and NZ Chinese Association vs Chinese Cultural Society NZUSA (students association) and NZ China Society; NZ recognises PRC, Republic of China Embassy departs
1973					PRC Embassy arrives: United NZ Chinese Action and Advisory Council planned, discontinued; Request for labour on gardens from Grower's Association; NZ Chinese Association (Auckland) submission over immigration; Annual Sports Tournament stopped
1974				Quota system for growers' relatives approved—50 per year	Easter Sports Tournament replaces Annual Sports Tournament on Double Tenth
1975				National party takes office-quota system stopped	
1976	8,081	6,779	14,860	Ministry of Recreation and Sports gives $74,530 to WCS & CC	WCS & CC starts construction on hall Chinese Anglican Church starts their project; CKT funds divided between WCS & CC, ACC
1977					Chinese Baptist Church and three locality Associations; WCS & CC building finished; Cantrebury Sports and Culture Center formed
1978					Auckland Chinese Community Centre opened
1979				Ministry or Recreation and Sports gives Anglican Church Centre $25,000	

Notes

1. The author gratefully acknowledges the help of Professor W.E. Willmott and Dr. David Thorns, both of the University of Canterbury who read and offered their advice on the draft of this article.
2. While Crissman uses the term segmentary structure he makes no attempt to link it to the large body of literature on segmentary systems which concentrate largely on lineage systems.
3. Wickberg is responding to what he sees as shortcomings in the models of associational development proposed by Freedman (1967) and the additional modifications posited by Crissman (1967) and Willmott (1969).
4. This term is borrowed from Cohen (1969 and 1974).
5. Appendix I provides a chronology of relevant events and population statistics for the Chinese community which are provided for future reference.
6. One possible explanation for this phenomenon, other than being totally the result of anti-Chinese feelings, relates to the internal and external political relations of New Zealand. In internal politics it was used by political parties to manipulate their electorates and it was used by an Upper and Lower House against each other as they fought to preserve their respective socioeconomic interests. In external politics it was used as a lever by a dependent colony to wrest autonomy from British Imperial hegemony. Britain did not want colonial immigration policy to jeopardise its foreign trade or treaty arrangements and to this end refused to accept some New Zealand legislation and imposed, in turn, acceptable forms like the Natal Act (1907). New Zealand retaliated in 1920 by removing the whole issue of immigration restriction from parliamentary debate making it instead the prerogative of Cabinet and the appropriate government department. In both contexts the issue of Chinese immigration could be debated and used safely in the absence of any substantive information on the Chinese Community, its organisation or activity, with the exception of three investigations into illegal activity (customs duty evasion, 1918; intermarriage with the indigenous Maori population, 1929; and illegal immigration 1957).
7. The Chinese population had declined as a percentage of the total population front 0.9% in 1881 to 0.24% in 1926.
8. News of the Japanese invasion in 1895 and the Boxer rebellion in 1900 had reached New Zealand leading to considerable debate in the Chinese community.
9. The Poon Fa Association represents people from the counties of Poon Yu and Fa Yuen; Kwong Chew Association represents people from Sun Wui (Seyip); and the Tung Jung Association represents people from Jung Sing and Tung Koon.

10 The number of Chinese women in the population increased from eighty-eight in 1911 to 271 in 1921 (see Appendix 1).
11 Temporary permit provisions had been passed in 1911 making it possible for merchants, tourists and students to come to New Zealand with a deposit of £10.
12 This was equal to the poll tax paid to the New Zealand government by Chinese front 1882 to 1919.
13 The Chinese Association in conjunction with the Consulate, the Chinese Churches and the Presbyterian Church had by 1947 pushed the government into accepting a Chinese minority in New Zealand, and 2,731 Chinese on temporary permits were given permanent residence status. By 1945, 41% of the Chinese community was under twenty-one years of age (see New Zealand Census, 1945 Vol. 8: 17-18).
14 Double Tenth had been an occasion for celebration by many New Zealand Chinese communities since 1912,
15 The final total cost of both projects was close to one million dollars which, excluding external contributions (about 10% of total), was to be financed by the activity and contributions of 3,500 people.

Chapter 7

The Chinese in New York City: Kinship and Immigration

Bernard Wong

Introduction

This paper is devoted to an examination of the adaptive patterns of the Chinese family in New York City life. I will demonstrate that the types of Chinese families developed in America and New York in particular are principally the result of patterns of immigration as well as the economic adaptive activities of the Chinese. The various types of Chinese family developed in America differ not only in size, but also in value orientation, intrafamilial relationships, adjustment problems, and cultural identities.

Chinese-American families differ from those in China and from American families. While the Chinese family in China was characterized by the strong bond between father-son (Hsu, 1953, 1959), Chinese families in America follow a variety of dominant dyads ranging from mother-child to father-son to husband-wife. Residential extended families are practically nonexistent among Chinese American families. However, Chinese American families are not uniformly Americanized. While the neolocal-nuclear family is the rule among Americans (Yorburg, 1973; Hsu, 1953), the Chinese developed a variety of family systems. Further, not all Chinese families are oriented to China; some are assimilated. Despite changes in Chinese American families, certain cultural continuities obtain. This paper will discuss the evolution of various Chinese families in New York City as well as the continuity and change of the Chinese family in the context of immigration and economic adaptation.

Data of the present study are derived from both fieldwork (in 1972, 1973, 1980, 1981)[1] and from written sources. Fieldwork activities included participant observation, interviews, and the collection of life history materials.

The Setting

New York City's Chinese population in 1980 was, according to the U.S. Bureau of Census, 156,331. There has been an increase of approximately 10,000 per year since 1980, bringing the number of Chinese in New York City in 1983 to about 186,000. This number includes all Chinese living in the metropolitan area of New York City. Half of the population concentrate in the Chinatown area at the lower east side of Manhattan. Other areas with sizeable Chinese populations are in the vicinities of Columbia University, Flatbush, Jackson Heights, and the Elmhurst section of Queens.

In the past 20 years, Chinatown-New York has become the largest Chinese population center in the U.S. Other cities that have large numbers of Chinese, in ranked order, are: San Francisco, Honolulu, and Los Angeles (J. Chen,1980). Since the 1870s, New York's Chinatown has developed into an important center for the Chinese. Today, Chinatown is not only a center of consumption, distribution, recreation for the Chinese, it is also the economic nerve of the Chinese in New York City. Economic lifelines of the Chinese are Chinese restaurants, garment factories, grocery stores, and gift shops. Of the 1000 enterprises in the area of Chinatown, 500 are garment workshops, 170 restaurants, 70 retail shops and wholesale businesses ranging from groceries to arts and crafts, and 15 banking institutions. The rest are stationery stores, travel agencies, movie houses, garment factory suppliers, and a variety of service-oriented stores (pharmacies, bakers, etc.).

The Chinese who live in the area of Chinatown depend on ethnic businesses for their livelihood. Professionals who can speak English tend to work in non-Chinese establishments as accountants, engineers, professors, doctors, and live outside of Chinatown. Thus, in a very general way, half of the Chinese are connected to Chinatown and the other half live in residential areas of Manhattan and the suburbs of New York City. Although these Chinese do not live in Chinatown proper, they frequent Chinatown regularly as a center of recreation, shopping, and even occasionally visit their friends and relatives who live there. Chinatown is also the information center for many suburban Chinese, for it publishes more than 10 different daily newspapers which carry city news, community news, international news, and news about China and Taiwan.

Chinatown is also a manpower center that supplies all the necessary personnel for Chinese restaurants in Brooklyn, Queens, and other parts of New York City. It is a heterogeneous community with many different social classes, diversified occupations, with people from different parts of China. In the pre-1965 period, the lingua franca for the community was Toysanese. Today, the standard Cantonese spoken in Hong Kong and the Guangzhou area is predominant. Other dialects such as Shanghainese, Mandarin and Fukienese can be heard in the streets and business establishments in Chinatown-New York.

The Chinese community of New York is heterogeneous in other aspects as well. There are many different types of families, ranging from the incomplete family (with one parent) to nonresidential extended families, with a variety of life styles and attitudes toward their ethnic identity. As will be demonstrated in this paper, these differences are mainly due to external circumstances and are results of immigration and the economic adaptation of the Chinese in a new land.

Immigration and the Chinese Family Patterns in New York City

Development of the Chinese family system in America is intricately related to the immigration pattern of the Chinese to the United States. Although family systems of other ethnic groups, such as the Anglo,

Italian, Irish, and other Europeans, are affected by immigration patterns in the sense that the second generation family differed from the first (Yorburg, 1973), none went through the same experience as the Chinese in America. The types of Chinese families and the quality of family life of the Chinese have been shaped and influenced by U.S. immigration laws applied to the Chinese.

1. The Chinese Exclusion Law and the Incomplete Family

The Chinese Exclusion Law of 1882, and the Immigration Act of 1924 specifically, prohibited immigration of Chinese women (Rung, 1962; Lee, 1960; Wong, 1982). Thus, a married woman would not be permitted to join her husband and many American Chinese families were separated. However, minor children could still gain entrance through the American-born parent. The family resulting from this immigration restriction is the *incomplete family,* consisting of one parent and children. Another factor aggravated the situation: the practice of Chinese men to return to China to get married and to sire children. Reasons for such a practice are: (1) the miscegenation law in effect prohibited Chinese from marrying white American women; (2) the imbalanced sex ratio, with males outnumbering females by a large margin as a consequence of the migration prohibition against women. Those who returned to China to sire children were of two kinds. One group hoped to return to China permanently after amassing a fortune. The other group hoped that their children could be brought to the U.S. Even if the children were admitted later, the mother often was not. As a result, many Chinese American families, until the 1940s, were separated. Some writers called this kind of family "mutilated" (Cheng, 1948; Chu, 1973). Consistent with the current usage in sociological literature, I call it the "incomplete family." Although there were Chinese with children and wives in New York's Chinatown in the 1940s, the majority of the men left their families behind in China. Hence, most Chinese in the U.S. in the 1940 era were male who were deprived of their family life.

According to the Bureau of Census statistics, out of 909 Chinese in New York state in 1880, only 12 were women. By 1890, when the Chinese population in New York state had increased to 2,935, only 33 were female. Male predominance persisted until 1965. For instance, in 1940 the sex ratio between Chinese male and female was almost six to one. The age group between 25 and 59 years made up 73.4 percent of the total Chinese population (Wu, 1958:24), and up to the end of World War II, New York's Chinatown was composed of adult, single males. Some authors referred to this as "bachelor society." Such labeling, although not inaccurate, is misleading, since the majority of this group were married, but their wives remained in China. According to Cheng-Tsu Wu (1958), in 1940 the ratio of married Chinese whose wives were not living in this country to those whose were living with them was six to one (see Table 1).

Table 1
New York City's Chinese Population by Sex

Year	Male	Female	Total
1910	5,060	210	5,266
1920	5,240	553	5,793
1930	8,649	1,060	9,665
1940	10,967	1,786	12,753
1950	13,702	4,703	18,404
1960	20,658	12,173	32,831
1970	37,504	31,820	69,324
1980	80,975	77,583	158,558

2. Immigration of War Brides

Improved U.S.-China relations in the 1940s started to change the quality of family life of the Chinese Americans. During the Sino-Japan War, the U.S. became the ally of China. Further, in the post World War II era, the U.S. joined many nations in the United Nation's pledge of self-determination. Moreover, China was not just a friend, she also became one of the five powers with the right to veto in the U.N. Changing attitudes towards China had a great deal to do with the repeal of the Chinese Exclusion Law in 1943. In the same year, the Act of 1924 was amended. Wives and/or unmarried children under 20 became eligible for admission to the U.S. as nonquota immigrants. These new provisions effected reunions of some Chinese families.

Immediately after World War II, another legislation — the War Bride Act of 1945 — facilitated immigration of Chinese women. Anyone who had served a minimum of six months in the U.S. armed forces could sponsor admission of his family. In fact, many Chinese ex-servicemen took the opportunity to return to China to bring back their wives and children, However, the sex ratio in 1950 was still imbalanced, with 13,702 males vs. 4,703 females (Table 1).

Lack of family life in Chinatowns during the period of 1882-1943 was responsible for the existence of family-name and hometown associations. It was also partially responsible for the Tong Wars as well. Many writers believed that the lack of outlets to participate in the larger society, coupled with lack of family life, propelled ambitious and rootless men into physical violence and racketeering activities (Lee, 1960; Kong, 1962; Chu, 1973). Some Tongs also monopolized illegal selling of "immigration slots" called "paper sons." From 1882 to 1950, many Chinese children born in China, but registered as "sons" of American citizens, could be admitted to the U.S. The practice was open to abuse, with many documents falsified and many "sons" only on paper. Cases were numerous enough, in fact, to cause concern in the U.S. Immigration Department.

The War Brides Act and the admission of Chinese families indeed improved the family life of the Chinese. The type of family resulting from the reunion was often the *conjugal or nuclear family*. According to Rose Lee (1 960), up to the end of 1950 about 6000 foreign-born Chinese women, accompanied by 600 young babies, entered the United States under the War Bride Act. Half of these (3000) were believed to have settled in New York's Chinatown (Chu, 1973). Even with the influx of Chinese war brides, the female and male ratio in 1950 was still far from even (see Table 1).

3. Stranded Chinese Scholars and the Wars in China

Rose Lee (1960) used the term *stranded* to refer to Chinese who came to the U.S. for education or other specific missions, but due to World War 11 and subsequent civil wars in China were not able to return to their homeland. Most of these Chinese were in the professions. Some came with their families, others married people of the same category after completion of their education. The third group of Chinese, considering the political chaos and instability in China, migrated to the U.S. with their families. Common among these three groups are: (1) all were highly educated; (2) most migrated from urban areas; (3) most worked outside the confines of Chinatown; (4) most lived outside of Chinatown; and (5) most were more westernized in their lifestyle and outlook.

The stranded family phenomenon occurred mostly during the 1940s and 1950s. The subsequent takeover of the Chinese mainland by Communism in 1949 promoted another action by the U.S. government. In 1953, the Refugee Act was passed, admitting another 214,000 refugees to the U.S., many of whom were Chinese. Some of these Chinese refugees settled in New York City. Thus, refugee families who arrived in the U.S. during this period had socioeconomic backgrounds similar to those of the stranded families, and many joined relatives in U.S. Chinatowns.

4. The New Immigrants

New immigrant is used in this paper to refer to people who migrated to the U.S. after 1965. The Immigration and Nationality Act Amendments in 1965 instituted a system of preference specifically for immigration of families and aliens with skills and talents. Since 1965, with the influx of new immigrants and their families, the sex ratio in the Chinese American population became more balanced. The New York Chinese population sex ratio in 1970 was 37,504 males : 31,820 females (see Table I) — another indication that family systems and family life are affected by U.S. immigration laws. In fact, the Chinese community in New York was so used to being without families that it found it difficult to deal with some of the problems created by new immigrant families — juvenile delinquency, schools, family quarrels, etc.

U.S.-China normalization since 1972 also facilitated the reunion of Chinese American families. Some Chinese made use of the friendly relations between the two countries to join their long-separated families. Some are still waiting in China and Hong Kong for their quota. While many Chinese Americans were counting their blessings, the U.S. Congress in 1982 proposed elimination of the 5th preference (admission of brothers and sisters of U.S. citizens), which aroused strong reactions from all the Chinese community. Residents of New York's Chinatown joined other nationality groups to register their protest in Washington, DC. For the sake of family reunion, they cooperated with other ethnic groups to lobby for retention of the 5th preference (i.e., migration of brothers and sisters to the U.S.)

On balance, Chinese Americans in the post 1965 era, especially since U.S.-China normalization, have benefited from more equitable treatment in the U.S. immigration laws. Many American Chinese families have been reunited or joined by more relatives from Hong Kong or China; these families with a newly-arrived parent or parents have been enlarged. The *enlarged families,* which consist of nuclear families and other relatives, have recently increased slightly.

Another effect of the recent immigration law is the emergence of *nonresidential extended families.* Parents who came earlier can now sponsor married children and their families. Migration of married children's families helped constitute the so-called "extended families." However, I must qualify that these extended families are not the traditional big-house family with many members and several generations living under one roof. They are nonresidential with families living separately. Likewise, parents and married children have individual households. These families, though independent consumption units, often have a common family business such as a restaurant or grocery store. In a sense, it is an economic productive unit with many individual families participating in establishment and maintenance of a family firm. The nonresidential type of extended family is another recent phenomenon related to the change of the immigration law of 1965 (Wong, 1974).

In summary thus far, the *incomplete, conjugal, enlarged, and nonresidential extended families* of Chinese Americans are part and parcel of the consequences of implementation of various immigration laws. Not only were the types of families related to immigration patterns, the quality of family life, numbers of families, and sex ratio between male and female were likewise affected by the various immigration laws.

Intrafamilial Relationships

The Chinese community of New York is heterogeneous in both family type and socioeconomic background, *Incomplete, enlarged, nuclear and nonresidential extended families* exist among Chinese of diverse socioeconomic backgrounds. However, proportionately we find more incomplete families among Old Immigrants and more nuclear families among American-born Chinese, New Immigrants, and professional Chinese. Extended families are practically nonexistent. However, there are relatively more nonresidential extended families among the New

Immigrants. The most prevalent for all groups of Chinese is the nuclear family. Census statistics of 1980 indicated that, out of 37,956 family households, 32,875 are married-couple (nuclear) families (see Table 2).

Table 2
Family and Nonfamily Households of Chinese in New York City

All households	47,762
Family households	37,956
Married-couple families w/children (87%)	32,875
Female household, wo/husband present,	
w/children (8%)	3,055
other (5%)	2,026
Nonfamily households	9,806
Persons per household : 3.28	
Persons per family: 3.77	

Source : U.S. Census of Population, 1980.

Married-couple families with children under 18 and younger account for 87 percent of all family households in New York City. Table 2 also shows that there are 3,055 families headed by female householders without husbands present, amounting to 8 percent of all family households. Further, 2,000 families are headed by males, accounting for 5 percent of all Chinese family households in New York City. The number of incomplete families in New York's Chinatown area is proportionately larger. While the exact number of incomplete families is not available in Chinatown, my rough estimate is that 25 percent of all family households in Chinatown are incomplete families. In 1970, *Chinatown (NY) Study Group* reported that more than 57.3 percent of Chinese families did not come to this country together, meaning that there are quite a few *temporary* incomplete families. Their family reunion has been achieved by a process of immigration relays (Sung, 1979; Asian American Field Survey 1977; see Table 3).

Intrafamilial relationships in Chinese families in New York City are highly diversified and complex since there are so many different types of families. In comparison to American families, which emphasize

Table 3
Family and Immigration

Question: Did your family come to the USA together?			
Yes	No	No Response	Total
174	260	20	454
38.3%	57.3%	4.4%	100%

independence, freedom, and privacy and are characterized by dominance of the husband-wife dyad (Hsu, 1953), Chinese American families in New York City followed many patterns of dominant dyads (father-son, mother-child, husband-wife, etc.) depending on patterns of immigration and socioeconomic backgrounds of the families.

1. Old Immigrant Families

The economic base of the old immigrants is strictly in the traditional ethnic niche of the Chinese: Chinese restaurants, garment factories, gift shops, groceries and laundries. *Old Immigrant families* refers to the first generation Chinese who arrived in the U.S. before 1965. To distinguish old immigrants from their descendants who were born in the U.S., I use the phrase *American-born Chinese* to refer to the latter. Old Immigrants are Chinatown-connected. Many of them started as employees and are now employers. They are Chinatown originals, in the sense that they came from socioeconomic backgrounds similar to those Chinatown old settlers/founders who arrived in the U.S. in the late 19th and early 20th centuries from four districts near Canton City in Kwangtung Province and speak the Toysan dialect. Social organizations were founded on bases of kinship, clanship, linguistic similarity, and regionalism and catered specifically to the needs of the old immigrants. These social organizations are still frequented by old immigrants today (Wong, 1978). In the pre-1965 era, some old immigrants had no intention of sponsoring relatives to the U.S. This group of old immigrants were sojourners who intended to return to China to join their families. Some old immigrants, however, sponsored their relatives to the U.S. The common pattern is to sponsor some members of the family first, normally the sons, and later other members of the family. Thus, the family reunion was completed in a period of time by a process of relay immigration.

A third group of old immigrants living in New York City have families. Benefiting from the War Bride Act or Refugee Act of 1943, they were able to sponsor their families in the 1940s and early 1950s to join them. These three groups of old immigrant families still exist in Chinatown. Thus, New York's Chinatown today has old immigrants who are separated from their families in China, those who have relay families, and those who have a war wife or refugee families. The latter two are relevant to this paper since they actually live with their families today in the U.S.

Common among all Old Immigrant families are their value orientation and their attachment to the Old World. Old Immigrant families retain the values of the Old World and filial piety is emphasized. Family authority is structured by age, sex, and birth rank. These families use traditional kinship terminology such as *Ge* (older brother), *De* (younger brother), *Che* (older sister), and *Mei* (younger sister). Boys are given more family authority than girls. The eldest son is the father's successor. The language used in the family is Toysanese. All major traditional festivals, such as the Chinese New Year, the Moon-cake Festival, and the Dragon Boat Festival are celebrated. The perpetuation of the family business is usually entrusted to the eldest son. In fact, fathers often sponsored immigration of their Chinese sons born on the mainland before they sponsored their wives. The idea was to ensure economic betterment for future generations by learning the family business and perpetuating it through the sons. Thus, many Chinese fathers wanted to start their sons in the family business while they were still young,

Both husband and wife are expected to maximize their savings through frugal living, but the wife in particular is expected to be a good housekeeper and spend little money. Frugality is highly valued among these families. Like the Chinese in the Philippines, Peru, and elsewhere, frugal living is the foundation of many entrepreneurial successes. Many of the older informants whom I interviewed constantly used the Chinese saying, *Chin Chien Chi Chia*, which means "frugality is the beginning of family success." Money saved is used for many purposes: (1) to expand the business; (2) to buy real estate; (3) to buy gold and diamond jewelry, which is believed to have more stability than money and could be converted readily to cash; and (4) to send children back to China to receive a Chinese education and to get married. Sending children to China now for education is out of the question. The money is spent in the U.S. for higher education of the children or to purchase household appliances when the children get married.

Children of old immigrant families were and still are encouraged to pursue higher education and be trained in practical fields: accounting, business management, engineering. For the delayed united old immigrant families, there is a tendency for mothers to have a great deal of influence on their children (Sung, 1979). In these delayed united families where children had lived with their mothers in China for many years before migrating to the U.S. the mother-child dyad was naturally predominant. Long years of separation from the father and the rest of the family posed many strains and difficulties of readjustment to new family life in the U.S. On arrival in the U.S., children often considered their fathers as "strangers," Since the child-rearing function and educational and disciplinary functions were entirely in the hands of mothers for years, arriving in the U.S. may not change the pattern. Mothers still play a central role in delayed united old immigrant families. Hence, a contradiction seems to exist among at least some old immigrant families. It is patriarchal in form but matriarchal in content (Sung, 1974). Among the more fortunate old immigrants who had their families in the U.S. from the very beginning or shortly after their marriage, there was little or no lengthy separation between the husband and the rest of the family. In this kind of family — certainly a minority — the dominant dyad is the traditional father-son relation. Thus, two patterns dominate within families of old immigrants, resulting principally from life chance and immigration experience: father-son vs. mother-child. Thus, the traditional father bond that guided social relations within the family in China is not applicable in all cases in old immigrant families in New York City. The dominant dyad of the traditional family in China between the father and son, which was important for descent and continuity of the traditional family system (Hsu, 1968), is not duplicated in all families. I also found weakening of the father-son bond, especially in American-born Chinese families. This diminished father-son bond is responsible for the disinterest among children of old immigrant families in practicing ancestor worship or joining any clan associations in Chinatown-New York today. In fact, children of old immigrant families, especially those who were native born, tend to move out of Chinatown and establish neolocal residence and nuclear families (families of American-born Chinese will be discussed later in this paper). Two other factors can account for their departure from Chinatown. One is education, which brought them more lucrative and prestigious professions in U.S. society. Second is the influence of the American way of life which emphasizes independence, freedom, and privacy. Differently put, the changed economic base of American-born Chinese has dissociated them from traditional family systems and the cultural influence of Chinatown.

2. New Immigrant Families

New immigrant families came to the U.S. after 1965. Many came together as families (see Table 3). The economic bases of new immigrant families, though varied, concentrate principally in the ethnic niche: garment factory, restaurant custom jewelry, grocery businesses, etc. Thus, they are Chinatown-connected and rely on traditional Chinese businesses. However, among new immigrants there are class or economic differences (Wong, 1976). Some are better educated and have English-speaking ability; others are less educated with no skills or ability in English. Educated children with skills will have more options. As time goes on, some will move out of Chinatown into other parts of New York to start Chinese restaurants or to work for American establishments after they have overcome initial adjustment problems or have accumulated enough savings. Some educated children will also stay in Chinatown for the unique opportunities they have carved out for themselves in real estate, accounting, TV-radio broadcasting, restaurant, or the various retail trades catering to residents of Chinatown. Families of well-to-do, well-educated New Immigrants differ from those of less affluence in many respects. Well-to-do new immigrant families pay special attention to children with regard to their homework and their future careers. Less affluent families have little or no time or ability to care for their children (Table 4).

Both less and more affluent new immigrant families prefer nuclear families and would like their children to straddle two cultures: Chinese and the U.S. However, intrafamilial relationships differ (Wong, 1974, 1976, 1982). Among the well-to-do, the traditional father-son bond typical in old China is now replaced by husband-wife relationships similar to those of the majority of American families. Both husband and wife contribute their time for childrearing and both parents also contribute financial resources for the maintenance of the family. However, the husband-wife relationship is not absolutely equal, with the latter leaning on the former for many family functions and decisions. In general, parents dominate their children rather than vice versa. It is not youth centered either, This seems to be another difference between children of the new immigrants and the majority of U.S. culture. Children always

Table 4
Dominant Dyads in Various Types of Chinese Families in New York City

Types of Families	Dominant Dyad	Cultural Orientation
Old immigrant families	Majority: father-son Some: mother-child	Old World
New immigrant families	Well-to-do/ well-educated : husband-wife	Chinese-U.S.
	Less affluent : children tend to dominate	
Families of American-born Chinese	Husband-wife	U.S.
"Stranded intellectual" or first-generation immigrant-professional families	Husband-wife	US.; U.S.-Chinese
Nonresidential extended families	In business: father-son In living : husband-wife	U.S. + Chinese

occupy second place in this kind of Chinese family. Parents love their children but also want to maintain control of their behavior, Thus, freedom among children of the well-to-do Chinese immigrant families is curtailed. In the selection of careers, children are strongly influenced by their parents. In fact, many teenagers have to follow the advice of parents in the selection of majors, schools, and even friends. It is common to see many college-age Chinese children supported by their parents for their college education and living with their parents in Chinatown. In fact, some parents told me that they do not want their children to "misbehave" and be "unduly influenced by their peers" and that they require their children to live at home. As students in public grade school and high school, many of the well-to-do children are required to attend the Chinese school on Saturdays and Sundays in Chinatown as their parents wish.

While affluent Chinese immigrants control their children, less affluent parents are sometimes controlled by their children — a role reversal for the parents (Sung, 1974). Not knowing English and the U.S. society, parents have to depend on their children for information. Children keep their parents away from school affairs by not interpreting some of the letters from the school. Due to the pressure of work, many children seldom see their parents as both work at menial jobs and are required to work long hours to support the family. Children of these families are without supervision. They make independent decisions about their use of leisure time and about school activities. Some do well; others do not. The latter become school "dropouts" or get involved in youth gangs. This kind of family resembles many of its counterparts among disadvantaged ethnic groups in the U.S. The disorganization of this type of new immigrant family has a great deal to do with poverty, which is a result of economic exploitation as well as lack of proper training or skills. Immigrants without English ability and other marketable skills often fill the ranks of menial labor and work long hours for less compensation. They help support profit aggrandizing activities of employers at the expense of a healthier family life. It is common to find both parents working 10-12 hours a day. The father's work is normally in the restaurant from 10 a.m. to midnight. The mother usually works as a seamstress in one of the garment factories for equally long hours. Thus, children of this kind of working family have little contact with or supervision from their parents. On the contrary, parents may have to turn to their children for help ; they need the English skill of the children as well as their knowledge of American culture. Instead of parents educating the child, roles are reversed in the less affluent new immigrant families. Children instruct their parents. Further, these young children cannot turn to their parents for guidance or direction, since the parents know little about the American way of life and the problems of growing up in America.

Unlike old immigrant families, all new immigrant families want to make the United States their permanent home. However from interviews and observation of new immigrant families, it is clear that the majority of the parents intend to instill in their children the traditional values of filial piety and teach them the Chinese language. At the same time, these parents want their children to learn English and receive college educations so that one day they may be *accepted* by the larger society. These parents hope their children will straddle both cultures — Chinese and American.

Although the husband is still expected to be the main provider, the wife also contributes to the common purse by working on her own or by assisting in the husband's business. Unlike the old immigrant families, where wives were expected to work either at home or within the family firm, wives of new immigrants have no such limitations. If the husband has a firm, the wife usually helps him with it. Otherwise she may seek employment in one of the Chinese garment factories or restaurants. Some even work as cashiers or secretaries for Chinese firms in Chinatown.

The value of thrift is emphasized in all new immigrant families. Both husband and wife strive to save as much as possible by working longer hours to earn extra income and by living frugally. It is common for new immigrants to reside in rundown or substandard housing in order to cut down on rent. However, these people are generous with their food budgets: they are not stingy about spending money in Chinese restaurants or purchasing food for family consumption because they believe one must maintain and improve one's health as the foundation of all gain-seeking activities. Extravagance in housing is not desirable because they believe that: (1) rent in New York is far too high, especially for good housing; (2) expensive housing is not necessary because they spend most of their waking hours at work and use their apartments only at night to sleep; (3) it is better to save more money for a rainy day or for future investment or expansion of one's business than to use the money "unprofitably" for lodging; and (4) living conditions even in Chinatown, the Bronx, or some other inexpensive neighborhood were no worse than what they encountered in Hong Kong.

All new immigrant families are Chinatown-connected for their economic well-being. Ethnic enterprises that help the achievement of the "American dream" also break the harmony and solidarity of some of the new immigrant families.

3. *Families of American-born Chinese*

Families of American-born Chinese are either second, third, fourth, or fifth generation Americans. They tend to fare better economically as a group because of their training and education. In the present-day Chinese community, some families are descendants of old immigrants, some descendants of stranded intellectuals, or descendants of first generation professionals. The economic base of these families is no longer the ethnic niche. Principally, they are in various professions — engineers, professors, scientists, computer scientists, doctors and lawyers. They work and live among the white middle class. Many values of the American middle class have been absorbed by American-born Chinese. These include neolocal households, independence, privacy, the habits of purchasing appliances on credit, materialism, emphasis on success, etc.

The husband-wife relationship in families of American-born Chinese differ significantly from that of old or new immigrants. First, although the husband is expected to be the provider and the head of the family, he is no longer the undisputed decision-maker. The husband is expected to consult his wife on major decisions. Frank discussions between husband and wife are more prevalent than in old and new immigrant families, The wife is often employed on her own, but the husband-wife bond is relatively strong. The measure of a successful marriage in families of American-born Chinese is the absence of divorce (Lee 1960).

The consumption pattern of families of American-born Chinese also differs from that of immigrant families. Thrift is not emphasized. American-born Chinese spend more money on recreation, furnishings, automobiles, housing, and electrical appliances. Even though some families have two wage earners and an income that is often greater than that of immigrant families, they do not have large amounts of savings or investments like new and old immigrants.

Families of American-born Chinese do not faithfully follow traditional Chinese customs. They cat some Chinese food and celebrate some Chinese festivals, but they do not speak Chinese in the family. Although their parents might have been relatively interested in retaining some traditional practices, such as addressing each other with traditional kinship terminology, children of these families prefer to follow the American way of addressing one another. I was told by some children that they are American first and Chinese second. There is more spontaneous discussion and communication in families of American born Chinese than in immigrant families. The latter also complained that American-born Chinese are not "strict" enough with their children and are not educating them in "civilized Chinese" manners.

From discussions with American-born Chinese, I learned that some second-generation Chinese were concerned with transmitting knowledge about Chinese cultural heritage to their American-born children. Their offspring, however, frequently wanted to be accepted by the larger society and were reluctant to learn the language and culture of China. To avoid conflict, an overwhelming majority of these parents compromised and tried not to impose their preferences on their children.

In American-born Chinese families, both father and mother share household chores and rearing of children. They also allow their children to make independent decisions concerning their mates, careers, and residence. Children date whom they like and marry partners of their own choice, whether they are white, black, or Chinese.

Parents in immigrant families (old or new) were not interested in joining organizations like the PTA; lack of time and lack of proficiency in English prevented such participation. American-born Chinese are quite active in the PTA. This does not mean that old immigrants were not interested in their children's education — Chinese of all categories emphasize higher education for their children.

Generally, immigrant families (both old and new) retained more Old World traditions than American-born Chinese. Sometimes the latter are labeled by the former as *Juk Sing,* meaning "bamboo-stick," which is used as a metaphor to indicate lack of roots in either Chinese or American culture. Sometimes they are also referred to as "bananas" by first-generation immigrants, meaning that they are "yellow" outside and "white" inside. These labels, though stereotypical, reflect a high degree of assimilation of American-born Chinese. In contrast, children of immigrant families who are born in China are referred to as *Juk Kak,* which means literally the "bamboo joint." It is a metaphor to indicate the cultural leaning of immigrant children born in China. They are rooted only in Chinese culture, not in American culture. The Chinese language is used in immigrant families, but only English is used in American-born Chinese families.

4. *Families of Professionals*

Families of professionals include all first generation Chinese who were either stranded in this country or voluntarily migrated to the U.S. for professional reasons or economic opportunities. The economic base of these Chinese is again outside of Chinatown. Many are intellectuals working at a university, research center, or library organization, or as engineers, accountants, architects, computer scientists, doctors, etc. They are westernized in their outlook and lifestyles. Many lived in major urban centers in China before settlement in the U.S. As mentioned earlier, some first-generation Chinese professionals were literally "stranded" in the U.S. because of the outbursts of civil war and political change in 1949 in China. Rose Lee called them "stranded families" (1960). The term stranded is no longer applicable, for some first-generation Chinese went through great difficulty to effect immigration into this country to practice their professions. I call all first-generation Chinese immigrant-professionals in this class *Chinese professionals*. They share many characteristics in common. They were better educated and were urbanized. Having lived in major urban centers in China before the revolution or in Hong Kong or Macao, many were westernized in their clothing, recreational, eating, and living habits. These individuals tended to come from wealthier families in China and as they originally came to the U.S. to further their careers for the sake of social mobility, they were not concerned with Chinatown's community affairs. Chinese ethnic enclaves, which were full of Chinese immigrants from southern China, bad little in common with the professional or stranded Chinese and their families. Additionally, there were differences in dialect, locality of origin, as well as orientation in the U.S. The families of professional Chinese live in suburbs of New York City or in the affluent residential areas of Manhattan and work and live among middle-class white Americans. Many professionals disdained Chinatown. They felt that Chinatown was not representative of China and considered residents of Chinatown to be low class and barbaric, since they were not highly educated and came from southern regions of China. This is particularly the case among "stranded" Chinese who came from northern China; they carried with them their regional ethnocentrism. For these reasons, a "distance" existed between Chinese professional families and Chinatown until the 1970s when a chance took place. Part of the reason for the change of attitude was the awareness of ethnicity and the ethnic movement. The Civil Rights movement of the larger society had a great deal of influence among all middle-class Americans, the professional Chinese included. Children and grandchildren of families of the professionals Chinese born in the U.S. became more democratic and egalitarian. The "class consciousness" and regional ethnocentrism of their parents and grandparents began to wear down, and some of these second and third generation American-born Chinese even returned to the Chinese community of lower Manhattan to organize community services for the poor and needy (Wong, 1977).

Families of professional Chinese also stress the husband-wife bond rather than the traditional father-son bond. Neolocal residence and nuclear family systems are preferred. With the opening up of China since 1972, many first-generation Chinese professionals took advantage of the relaxation of immigration constraints to sponsor their parents to come to the U.S. Thus, some nuclear families now became enlarged families.

Since the majority of family heads were born in China and had been educated in China, certain cultural roots had been planted. Values such as filial piety, frugality, hard work, hospitality, propriety are still deep in their thinking. On the other hand, because of Western education and contacts with Westerners, they were also westernized. Some were Christian converts and subscribed to many Western cultural practices. They were for democracy in government, equality among men, women's liberation, and romantic marriages. Their marriages as well as those of their children were entirely their own choice. In selecting mates, the concern is with companionship, common attraction, common interests, and mutual affection. Their attitudes toward careers differ little from other middle-class Americans. An achievement orientation is inculcated among the children. Siblings are no longer required to address each other by reverential kinship terminology. Although parental authority is still strong among some of the more tradition-minded professional Chinese families, there is more democracy and also more exchange among family members.

In terms of cultural orientation, there is no consensus among all Chinese professionals who are first generation immigrants. One group is for complete Americanization; their attitude is "while in Rome, behave as Romans do". The other group retains a dual attitude and prefers to straddle two cultures — Chinese and American. This second group of Chinese professionals hope that their children will master both Chinese and English and acquire a synthesis of both cultures. However, their American-born children tend to be completely Americanized disregarding the efforts of their first generation parents. Perhaps this is due to peer group pressure as well as their concern for professionalism. It seems that they are so highly dedicated to pursuing their professional life that they have no time to synthesize a Chinese-American lifestyle. While in school, they propelled all their energy into scholastic excellence. While at work, they are dedicated to work and to improvement of their careers. Hence, it is difficult for them to learn Chinese language and culture.

Intermarriage with white Americans occurs among some professional Chinese. This is due to the stress on common interests and compatible lifestyles. In the case of children of intermarriages, they identify only with the United States. This phenomenon is common among other racial-ethnic groups in America. Through interracial and interethnic marriages, the "melting pot" type of Americanization (Gordon, 1964) has been achieved among many ethnic groups in the U.S. My personal research in

Peru (Wong, 1979) indicated that the rapid process and high degree of assimilation of Chinese into Peruvian society had a great deal to do with intermarriage between Chinese and Peruvians. Many other social scientists also believe that interracial marriage is an important factor for assimilation of various immigrant groups into the mainstream of host societies (Lee, 1960 ; Kong, 1962 ; Wagley and Harris, 1958 ; Blalock, 1967 ; Mitchison, 1961 ; Lyman, 1968). However, the number of interracial marriages between Chinese and whites in New York City or elsewhere in the U.S. has not been significantly large (Weiss, 1973). Descendants resulting from these marriages in New York City are not more than 1000 (Wong, 1978).

In general families of professional Chinese are more assimilated than those of old and new immigrant families mentioned earlier. The major reasons for their high degrees of assimilation (Gordon, 1964) are because they are not Chinatown-connected. They work and live among white Americans. Their economic base has allowed them to have more contacts with U.S. society through education, institutions, careers, neighborhood connections, professional associations, churches, and other secondary institutions. Their lifestyle is principally a product of their careers, which are intimately connected with the American economy and society.

5. Nonresidential Extended Families

The ideal of traditional Chinese families to have many generations living 'under one roof remained an ideal in both China and outside China. Many studies on China confirmed that the average family size in traditional China was 5.7. Of the three communities (Manila, NYC and Lima) I studied, only the Philippines saw the occurrence of the big-house type of extended family. Even among Philippine Chinese, the number of such families remains small. Chinese in Peru and the U.S. have practically no residential extended families.

In all three Chinese communities (Manila, Lima, and New York) however, nonresidential extended families exist. Thus, brothers with their married wives and respective children may live in the same neighborhood or in the general vicinity of each other. Each of these families maintains their own kitchen and is an independent consumption unit. Social and economic interaction among these families are intense. Information about children, schooling, and health care is exchanged. Economic interaction may take the form of partnerships. Thus, members of non-extended families may own a business as partners or work together in the firm of their parents. Socially, they celebrate many traditional holidays together and participate in family rites of passage and social activities of the family firm. The existence of nonresidential families seems to be dictated by two major factors (Wong, 1974). One is resources. Lack of capital and manpower resources dictated close cooperation of all family members, Second is the urban environment which makes it difficult to find space to house many people in one household. Other reasons include ease of living in a smaller family unit and the power of women in modern societies. The father-son dyad is gradually being replaced by the husband-wife dyad which influences day-to-day activities of one's family. In a sense, this change was brought about by the modern economy and by changes in host societies (such as the Women's Liberation Movement, industrialization, urbanization), as well as by the generally increased status of women in modern society. Women often have economic power and with it they are less hesitant to assert their independence. They are less likely to put up with in-laws and the dictatorship of husbands.

In New York City, nonresidential extended families exist principally among new immigrants who needed both financial and labor resources for establishing and maintaining traditional ethnic businesses. Both garment factories and Chinese restaurants are labor-intensive. Profit maximization depends on flexibility, hard work, and trust (Wong, 1974, 1979, 1982). The relationship in the firm is an extension of that of the traditional extended family. In a garment factory that I observed, I noted that all four sisters of the owners were supervisors of four important sections of the firm. They were, however, coordinated by the oldest brother who was the major decision maker. Action was taken without much consultation. All the sisters trusted him and followed his direction without question. During his absence, the older sister would be in charge of the operation. Similarly, in a family restaurant, I saw the management pattern along kinship lines. The father was the patriarch who decided what to buy and sell and what the salary schedules would be of all employees. The father also assigned key positions to the sons. All the daughters and daughters-in-law served as waitresses. The expansion of the firm also followed the traditional kinship pattern. Thus the first branch of the restaurant was headed by the eldest son. The second son managed the second branch, and so on. When it came to individual family affairs, it depended on the constituent families. Married sons and daughters each lived independently with their spouses and children in nuclear households.

Thus, the extended family is not a residential unit; it functions as a firm family, as an economic-productive unit. It is an economic adaptive strategy dictated by economic needs and by the type of businesses pursued by Chinese. Professional Chinese, on the other hand, are wage-earners, employed by various American firms. They do not have to establish nonresidential extended families to pool financial and labor resources to maintain an economic unit. However, among new Chinese immigrants, it is desirable to have family cooperation for the establishment of labor intensive enterprises. They also find it easy to pool their capital than to borrow from banks. As new immigrants, many are without credit references and necessary collateral and they will not be able to obtain loans to finance their businesses. Restaurants and garment factories are tedious and require trusted and hard-working laborers. Family members are the best laborers to fill the needs. Many informants lamented that they do not have enough trusted help to manage their business because they simply do not have enough kinsmen.

The number of nonresidential families could not be ascertained since official census statistics in the U.S. have no such category. Of a sample (30) of Chinese restaurants I studied, one-third were run by nonresidential extended families, and all were highly successful.

The intrafamilial relationship or each constituent nuclear family is similar to those of the nuclear families of new immigrants, which was discussed earlier and will not be repeated here.

Wider Kinship

Kinship relationships outside of families are various types of fictive kinships and clanships. Both of these are influenced by the larger society as well as by the mother country. The use of lineage and clanship for organization of association networks is particularly strong among the Chinese in the Philippines (Amyot, 1973). In this respect, the Chinese in Peru are the weakest, and the Chinese in the U.S. are ranked in the middle.

Lineage association based on patrilineal kinship in China is adopted by overseas Chinese. In the Old Country, a lineage is an exogamous kinship unit in which members can trace blood relationship to an ancestor associated with a given locality (Hu, 1948). However, lineage associations among overseas Chinese are based on surname, without a necessarily demonstrable blood relationship. Hence, it seems to be anthropologically appropriate to call these lineage associations clan associations. There are also multisurname associations that were formed according to historical alliances or traditional sworn-brotherhoods. In Manila, there are more than 47 clan associations, representing 76 surnames. Each of these association averages about 700 members (Amyot, 1973: Wong, 1968).[2] Among the Chinese in New York, there are 24 family-name (clan) associations, representing 60 family names (Wong, 1974). Membership in New York Chinatown family-name associations is small, ranging front 50 to 500. In Lima, there is only one multifamily name association that claimed to have 200 members. In terms of activities, there is ancestor worship in all clan associations. Other functions include settlement of disputes, celebration of major Chinese holidays, and providing mutual help in financing and employment as well as temporary lodging. From my observation of the three Chinese communities, it appears that there is more intensity in Chinese clan associations in Manila. They have more clan associations, members, and more activities. Further, the clan associations in Manila organize other activities such as scholarship fund drives, the granting of credit, and sponsorship of charity functions for the benefit of the needy. In New York's Chinatown, rotating credit clubs and recreational clubs are also formed within some clan associations. However, most of those who use the clan association facilities in New York's Chinatown are senior citizens. Participation among new immigrants, professionals, and American-born Chinese is low (see Table 5). Seventy-eight percent of the Chinese in New York-Chinatown do not

Table 5

Participation in Chinatown's Family-Name (Clan) Associations

Question: How many members of your family participate in family-name associations?		
	N = 565	100%
None	442	78.2%
One member	59	10.4
More than one member	48	8.5
No response	16	2.9

Source: *Chinatown Study Group Report, 1970.*

participate in clan associations. The clan association in Lima is most inactive and has become more like a social-recreational club than a kinship-mutual help club.

Clan associations in Manila do have some members who actually belong to similar lineages. Thirteen of the surname groups among the Chinese in Manila have more than one association for the same surname. Thus, for instance, Ch'en has four; Shih and Lin each has three; Ts'ai, Li, Yang, Kuo, Ting, Ma, Hsu, Liu, Chang, and Hsieh each have two associations. These associations are segmented according to dialect, regional, and blood ties (Amyot, 1973).

Among the Chinese in New York-Chinatown, anyone who possesses a family name Huang can join the Huang Association. Members could have migrated from different parts of China, with no traceable blood tie, yet they are still eligible to join their respective associations. Thus, there are more genealogical distances in New York Chinese family-name (or clan) associations than in their counter-parts in Manila.

Old immigrant families of New York's Chinatown used the family-name association as well as other methods to enlarge their kinship circle, Similarity in the writing of a surname (e.g., Tan Tom, Hsu, Tse), historical neighbors (e.g., Wu, Chay, Chou; Lay, Fang, Kwang), old friendship (e.g., Chan, Wu, Yuang, Yuen), sworn brotherhood (Liu, Kwan, Chang, Chow), hometowns (e.g., Fukien, Ming Yang), old schoolmates (Ling Name University Alumni Association, etc.) were used widely by old immigrants to create friendship and pseudo kinships groupings. This practice of extending one's circle of kinsmen and friends through clanship association is not common among new immigrants or professionals.

New immigrants or Chinese professionals use principally the dry parenthood or Christian rituals of baptism and confirmation to extend their personal and kinship network. However, increasingly friendship supersedes primordial ties. It is common that some Chinese have closer friends among white Americans than among the Chinese. The social solidarity is based more and more on similarity of profession, collegiality, and sentiment.

American-born Chinese have little to do with the Chinese in Chinatown. Their friends tend to be drawn from other Chinese born in America or from their white peers, neighbors and colleagues. Some of them also use the Christian ritual of baptism to enlarge their kinship circle.

Conclusion

The Chinese family in New York differs from that of the dominant society in the quality of family life as well as in the dynamics and development of various types of family systems. Immigration policies have affected Chinese more than any other immigrant group, for the Chinese were the first to be singled out for wholesale discrimination in the form of "exclusion." The Chinese Exclusion Law and the denial of admission of Chinese women created a "bachelor society" in many Chinatowns for a period of time, and New York's Chinatown was no exception, Separation resulted not simply in incomplete families, but also in the reversal of the role of mothers. Many U.S. immigrant Chinese children were raised in a motherfocal household for years in China without their fathers. After reunion years later with fathers, this pattern of mother dominance still persisted, especially in the old immigrant families. Recent immigration policy changes — notably the 1945 War Brides Act, the 1950 Refugee Act, and the new 1965 Immigration Law brought some positive changes as far as family life for Chinese is concerned. Many migrated with their respective families, others effected the migration of their families in China. The infusion of families changed the demographic pattern of Chinatown-New York as well as the socioeconomic life of the Chinese in New York City in general.

Migration of large numbers of families to the Chinese community in New York City also caught the community by surprise. Many new problems arose, such as juvenile delinquency, education, employment, health care, and housing. Some new immigrant families experienced sudden changes in their family life as well. Not being able to render supervision of their children as a result of economic pressure, they have willingly or unwillingly let the children slip away from their control. Parents were left in the dark about activities of children. Further, intrafamilial relationships also changed from parent-dominated to children-dominated. The children became the center from whom parents had to learn about American culture.

As a result of immigration policies and economic adaptation, the Chinese in New York City developed a variety of family systems: the old immigrant families, new immigrant families, American-born Chinese families, the families of Chinese professionals, and nonresidential extended families. Some of these families are more Old World oriented, others are U.S. oriented. Some straddle two cultures — Chinese and American.

Common among all of them is their diligent pursuit of the "American dream." All emphasize higher education in practical fields. On the other hand, there is no one uniform pattern of intrafamilial relationship applicable to all. Some are characterized by dominance of the traditional father-son dyad, others the mother-child dyad, and still others the husband-wife dyad. Old World influence is stronger in immigrant families (both new and old) and weaker in the rest. Thus, birthplace and length of residence have obvious impacts on adherence to Old World traditions. New World influences such as dominance of the husband-wife dyad, the preference for nuclear family households, the pursuit of affluence and happiness, and emphasis on women's equality are stronger among families of American-born Chinese families and the families of professional Chinese. Non-Chinatown-connected careers, the American education system, and residential patterns of these Chinese families seem to be major factors of Americanization. Chinatown-connected immigrants who depend on the traditional ethnic niche are thus less assimilated than those who work and live among white Americans.

New immigrant families keep up some of the traditions, still fresh among them because of their recent arrival. The majority are oriented to the U.S. and intend to stay permanently. Affluent Chinese want to have the best of both cultures: Chinese and American. They want the Chinese family system but American affluence. In the process of making a living, some still have to rely on capital and labor resources of the family. Hence, the emergence of nonresidential extended families is to meet some practical needs. Even among these business families, certain changes have occurred. They are economic-productive units, but not consumption-residential units like the traditional big-house families. The housing situation in the urban environment and the preference for privacy and independence encourage living separately. Thus, the nonresidential extended family is a special adaptation to economic needs as well as to the urban environment.

Though the traditional Chinese family system has been changed and modified in New York City, some traditions linger on among all Chinese. All seem to value personalism and familism. All want to incorporate friends into their kinship network. Though the exact method of enlarging one's personal/kinship network differs, all resort to some kinds of ritual and fictive kinship. Chinatown-connected immigrants follow traditional methods: Old World connections, dry parenthood, etc. Non-Chinatown-connected Chinese enlarge their personal/kinship networks through

Christian types of godparenthood or professional associations as well as through collegiate, colleague-like old-boy networks.

Of all the different family types discussed in the paper, it appears that American-born Chinese families are assimilated faster into American society. Other trends of development are replacement of the father-son bond by husband-wife bond, the substitution of patrilocal, patrilineal kinship system with the neolocal-nuclear family system with little connection to lineage and clanship. These trends will quicken as the economic opportunity structure widens with the Chinese moving into the careers of middle-class Americans and into neighborhoods of white people. Meanwhile, family life and experience are not comparable among all Chinese in New York City, as they still live and are raised in a variety of families. The quality of family life and evolution of the Chinese family system in New York will continue to depend on two forces that affected them in the past: immigration policies and economic opportunity.

Notes

1 Fieldwork research was supported by a grant (GS-352q) from the National Science Foundation and a fellowship in ethnic studies from The Ford Foundation. A recent follow-up field study was aided by a grant from the University of Wisconsin System Ethnic Studies Coordinating Committee.
2 The field research project on the Chinese was part of *Cognitive Mapping in Manila,* sponsored by the Institute of Philippine Culture (Ateneo de Manila University, 1966-1968).

Chapter 8

Chinese Immigrant Children in New York City: Bicultural Conflicts

Betty Lee Sung

The Chinese now make up one of the largest immigrant groups to the United States. In the decade from 1984 to 1993, immigrants from the People's Republic of China, Taiwan and Hong Kong exceeded half a million. Additional thousands of Southeast Asian refugees as well as secondary migrants from Canada and Latin America entering the country may be of Chinese ethnic origin. Of these newcomers, approximately one out of six are children and youths under 19 years of age. Most studies of immigrants focus upon the adult; few upon the younger generation. A review of the literature reveals almost a total vacuum in studies on how children weather the immigrant experience. Children are considered appendages of the adults. They go where the parents take them. They live where their parents decide. They eat what their parents can provide. Yet children do have concerns of their own, and they react differently. Their experiences deserve to be delineated and looked at separately.

What happens in the lives of Chinese immigrant children and youths when they make that transoceanic leap from the Orient to American soil? More than geography is involved. The language, ways of thinking, behavior, responses, customs, and fundamental beliefs of the two cultures are poles apart. The entire body of culture with which the immigrants are cloaked is called into question. The children must unlearn as well as learn. Even though they may find some aspects of the old culture obsolete, they are loathe to give up that which is part of them. How much of the new must they take on to function adequately? How much are they handicapped at first? How long does it take to acquire some of the new ways?

The moment a child is born, he begins to absorb the culture of his primary group. These ways are so ingrained they become second nature to him. Imagine for a moment how wrenching it must be for an immigrant child who finds his cumulative experiences completely invalidated and who must learn a whole new set of speech patterns and behavior when he settles in a new country. The severity of his culture shock is made all the more apparent by Teper's definition of culture.

> Culture is called a habit system in which 'truths' that have been perpetuated by a group over centuries have permeated the unconscious. This basic belief system from which 'rational' conclusions spring may be so deeply ingrained that it becomes indistinguishable from human perception — the way one sees, feels, believes, knows. It is the continuity of cultural assumptions and patterns that gives order to one's world, reduces an infinite variety of options to a manageable stream of beliefs, gives a person a firm footing in time and space, and binds the lone individual to the communality of a group. (1977:20)

In their adjustment, the language barrier was the problem most commonly mentioned by Chinese immigrant children. Language looms largest because it is the conduit through which we interact with other people. It is the **means** by which we think, learn and express ourselves. Less obvious is the **basis** upon which we speak or act or think. If there are bicultural conflicts, these may engender problems and psychological difficulties, which may not be immediately apparent, but may nevertheless impact on the development of immigrant children.

In this article, we want to point out some of the cultural conflicts that commonly confront the Chinese child in the home and particularly in the schools. Oftentimes, teachers and parents are not aware of these conflicts and ascribe other meanings or other motives to the child's behavior, frequently in a disapproving manner. Such censure confuses the child and quite often forces him to choose between what he is taught at home and what is commonly accepted by American society. In his desire to be accepted and to be liked, he may want to throw off that which is second nature to him. This may cause anguish and pain not only to himself but also to his parents and family. A few specific examples of bicultural conflict are presented to show how everyday occurrences can result in dilemmas for Chinese immigrant children.

Political Environment

It is common knowledge that people from Mainland China have lived under oppressive government control for years with only a little bit of let-up in the 1990s. China continues to be a totalitarian state. Taiwan was called Free China, but it, too, was governed by martial law until 1987. The people of Hong Kong may have enjoyed personal freedom, but being a British colony (until 1997) the Chinese had no voice in the government. In China, the people lived by the communist ideology and a highly centralized controlled economy. Coming to the United States, Chinese immigrants find themselves in a vastly different political environment. This country is a democracy with freedom of speech and participatory government. One can criticize public figures without fear of retribution. One can voice one's opinion freely. One is expected to take an active part in social and political activities.

Chinese immigrants have to get used to a more open society Parents are constantly admonishing their children to be more guarded and careful about their speech and behavior. The children are unaccustomed to voicing their opinion and do not take part in class discussions. Teachers may think they are dumb because they do not open their mouths. Freedom is difficult to cope with when choices must be made. In the habit of having had decisions made for them and obligated to obey, it is hard to deal with decisions and choices. People brought up in the United States find it hard to understand this. They have enjoyed democracy for so long.

Aggressiveness

A Chinese proverb says, "Good iron is not used to make nails. Good men are not used for soldiers." The soldier or the man who resorts to violence is looked down upon. The sage or gentleman uses his wits, not his fists. So the Chinese child is taught not to fight, whereas the American father will take his son out to the backyard and give him a few lessons in self-defense at the age of puberty. He teaches his son that the ability to fight is a sign of manhood. The Chinese parent teaches his son the exact opposite. Stay out of fights (Sollenger, 1968:17). Yet, when the Chinese child goes to the school playground, he becomes the victim of bullies who pick on him and call him a sissy. Teenagers can be pretty tough and cruel. If the child goes home with a black eye and bruises, his parents scold him and chastise him. If he does not fight back, he is considered a coward. What is he to do? The unresolved conflict about aggressive behavior is a major problem for Chinese American males. They feel that their masculinity has been affected by their childhood upbringing.

What do teachers or monitors do? In most instances, they are derisive of the Chinese boys. "Why don't you Chinese fight back?" they exclaim. "Why do you just stand there and take it?" This derision only shames the Chinese boys, who feel that their courage is questioned. This bicultural conflict may be reflected in the self-hatred of some Asian American male activists who condemn the passivity of our forefathers in response to the discrimination and oppression they endured. Ignorant about their cultural heritage, the activists want to disassociate themselves from such "weakness," and they search for historical instances in which Asians put up a brave but costly and oftentimes futile fight to prove their manhood. The outbreak of gang violence may be another manifestation of the Chinese male's efforts to prove that he is "macho" also. He may be overcompensating for the derision that he has suffered.

Sexuality

In American schools, sexuality is a very strong and pervasive force. Boys and girls start noticing each other in junior high; at the high school level, sexual awareness is very pronounced. School is as much a place for male/female association as it is an institution for learning. Not so for the Chinese. Education is highly valued, and it is a very serious business.

To give their children an opportunity for a better education may be the primary reason why the parents push their children to study, study, study. Interest in the opposite sex is highly distracting and, according to some old-fashioned parents, is improper. Dating is an unfamiliar concept and sexual attractiveness is underplayed, not flaunted as it is according to American ways.

This difference in attitudes and customs poses another dilemma for both the Chinese boys and girls. In school, the white, black, and Hispanic girls like to talk about clothes, makeup, and the dates they had over the weekend. They talk about brassiere sizes and tampons. The popular girl is the sexy one who dates the most. She is the envy of the other girls.

For the Chinese girl, the openness with which other girls discuss boys and sex is extremely embarrassing. Chinese girls used to bind their breasts, not show them off in tight sweaters. Their attitude toward the opposite sex is quite ambivalent. They feel they are missing something very exciting when other girls talk about phone calls from their boyfriends or about their dates over the weekends, yet they will shy away and feel very uncomfortable if a boy shows an interest in them.

Most Chinese parents have had no dating experience. Their marriages were by and large arranged by their own parents or through matchmakers. Good girls simply did not go out with boys alone, so the parents are very suspicious and apprehensive about their daughters dating, and they watch them very carefully. Most Chinese girls are not permitted to date, and for the daring girl who tries to go out against her parents' wishes, there will be a price to pay.

It is no easier for the Chinese boys. The pressure to succeed in school is even greater than for girls, and parental opposition to dating is even more intense. Naturally, the parents want their children to adhere to the old ways, while some children do not agree with their parents and have to carry on their high school romances on the sly. These children are bombarded by television, advertisements, stories, magazines, and real-life examples of boy-girl attraction. The teenager is undergoing puberty and experiencing the instinctive urges surging within him or her. In this society teenagers are titillated, whereas in China they are kept under wraps until they are married.

The problem is exacerbated when the teachers make fun of Chinese customs and the parents. In one instance at a school in Chinatown, a Chinese girl had been forbidden by her parents to walk to school with a Puerto Rican boy, who was in the habit of accompanying her every day. To make sure that the parents were being obeyed, the grandmother would walk behind the girl to see that she did not walk with the boy. Grandma even hung around until her granddaughter went into class, and then she would peer through the window to make sure all was proper before she went home. Naturally this was embarrassing for the girl, and it must have been noticed by the teacher. He exploded in anger at the little old lady and made some uncomplimentary remarks about this being the United States and that Chinese customs should have been left behind in China. This teacher's remarks could only alienate the daughter more from her parents. He could have explained to the girl and even to the entire class the cultural values and traditions of the parents so that the girl could understand why they behaved in such a fashion. Putting down the parents and their customs is the worst thing he could have done.

Sports

The Chinese attitude toward sports is illustrated by an oft-told tale about two Englishmen who were considered somewhat mad. The two lived in Shanghai where they had gone to do business. In the afternoons, they would each take a racquet, go out in the hot sun, and bat a fuzzy ball across the net. As they ran back and forth across the court, sweat would pour down their faces, and they would be exhausted at the end of the game. To the Chinese onlookers, this was sheer lunacy. They would shake their heads in disbelief and ask: "Why do these crazy Englishmen work so hard? They can afford to hire someone to run around and hit the ball for them." The Chinese attitude toward sports has changed considerably, but it still does not assume the importance that it enjoys in American life.

Turn on any news program on radio or television, and you will find one-third of the air time devoted to reporting sports news. Who are the school heroes? The football quarterback, the track star, the baseball pitcher. What are the big events in school? The games. What is used to rally school spirits? Sports.

Yet in the traditional Chinese way of thinking, development of the mental faculties was more important than development of the physique. The image of a scholar was one with a sallow face and long fingernails indicating that he spent long hours with his books and not having to do physical labor. Games that require physical prowess, such as football and boxing, were not even played in China. *Kung fu* or other disciplines of the martial arts did not call for physical strength as much as concentration, skill, and agility. In the minds of many Chinese, sports are viewed as frivolous play and a waste of time and energy. Add to this the generally smaller physique of the Chinese immigrant student in comparison to his classmates, and we do not find many of them on any of the school teams.

What does this mean to the Chinese immigrant students, especially the boys? On the one hand, they may think that the heavy emphasis upon sports is a displaced value. They may want to participate, but they are either too small in stature or unable to devote the time necessary for practice to make the school teams. If the jocks are the big wheels, the Chinese student will feel that his kind is insignificant. But most important of all, an entire dimension of American school life is lost to Chinese immigrant children.

Demonstration of Affection

A commonly voiced concern among Chinese children is: "My parents do not love me. They never kiss or hug me. They are so cold, distant, and remote." The children long for human warmth and affection because they see it on the movie and television screens, and they read about it in books and magazines. Because their experiences with father, mother and other members of the family as well are so formal and distant, they come to the conclusion that love is lacking. In China, where such behavior is the norm, children do not question it. But in this country, where expressions of affection are outwardly effusive and commonly exhibited, they feel deprived.

This lack of demonstrative affection extends to spouse and friends. To the Chinese, physical intimacy and love are private matters never exhibited in public. Even in handshaking, the traditional Chinese way was to clasp one's own hands in greeting. Kissing and hugging a friend would be most inappropriate, and to kiss one's spouse in public would be considered shameless.

Nevertheless, Chinese children in this country are attracted to the physical expressions of love and affection. While they crave it for themselves, they are often unable to reciprocate or be demonstrative in their relations with their own friends, or later on with their own spouses and children because of their detached emotional upbringing.

In the schools, this contrast in culture is made all the sharper because of the large number of Hispanic children in the same schools. In general, the Hispanics are very outgoing and are not the least bit inhibited about embracing, holding hands, or kissing even a casual acquaintance. Chinese children may interpret these gestures of friendliness as overstepping the bounds of propriety, but more often than not, they wish they could shed their reserved shells and reach out to others in a more informal manner. On the other hand, the aloofness of the Chinese students is often wrongly interpreted as unfriendliness, standoffishness, and a desire to keep apart. If all the students were made aware of these cultural differences, they would not misread the intentions and behavior of one another.

Education

Under Communism, attitudes toward education in China changed from positive to negative. During the Cultural Revolution, scholars, writers and professionals were reviled and attacked as elitist. Some of the immigrant parents lived through this period where it was better to be "red" than "expert." Schooling was inferior and devalued. American teachers who were used to highly motivated Chinese students were stunned by immigrant children who came from China after the Cultural Revolution. Fortunately, the high value placed on education has re-asserted itself with the parents. However, the children confront another challenge to this cultural dilemma.

The fact that Chinese children generally do well academically may be due to the hard push parents exert in this direction. None of this means, however, that these children do not experience bicultural conflict regarding education when they see that the bright student is not the one who is respected and looked up to in American schools. Labels such as "bookworm", "nerd", and "teacher's pet" are applied to the intelligent students and these terms are not laudatory but derisive. When parents urge their children to study hard and get good grades, the children know that the payoff will not be social acceptance by their schoolmates. The rewards are not consistent with the values taught at home.

Nevertheless, in a survey, Chinese immigrant high school students indicated that they prized the opportunity to get an education. Education was not easily available to everyone in China, Hong Kong or Taiwan. Poor families could not afford to send their children to school, and disqualifying factors were many. In this country, school is free through high school and even compulsory up to a certain age. It is not a matter of students trying to gain admittance by passing rigorous entrance exams, but a matter of authorities trying to keep the dropout rates low that characterizes the educational system here. Since education is free and easy to get, it is often taken lightly.

New York public school academic standards are lower than those in Hong Kong or Taiwan, and the school work is easier to keep up with. As a result, there is less distinction attached to being able to stay in school or graduate. What the Chinese immigrant students prize highly has less value in the larger society. As newcomers to this country, they start to have doubts about the goals that they are striving for.

Tattling

Should one report a wrongdoing? Should one tell the teacher that a schoolmate is cheating on his exam? Should one report to the school authorities that a fellow student is trying to extort money from him? The American values on this score are ambiguous and confusing. For example, in the West Point scandal a few years ago, most of the cadets involved were not cheaters themselves but they knew about others cheating and did not report it to the authorities. Their honor code required that they tell, but the unwritten code among their fellow cadets said that they should not tattle or "fink." If they had reported the cheating of their fellow cadets, they would have been socially ostracized. There is a dilemma for the American here as well.

This bicultural conflict was noted by Denise Kandel and Gerald S. Lesser in their book, *Youth in Two Worlds* (1972) in which their reference groups were Danish and American children. The Danish children, like the Chinese, feel duty bound to report wrongdoing. There is no dichotomy of consequences here. Authorities and peers are consistent in their attitude in this respect, and this consistency helps to maintain social control. The teacher cannot be expected to have four pairs of eyes and see everything. The parents cannot be everywhere at once to know what their child is doing during the day. If the siblings or schoolmates will help by reporting wrongdoing the task of teaching the child is shared and made easier for the adults. But when social ostracism stands in the way of enforcing ethical values, an intense conflict ensues and contributes to the breakdown of social control.

Thrift

About thirty banks are found within the ethnic enclave known as Chinatown in New York City. When Manhattan Savings Bank opened a new branch, it was able to attract three million dollars in deposits within a few months. Most of the large banks are aware that Chinatown is fertile ground for the accumulation of capital because the Chinese tend to save more of what they earn than other ethnic groups in America in spite of the fact that their earnings are small. Their savings grow because of two major factors. One is the sense of insecurity common to immigrants who need a cushion for the uncertainties that they feel acutely. The other is the esteem with which thrift is regarded by the Chinese. A person who is frugal is thought of more highly than one who can sport material symbols of success.

The value placed upon thrift poses acute bicultural conflict for Chinese immigrant children who see all about them evidence of an economic system that encourages the accumulation and conspicuous consumption of material possessions. A very important segment of the consumer market is now the teenage population. The urge to have stylish clothes, a stereo, a camera, sports equipment and a car creates a painful conflict in the child who is enticed by television and other advertising media, but whose parents reserve a large percentage of their meager earnings for stashing away in banks.

In school, the girl who spends money on fashionable dresses and the latest rock record feels more poised and confident about herself than do her less materially fortunate classmates. She is admired, complemented and envied. In the Chinese community, on the other hand, a Chinese girl who spends a lot of money on clothes and frivolities would soon be the object of grapevine gossip and stigmatized as a less-than-desirable prospective wife or daughter-in-law, whereas praises would be sung for the more modestly dressed girl as being careful with money.

A commonly voiced complaint by students against their parents is that they are "money-hungry." The parents give their children very little spending money. In fact, money earned by the children must be handed over to the parents who do not buy fashionable clothing. Rather they buy only serviceable garments which the children are ashamed to be seen in. The Chinese home is generally not furnished for comfort or aesthetics so when Chinese children visit the homes of their non-Chinese friends and compare them with their own living quarters, they feel deprived and ashamed of their parents and their family. They certainly do not want to bring their friends home to play, and the teenagers may stay away from home as much as possible, feeling more comfortable with their peers in clubhouses or on the streets. The contrast in spending attitudes between the underdeveloped economy from which many Chinese immigrants have come and the American economy which emphasizes mass and even wasteful consumption is very sharp, and it creates many an unresolved conflict in children, who do not realize that cultural differences lay behind it. They think that their parents value money more than they care for their children and exhibit this by denying them material possessions that give them pleasure and status in the eyes of their peers.

Credit is another concept foreign to immigrants from China. If one does not have money, one should not be tempted to buy. Credit is borrowing money, and borrowing should be resorted to only in extreme emergencies. The buy-now, pay-later idea goes against the Chinese grain. So the Chinese families postpone buying until they have saved up enough to cover the entire purchase price. This attitude is fairly common even when it comes to the purchase of a home. The family will scrimp and economize, putting aside a large portion of its income for this goal, denying itself small pleasures along the way for many, many years until the large sum is accumulated. To the Chinese way of thinking, this singleness of purpose shows character, but to the more hedonistic American mind, this habit of thrift may appear asinine and unnecessary.

Individualism

Francis L.K. Hsu has written extensively about individualism as a prominent characteristic of American life. According to Hsu, the basic ingredient of rugged individualism is self-reliance. The individual constantly tells himself and others that he controls his own destiny and that he does not need help from others. The individual-centered person enjoins himself to find means of fulfilling his own desires and ambitions.

Individualism is the driving force behind the competitiveness and creativity that has pushed this nation forward. Loose family ties, superficial human relationships, little community control, and weak traditions have given the individual leeway to strike out on his own without being hindered by sentimentality, convention, and tradition. Self-interest has been a powerful incentive.

In contrast, Hsu contends, the Chinese are situation-centered and more collective-minded. Their way of life encourages the individual to find a satisfactory adjustment within the external environment of men and things. The Chinese individual sees the world in realistic terms. He is dependent upon others and others are dependent upon him. Like bricks in a wall, one lends support to the other and they all hold up society as a whole. If even one brick becomes loose, the wall is considerably weakened; interlocked, the wall is strong. The wall is the network of human relations. The individual subordinates his own wishes and ambitions for the common good (Hsu, 1960; 1972).

Kenneth Abbott, in his book *Harmony and Indiviidualism* (1970) also points out that Western ideas of creativity and individualism are not accented in Chinese and must be held within accepted norms. One of the reasons for this is the importance ascribed to maintenance of harmony. Harmony is the key concept in all relationships between god(s) and man and between man and man. It is the highest good.

To the Chinese, the sense of duty and obligation takes precedence over self-gratification. It is not uncommon to find Chinese teenagers handing over their entire paychecks to their parents for family use or for Chinese students to pursue a course of study chosen for them by their parents rather than one of their own choosing. Responsibility toward distant kin is more keenly felt by the Chinese than by other Americans. Honor and glory accrue not only to the individual but to all those who helped him climb the ladder. This sense of being part of something greater than oneself gives the Chinese a feeling of belonging and security in the knowledge that they do not stand alone. On the other hand, individual freedom of action is very much restricted.

Dependency

This cultural heritage of collectivism and family orientation tends to prolong the period of dependency of Chinese immigrant children. In her study, "Socialization Patterns Among the Chinese in Hawaii," Nancy F. Young noted the following:

> Observations of Chinese families in Hawaii indicate that both immigrant and local parents utilize child-rearing techniques that result in parent-oriented, as opposed to peer-oriented behavior . . . Chinese parents maximize their control over their children by limiting their experiences with models exhibiting non-sanctioned behavior (1972:36)

Immigrant mothers exercise constant and strict supervision over their children. They take the children wherever they go, and baby sitters are rarely used. They prefer their children to stay home rather than go out to play with their friends. Friends are carefully screened by the mother, and the child is not expected to do things for himself until two years beyond the mean age that a Jewish mother would expect her child to do for himself (8.85 years versus 6.83 years).

On the other hand, American-born Chinese parents expect their children to cut the apron strings sooner than any of the other ethnic groups surveyed (mean age 6.78 years). Upon close reflection, Young's findings substantiate my own experience and that of many of my peers in child-rearing. We, who are American-born, have assimilated the American values of independence at an early age and even have gone overboard in rearing our own children toward these ends.

The extremes exhibited between the American-born and immigrant Chinese may be indicative of the bicultural conflict that the Chinese in this country feel. When they were children, they may have felt that their parents were overprotective. This was frequently mentioned by the teachers to whom we talked. We saw evidence of this in the elementary schools in the practice of mothers coming to the school from the garment factories during their own lunch hours to feed their children lunch. Many walked their children to and from school even to junior high school. It was not clear to us whether the parents were justifiably afraid for their children's safety from the gangs or whether they were being overprotective. The teachers thought the mothers were smothering the children and restricting their freedom of action. By adolescence, the children must have felt the same. They were chafing against parental control over what they presumed to be their own business, while the parents thought they were merely doing their parental duty. Teachers and parents do not agree on this score, with the result that parental authority is often undermined by a teacher's scoffing attitude.

Respect for Authority

Challenge against established authority has been a notable feature of American youth culture over the past three decades. Parents, teachers, police, the government, the church — all authority figures in the past — have been knocked down and even reviled. Violence against teachers is a leading problem in schools across the nation. If the students do not have respect for the teacher, neither will they have respect for the knowledge that the teacher tries to impart.

A similar phenomenon occurred during the Cultural Revolution in China. Thank goodness this period was short-lived (1965 to 1976) and the Confucian values of respect for one's elders and those in authority have returned. There is a very strong tendency for Chinese children to accept authority without question. Students seldom disagree with or challenge a teacher. They memorize texts without questioning the premise. Students in this country are encouraged to probe, to question, to seek new solutions. The approaches are quite different.

Heroes and Heroines

Who are the people who are praised, admired, looked up to, and revered? The idols of different cultures are themselves different types of people, and the values of a society may be deduced from the type of people who are respected and emulated in that culture. In the United States, the most popular figures are movie, television and stage stars; sports figures; politicians; successful authors, inventors, scientists; and the rich. Who are the heroes and heroines of China? If we use literature as a guide, they are the filial sons and daughters, the sacrificing mother; the loyal government minister; the patriot or war hero who saves his country; and revolutionaries who overthrow despotic rulers and set up their own dynasties. Under Communism, the persons honored were self-sacrificing workers and the Communist leaders.

Priests, ministers, and rabbis once commanded prestige in this country, but the status of these men of God has declined. In China, monks or priests have always occupied lowly positions. In contrast to the United States, actors were riff-raff. Women did not act in the theater, so men had to play female roles. Western influence and the media has brought about vast changes, so that today, movie and television stars in Hong Kong and Taiwan are celebrities like in the United States.

As a rule, Chinese heroes and heroines were people of high moral virtues, and they set the standards of conduct for others. In this country, the more sensational the exposé of the private lives of national leaders or entertainment figures, the more fanfare they get, and their box office value goes higher. How movie stars retain their popularity in spite of the relentless campaigns to expose them is very difficult for someone not brought up in the United States to comprehend. An old adage says, "No man is a hero to his valet." Yet the fact that American heroes and heroines survive and thrive on notoriety and self-confession can only mean that the American people secretly admire such behavior. One might say: Chinese heroes are saints. American heroes are sinners.

The above are but a few examples of bicultural conflict that Chinese children experience. Not all Chinese children experience conflict to the same degree because they do not come from the same social and economic environment. Those from Hong Kong, and to a lesser degree those from Taiwan, have been exposed to very strong Western influence, and their parents may have moderated Chinese values to some degree. Those from Mainland China have lived by a totally different set of standards imposed by the government, and their gap is much wider to bridge. At several periods the Chinese government waged anti-"spiritual pollution" campaigns to rid Chinese culture of Western influence.

Marginality

There are two divergent trains of thought regarding bicultural conflict. Robert E. Park first coined the term "marginal man" for this predicament. Park stressed that "marginal men are — precisely because of their ambiguous position from a cultural, ethnic, linguistic, or sociostructural standpoint — strongly motivated to make creative adjustments in situations of change, and in the course of this adjustment process, to develop innovations in social behavior" (Gould 1964:407). However, the evidence is not clear. Marginal individuals are more prone to succumb to anomie and thus become carriers of social disorganization rather than creative change. Everett Stonequist in his work, *The Marginal Man,* brings out the latter viewpoint. He wrote:

> The marginal personality is most clearly portrayed in those individuals who are unwittingly initiated into two or more historic traditions, languages, political loyalties, moral codes or religions. This occurs for instance as a result of migration. . .

> When the standards of two or more social groups come into active contrast or conflict, the individual who is identified with both groups experiences the conflict as an acute personal difficulty or mental tension. . .(1937:3-4)

> So the marginal man . . . is one who is poised in psychological uncertainty between two (or more) social worlds; reflecting in his soul the discords and harmonies, repulsions and attractions of these worlds, one of which is often 'dominant' over the other; within which membership is implicitly if not explicitly based upon birth or ancestry (race or nationality); and where exclusion removes the individual from a system of group relations (1937:8)

Adults tend to perceive their marginality as a sense of wanting to be an accepted member of a group or groups and conversely a sense of exclusion from such groups. Children, on the other hand, perceive of their marginality as a dilemma. They are faced with a situation where courses of action are diametrically opposed or radically different. They do not see the dilemma as rising from cultural differences; they just see it as an impasse. The choices are painful and more often than not immobilizing. Not having the maturity to evaluate or modify their courses of action or to adjust their values, they do nothing. The vacuousness of their indecision or their inability to decide is extremely draining emotionally.

For Chinese immigrants who live in cities with large Chinese communities, these conflicts are moderated to a large degree because there are other Chinese children to mitigate the dilemmas that they encounter. When they are among their own, the Chinese ways are better known and better accepted. The Chinese customs are not denigrated to the degree that they would be if the immigrant child were the only one to face the conflict on his or her own. Even so, teachers and parents should be made aware of these conflicts to avoid exacerbating the differences and to inculcate in both the Chinese and non-Chinese a healthy respect for cultural differences.

Chapter 9
ಬಂಡ

Chinese Around the World: The Familial and the Familiar

Hendrick Serrie

This paper is concerned with all local social organizations described in thirteen ethnographies of geographically separated and socioeconomically differentiated Chinese communities. It compares the principles of recruitment of these organizations and the services they offer, and analyzes their structural and functional constancy and variation. It then relates these findings to the Hsu attributes of continuity, inclusiveness, authority, and asexuality, and tests the persistence of these attributes against a preliminary picture of global Chinese culture.

The Hsu Attributes

In a series of works spanning the past four decades, Francis L. K. Hsu has developed a psychocultural analysis of Chinese culture in contrast and comparison with several other literate traditions (Hsu 1948 and 1967;

1953 and 1970; 1963; etc.). In his hypothesis of dyadic dominance, Hsu concludes that the father-son dyad, dominant in traditional Chinese culture, infused it with inherent father-son attributes of continuity, inclusiveness, authority, and asexuality (Hsu 1965; 1971; Hsu-Balzer, Balzer, and Hsu 1974). Hsu maintains that these four attributes have persisted in Chinese culture since ancient times, and, allowing for variations in time and space, are more or less universal within it.

Hsu defines continuity as "the condition of being, or the attitude of desiring to be, in an unbroken sequence or connection with others," and it is indicated by relative durability of relationships. Inclusiveness is "the act of incorporating, or the attitude of wishing to be incorporated," and is indicated by a widening circle of relationships derived from a continuous original relationship. Authority is defined as "personal power that commands and enforces obedience, or the belief on the part of subordinates of the legitimacy or the necessity of obeying commands and of a superior's right to issue them." Asexuality is simply "the condition of having no connection with sex" (Hsu 1965 : 642 - 644), or "the relegation of sex to a particular area of society (like marriage and prostitution) and its non-diffusion to other areas of society" (Hsu 1980 : personal communication).

Hsu finds that the Chinese patrilineal extended family as well as the most important social organization beyond it-the lineage or clan-are both expressive of the father-son dyadic attributes of continuity, inclusiveness, authority, and asexuality. Many clans were perpetuated over centuries of time. Although family division was the rule, some extended families fulfilled the "big family" ideal and persisted, often with several generations under the same roof.

Selection of Variant Cases

From the available cases of Chinese communities, the most variant were chosen. These include: Taitou, Shantung (Yang 1945); Kaihsienkung, Kiangsu (Fei 1939); Phenix Village, Kwangtung (Kulp 1925); West Town, Yunnan (Hsu 1948 and 1967); the Boat People, Hong Kong (Anderson 1970a); Hang Mei, Hong Kong (Potter 1968), K'un Shen, Taiwan (Diamond 1969); Phnom Penh, Cambodia (W. E. Willmott 1967 and 1970), Bangkok, Thailand (Coughlin 1960); Semarang, Indonesia (D. E. Willmott 1960); Sacramento, California (Weiss 1974), Mississippi Delta (Loewen 1971); and London, England (Ng 1968).

Chinese Around the World: The Familial and the Familiar   191

The selection of cases attempted to capture whatever differences might obtain between mainland, offshore, and overseas communities, and between further regional distinctions within those categories. The range of cases includes rural agricultural villages of 650-1450 people, two of them wealthy and composed of a single lineage in each; a market town of 8,000; a shallow-water fishing village of 3,000 with lineages devoted to shamanistic cults; deep-sea fishermen who live all their lives on boats and have little social organization beyond the extended family; concentrated urban minorities of 1.3% in California to 50.0% in southeast Asia with populations of 10,500 to 500,000; and dispersed minorities of O.07-0.3%, operating grocery stores in the American Deep South and operating Chinese restaurants scattered throughout a British city of eight million.[1]

Types of Chinese Social Organization

Social organizations beyond the level of the family in the thirteen Chinese communities can be categorized into five types. on the basis of whether members are recruited in terms of kinship, surname, residence, origin or contract (Table 1).

1. Kinship organizations, which recruit members through birth or marriage, may be elaborated beyond the level of the family into clans or lineages *(tsu),* which sometimes subdivide into branches *(fang).* They are found in all mainland and offshore communities in the sample, with the exception of the Boat people. They are also mentioned in passing in the data on the overseas community in Semarang. As mentioned previously, these familial organizations are the embodiment of the Hsu attributes of continuity, inclusiveness, authority. and asexuality.

2. Surname organizations, found in Phnom Penh, Bangkok, Semarang, and Sacramento. are open to all persons of a given surname, and have overtones of kinship in that many Chinese believe that people of the same surname are patrilineally related, however undemonstrable or distant the connection. In these organizations, the familiarity of a person's own surname is sufficient as a principle for uniting Chinese persons who otherwise may be strangers. Multiple surname organizations, such as were formed in Sacramento, may group people of several *unrelated* surnames within a single organization. In one example, the four surnames of the association are those of four closely associated military heroes in the post-Han Dynasty decades celebrated in *The Romance of the Three*

Table 1
Secondary Social Organizations and Recruitment Types in 13 Chinese Communities

secondary social organization (=beyond level of family)	recruitment type	Taitou	Kaihsienkung	Phenix Village	West Town	Boat People	Hang Mei	K'un Shen	Phnom Penh	Bangkok	Semarang	Sacramento	Mississippi Delta	London
1 Branch	Kinship	x		x		x								
2 Lineage	Kinship	x	x	x	x		x	x			x			
3 Single Surname Association	Surname									x	x	x	x	
4 Multiple Surname Association	Surname												x	
5 Neighborhood	Residence	x	x					x						
6 Community-wide Organization	Residence	x	x				x	x						
7 Government Local Organization	Residence	x	x		x		x	x						
8 District Association	Origin								x	x				
9 Dialect Association	Origin								x	x	x			
10 Secret Society	Contract										x	x		
11 Subsistence Organization	Contract		x	x		x	x	x	x	x	x			x
12 Credit Society	Contract		x	x		x	x	x	x		x			
13 Burial Society	Contract			x			x	x			x			
14 Benevolent Society	Contract								x	x		x		
15 Political Organization	Contract						x			x	x	x	x	x
16 Contractual Religious Organization	Contract								x	x	x	x	x	x
17 Contractual Educational Organization	Contract	x						x			x	x		
18 Cultural Club	Contract	x		x				x	x			x	x	
19 Athletic Club	Contract			x						x	x	x	x	
20 Gaming or Gambling Club, Den	Contract				x						x			x
21 Social Club	Contract										x	x	x	x

Chinese Around the World: The Familial and the Familiar 193

Table 1 (Contd.)
Secondary Social Organizations and Recruitment
Types in 13 Chinese Communities

Sources : Yang, x, 16, 32, 38, 67, 70, 74, 83, 114-115, 134-138, 141-144, 148, 150-152, 157-158, 163-165, 173, 181, 194, 197, 234, 236-238, 257-263; Fei, 17-18, 20-21, 23-24, 57, 75-76, 84-86, 98-99, 102-106, 114, 129, 204, 216, 219, 223-225, 241, 267, 273; Kulp, xxiv-xxv, xxviii, 13, 101, 110, 121, 124, 142-143, 145-146, 148, 189, 196-199, 202-203, 206-210, 218, 221, 260, 289, 302, 310, 321, 323; Hsu, 16, 24-25, 109, 112, 117, 123-125, 127-129; Anderson, 3, 28, 33, 37-39, 43, 47, 62, 68, 81-82, 87-90, 92, 94, 101, 114, 120-123, 173; Potter, 12-13, 15, 17-18, 20-22, 25, 27-30, 59, 91, 95-96, 101-104, 106, 108, 111, 115-116, 143, 156, 165-169; Diamond, 23, 36-37, 62-65, 68-69, 72, 74-82, 84-86; W.E. Willmott, 1967, 84-87; 1970, 7, 13, 36-37, 44, 49, 55, 65-67, 70-74, 78-79, 81-84, 87-89, 91, 100, 102, 105, 108-112, 114-117, 143; Coughlin, 6-7, 33-34, 38-45, 47-57, 59, 70, 98-99; D.E. Willmot 26-28, 50, 53-55, 60, 62, 64-66, 71, 83, 88, 99-103, 115, 119, 122, 129-136, 138-141, 144-145, 161, 167, 170-175, 179, 211, 228, 230-234, 247-252, 260-261, 263, 285-286, 300; Weiss, 8, 80, 87-88, 90, 92-94, 128, 130, 151, 159-161, 163, 175, 178, 181, 184-188, 190, 192, 194, 201, 203, 211, 214, 221-224, 226, 229, 237; Loewen, 33-34, 36-38, 51, 60-61, 71, 83-84, 88-89, 91-93, 109, 112; Ng, 19, 29, 33, 49-60, 65-69, 71-74. Itemized references cited in Serrie, 1976.

Kingdoms, in another example the different characters for each of the four surnames of the association have a seven-stroke radical in common. Surname organizations are found in overseas communities in which most Chinese persons are oriented at least initially as sojourners and usually have few kinsmen. Surname organizations seem to be substitutes for kinship organizations; indeed, they are often considered in the literature to be exactly like clans. They are not exactly like Chinese clans and lineages however, in that the kinship ties are merely conjectural or literary, and the organization is consciously established *de novo.* (On the other hand, even traditional lineages or clans could be quite imaginative, as in claiming ties to notable persons.) In any case, this sometimes extraordinary extension of kinship found in surname organizations illustrates the Hsu attributes of continuity and inclusiveness.

3. Residence organizations, which recruit members on the basis of the territorial proximity of their homes, include traditional neighborhood and community-wide institutions, and also those organized locally by the Nationalist (KMT) government. As a principle of recruitment, residence has nothing to do with kinship and is grounded in familiarities built upon the simple convenience of propinquity. In Taitou and Kaihsienkung, small informal groupings of immediate neighboring individuals and families share far more intensively in the daily activities, the celebrations, and the crises of life than do the larger kinship organizations; and this intimate, face-to-face daily interaction represents a social organization that is directly supplemental to the family. The tendency to formalize this common impulse may be seen as a manifestation of the Hsu attributes of inclusiveness and continuity.

Neighborhoods defined by tradition include the *hu-tung* of Taitou, the *shanlin* and *de* of Kaihsienkung, and the unnamed neighbor groups in K'un Shen. Beyond the neighborhood, community-wide organizations include the village temples that territorially bisect Kaihsienkung and unite Hang Mei and K'un Shen; and the village defense and crop watching programs in Taitou and Hang Mei. Local government organizations include, at both the neighborhood and community levels, the Kuomintang's *pao-chia* system in Taitou, Kaihsienkung, and West Town and its subsequent *lin-li* system in K'un Shen; and local government schools. The government neighborhood organizations *(pao, lin)* do not coincide with traditional residential neighbor groupings, but the idea is the same.

4. Origin organizations, uniting overseas people on the basis of common origin in a part of China, include district and dialect associations. Based in the commonalities of former residence "near" to one another in the homeland, they are rooted in a wider area beyond the original neighborhood or village. Again, the formal institutionalization of such sentiments represents the Hsu attributes of continuity and inclusiveness. District associations, based on immediate or extended ties of prior residence in a particular locality in China, are found in Phnom-Penh and Bangkok. Dialect associations composed of people speaking a particular variant of Chinese (typically specific to a given region in China), are found in Phnom Penh, Bangkok, and Semarang. Among the Bangkok Chinese, district associations are a way of subdividing dialect associations that are very large. There are no origin organizations in Sacramento, perhaps because most Chinese are derived from the same place of origin (the Sze-Yap-speaking County of Toishan in Kwangtung).

5. Contractual organizations, found in all communities in the sample, are ostensibly free of prior connections that extend from family or domicile. They recruit members on a voluntary basis of common interest, and serve needs of subsistence, credit, burial, benevolence, politics, religion, education, culture, sports, gambling, and sociability. In actual practice, however, Chinese contractual organizations often recruit members on the basis of kinship, surname, residence or origin.

Organizations aiding subsistence efforts include the Cooperative Silk Factory in Kaihsienkung; the Irrigation Cooperative Society and the Sugar Manufacturing Association in Phenix Village; daily fishing fleets and nightly docking clusters among some of the Boat People; the marketing cooperative in Hang Mei, the Fishermen's and the Farmers' Associations in K'un Shen; Chambers of Commerce, merchants' associations and trade and professional guilds in Phnom Penh, Bangkok, Semarang, Sacramento, and London; and workers' associations and unions in Bangkok, Semarang, and London. The village organizations include only local people, many or them kinsmen and neighbors. Among the urban Chinese overseas, there is a pronounced tendency for origin groups to monopolize particular occupations and the corresponding organizations.

Small Mutual Aid Clubs with elaborate rules for pooling meager resources and requiring a series of banquets are widespread among Chinese as credit organizations, typically involving only friends. Burial Associations serve to guarantee their members both the cost of and sufficient mourners for funerals acceptable to Chinese standards, and Benevolent Associations provide these and other welfare benefits to needy nonmembers. In some southeast Asian communities welfare benefits provided by Chinese organizations are distributed to needy non-Chinese people as well.

Political organizations include the Ping Shan Kung So, a Hong Kong party based in Ping Shan, the cluster of eight villages of which Hang Mei is the largest, wealthiest, and most powerful. Kuomintang branches are mentioned for Semarang and Sacramento; pro-communist organizations include the Sin You She in Semarang and the T'ai P'ing Club in London. In Semarang BAPERKI, a predominantly Chinese party with an assimilationist orientation, takes an active part in Indonesian politics. Besides the KMT branch, the Sacramento Chinese have an Anti-Communist League, a Chinese Women's New Life Movement, and local Democratic and Republican Clubs.

Contractual religious organizations (differentiated here from those organized in terms of kinship or residence) include the "Buddhist" and other temples of Phnom Penh and Semarang; the "Confucian" and other societies in Bangkok, Semarang, and Sacramento; and the Christian churches and missions in Semarang, Sacramento, Mississippi, and London. Contractual educational organizations (differentiated from those organized by kinship groups or the government) maintain Chinese or Christian schools and include a Parent-Teacher's Association in K'un Shen.

Cultural clubs are involved with Chinese opera, theater. dance, music, literature, lion and dragon outfits, and drum and bugle corps. Athletic Clubs, traditionally focused on boxing, now also include ping pong, badminton, tennis, golf, soccer, basketball, bowling, skiing, and swimming. Strictly social clubs include various unnamed groups in Bangkok; Societat and Rotary, among others, in Semarang; and posts of the American Legion and Veterans of Foreign Wars in Sacramento and Mississippi.

The secret society or brotherhood *(tong),* identified with criminal and ceremonial activities in Semarang and Sacramento, is an additional category. In these organizations, all members become pseudo-kinsmen no matter what their prior relations. Secret societies used to exist in Mississippi and London, but they have reportedly died out.

In summarizing the structural types of Chinese social organizations, the Hsu attributes of continuity and inclusiveness are apparent in those organizations that recruit members on the basis of kinship, surname, residence, and origin. Contractual organizations, although seeming in principle to have little to do with prior connections among members, in actuality often recruit members along the same lines of kinship, surname, residence, and origin.

Constancy and Variation in Chinese Social Organization

On the basis of the data from these thirteen communities, three generalizations obtain. First, contractual organizations serving subsistence, credit, political, educational, cultural, athletic, and gambling interests are found in Chinese communities around the world. Second, lineages or clans, neighborhoods, residentially based temples, and local government organizations predominate in mainland and offshore rural villages. Third, surname, district and dialect associations, secret societies, benevolent societies, contractual religious organizations. and social clubs predominate in overseas communities. Some of these kinds of organizations are also common in precommunist mainland cities (Ho 1968:34).

Overseas, a dearth of kinsmen and sojourner orientation account for the absence of lineages or clans, and for the creation of surname organizations as a substitute for extended kinship ties. The absence of lineages is relative, for they are mentioned though not described for Semarang and exist elsewhere-e.g., the Philippines.

Structural Patterns in Chinese Communities

No Chinese community in this sample, including the single-lineage villages of Phenix Village and Hang Mei, is organized in terms of kinship only. From the typology of social organizations based on principle of recruitment, three patterns emerge (Table 2). First, small rural Chinese

Table 2

Recruitment Types of Secondary Social Organization in 13 Chinese Communities

community	recruitment types of secondary social organization
Taitou	Kinship, Residence,[1] Contract
Kaihsienkung	Kinship, Residence, Contract
Phenix Village	Kinship, Contract
West Town	Kinship, Residence,[1] Contract
Boat People	Contract
Hang Mei	Kinship, Residence, Contract
K'un Shen	Kinship, Residence, Contract
Phnom-Penh	Surname, Origin, Contract
Bangkok	Surname, Origin, Contract
Semarang	Kinship,[2] Surname, Origin, Contract
Sacramento	Surname, Contract
Mississippi Delta	Contract
London	Contract

1 Local government organizations only.
2 Mentioned but not described in ethnography.

communities are organized in terms of kinship, contract, and sometimes residence. Second, the large urban Chinese communities in overseas cities are organized in terms of surname, origin, and contract, Third, demographically marginal communities are organized only in terms of contract.

The Boat People, the Chinese in the Mississippi Delta, and the London Chinese are demographically or sociologically marginal Chinese communities. The Boat people live in large propinquitous aggregates along the waterways of south China, and, in this case, along the rim of Castle Peak Bay where around 7,000 people cram together in night-time docking. With no social organization beyond the daily fishing fleets and night-time docking clusters, this amorphous population constitutes a community in an extremely minimal sense. An endemic inconstancy of residence among the Boat People, with frequent, sudden trips to other moorings, other ports, adds a further element of marginality. Although the absence of lineages among the Boat People seems extraordinary, it is only one aspect of a general lack of social organizations — kinship, residence, or contract — beyond the level of the family and work group.

In Mississippi and London, the Chinese have relatively sparse and dispersed populations: 5,640 Chinese constitute 0.07% of the population of London, anti 1,145 Chinese constitute 0.3% of the population of the Delta. In both cases, the Chinese are scattered thinly over the entire area, living near the restaurants and grocery stores that are their source of livelihood rather than living in a concentrated territory. The largest population of Mississippi Chinese amounts to only 110 in the largest town.

London Chinese of prewar times, mainly ex-seamen from Kwangtung, were once residentially concentrated but were forced to move when the bombed-out East End underwent urban renewal in the '50s: since then they have been dying out and their children or grandchildren intermarrying and assimilating into British society and culture. The postwar Chinese in London, primarily involved with the two hundred or so Chinese restaurants in the city, are for the most part still sojourners, oriented toward accumulating savings and returning to their villages in the New Territories.

Chinese Structural Substitution

The three structural patterns suggest a principle of substitution in the formation of social organizations in Chinese communities, wherein the familiar is the most preferred surrogate for the familial (Chart 1). This principle is a further manifestation of the Hsu attributes of continuity and inclusiveness.

Chart 1
Patterns of Structural Preference in Global Chinese Social Organization

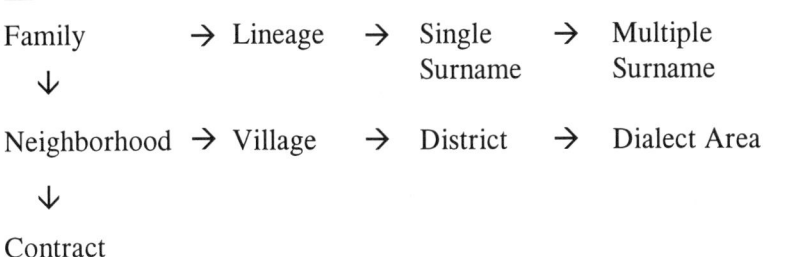

We start with the single household, extended or supranuclear family as the building block of Chinese community. In precommunist mainland and offshore rural villages, close neighbors are drawn into the daily life of the family, especially by women, who have little access to friendship other than that offered by propinquity. Widening circles of affiliation beyond these two intimate groups include, within kinship, those relatives with mourning obligations, perhaps a lineage branch, and the lineage or clan itself.

With regard to residence, the widening circles of affiliation include the larger neighborhood, perhaps a bifurcation of the village, and the village itself. Such needs as arise that cannot be met through kinship or residence principles are handled through contractual organizations, which seem to be relatively minor, and which informally recruit members who are familial or familiar anyway.

In overseas communities, widening circles of affiliation based on kinship run into severe obstacles. Many sojourners have no immediate family, and few of the long-term residents may have sufficient relatives to form a branch of their lineage. As a substitute for demonstrated kinship, the un-demonstrated, presumed kinship of common surname is resorted to. An insufficiency of persons with the same surname may lead to the formation of multiple surname groups, in which the different surnames have no presumed kinship connection at all. At this point almost any convention demonstrating a historic or literary familiarity will suffice to unite the different surname groups.

Similarly, in overseas communities the sojourner orientation, urban mobility and ethnic diversity may make the formation of neighborhoods and other formal residence organizations difficult to achieve. The widening circles of affiliation, which on the mainland move from immediate neighbors to wider neighborhood to village, in overseas communities must go beyond these small territorial entities to the larger district, or further to the general region within which the same dialect of Chinese prevails. Just as overseas surname groups involve a good deal of stretching of the kinship principle, so do overseas district and dialect organizations stretch the principle of residence, since it is not actual overseas residence, but a residence of remembrance back in the home country. Again, as with mainland and offshore rural communities, when the familial/familiar principles of kinship/surname and residence/origin give out, contract becomes the organizing principle. In urban communities contractual organizations are very important, but like the villages they often include elements of the familial and familiar on an informal basis.

Demographically marginal communities do not seem to dispute this principle. Although much has been made of the absence of lineages among the Boat People (Anderson 1970b), it is but part of a general absence of social organizations beyond the family and work group level, and does not indicate a lack of concern with kinship per se. Indeed, the Chinese family among the Boat People must bear an even heavier load in the absence of other supporting organizations, but in general shows similarity to Chinese families elsewhere. In like manner, the extremely sparse Chinese communities in the small towns of the Mississippi Delta and scattered throughout the city of London simply have too few people in any one location to enable much elaboration of social organizations according to kinship, surname, residence, or origin, and for this reason the sole principle of contract is used.

Functions of Chinese Social Organization

Based on the data furnished by the thirteen ethnographies, the functions of Chinese social organizations are seen to include management of property assets, coordination of labor, economic controls. credit, welfare, political controls, education, ancestor worship, nonancestral religion, sociability and recreation, and the preservation of ties to China. Table 3 summarizes all functions of secondary social organizations and specifies the recruitment types of organization that handle each function in each of the thirteen communities.

Some functions vary with the mode of subsistence. Coordination of labor for emergencies and periodic tasks is found in all the rural villages, and rarely elsewhere; much of this is explained by the historic vulnerability to bandits and thieves, and the demands of the yearly agricultural round. Three villages also coordinate labor in entrepreneurial ventures. In contrast, economic controls guaranteeing quality and integrity, circulating economic information, regulating prices, and controlling business competition are found in the commercially oriented overseas communities. In Mississippi, an exception, these controls are powerful but are handled informally.

Formal organizations providing credit are found in almost all the mainland cases, but seem rather limited within the overseas communities. However, although informal in Mississippi and London, interpersonal loans were of major importance in helping young immigrants and entrepreneurs get a start.

Formal concern with providing welfare benefits, which typically focus on protection from starvation and provision for a minimally acceptable burial, is rather limited within mainland and offshore communities. In contrast, perhaps reflecting greater community affluence, or heightened insecurity in an alien environment without substantial numbers of close relatives, concern with welfare and immigrant assistance is more prevalent among the overseas Chinese. In Mississippi and London, marginal Chinese communities lack formal organization of these functions, but do a great deal on an informal basis. A Sacramento organization offers services as an employment agency. Some overseas communities offer

Table 3
Functions, Recruitment Types of Secondary Organizations in 13 Chinese Communities

recruitment type of secondary social organization
K=Kinship; S=Surname; R=Residence; O=Origin; C=Contract

function	Taitou	Kaihsienkung	Phenix Village	West Town	Boat People	Hang Mei	K'un Shen	Phnom-Penh	Bangkok	Semarang	Sacramento	Mississippi Delta	London
Property Assets													
owns, manages agricultural land	.	.	K.	.	.	KR.	.	.	.	.	.	.	.
owns, maintains secular building	.	.	K.	.	.	K.	.	OC	SO.	OC	SC	C	C
Coordination of Labor													
coordinates members' labor in emergencies	R.	R.	.	.	.	R.	R.	.	.	.	.	.	.
coordinates members' labor for periodic tasks	R.	.	K.C	.	.	RC	R.	.	.	.	.	.	.
engages in economic ventures	.	.C	K.C	.	.	.C	.	.	.	.	.	.	.
Economic Controls													
serves as employment agency	.	.	.	.	.	.	.	.	.	.	S.	.	.
guarantees quality of members' products	.	.	.	.	.	.	.	OC	.	.C	.	.	.C
guarantees integrity of members' dealings	.	.	.	.	.	K.	.	OC	.	.C	.	.	.C
circulates economic information	.	.	.	.	.	.	.C	OC	.C	OC	.	.	.C
regulates prices in products, labor	.	.	.	.	.	.	.	.	OC	.C	.	.	.C
controls business competition	.	.	.	.	.	.	.	.	OC	.C	.	.	.C
Credit													
offers loans to members	.	K.C	K.	.	.C	.	KRC	.C	.	.C	.	.	.
offers loans to members at low interest	.	.C	.	.	.	.C	.	.C	.	.	.	.	.
offers loans to members at no interest	R.	.R	.C	.	.	.	.	.	.	.	.	.	.

Chinese Around the World: The Familial and the Familiar   203

Function	C1	C2	C3	C4	C5	C6	C7	C8	C9	C10	C11	C12	C13	C14
Welfare														
provides welfare benefits to members	K.		K.					R.	SOC	SOC	.C	S.		.C
contributes to local charities									O.	SO.	.OC	.C	.C	
operates, contributes to hospital, clinic			K.						.C	O.				.C
offers assistance to immigrants									O.	O.		S.		.C
provides charity burials			K.						O.	S.C		S.		.C
Political Controls														
judges, punishes offenses of members	K.		K.			K.			SOC	SOC	.C			.C
mediates disputes involving members		.R.	K.			K.					.C	S.C		.C
provides legal assistance to members			K.									S.		.C
acts for community as a whole			K.			K.		.R.		.C	.C	.C		.C
negotiates with government			K.			K.					.OC	S.		.C
Education														
owns, maintains school	KRC	.R.	K.	.R.				.R.	OC	OC	.C	.C	.C	
contributes to local school				K.								S.		
offers financial aid to students			K.						O.					
honors successful students			K.									S.C		
Sociability and Recreation														
members gather to talk	.R.	.RC	.C					RC		SO.	O.	S.C	.C	.C
offers formal meeting facilities	.R.	.R.								O.	O.	S.C	.C	.C
members gather to eat			.C						.C	S.				
organizes banquets for members	KR.	KRC	.C						SOC	SO.		S.C		.C
members gather for literary, artistic, cultural activities									.C		O.	S.C		
offers reading facilities									.C	S.	O.	S.		.C
members gather for music, dance			.C					RC	.C	.C		.C	.C	.C

Table 3 (Contd.)
Functions, Recruitment Types of Secondary Organizations in 13 Chinese Communities

function	Taitou	Kaihsienkung	Phenix Village	West Town	Boat People	Hang Mei	K'un Shen	Phnom-Penh	Bangkok	Semarang	Sacramento	Mississippi Delta	London
members gather for games, gambling				.C					OC	O.	S.		.C
members gather for sports			.C						SO.	O.	.C		.C
organizes outings for members											.C		
organizes celebrations	R.	.R	.C				.R		.O	.C	S.C		
Ties to China													
offers media materials from China											S.C		.C
organizes courses in Chinese language, culture for members											.C		.C
organizes trips to China for members													
provides facilities for storing human remains bound for China									.O		S.		
Ancestor Worship													
owns, maintains ancestral temple	K.		K.	K.		K.	K.		.O	S.			
owns, maintains genealogical records	K.	.R	K.	K.		K.	K.	SOC	S.C	S.	S.		.C
organizes ancestral ceremonies	K.	KR	KC	K.		K.	K.	SO.	SO.	.C			.C
owns, maintains grave site			K.					.O		OC			
guarantees funerals of members			.C			K.C	.C						

recruitment type of secondary social organization
K=Kinship; S=Surname; R=Residence; O=Origin; C=Contract

Nonancestral Religion										
owns, maintains nonancestral religious building	...	...	...	R.	...	R.	.R.	.OC	O.	.OC	..C
contributes to nonancestral religious organization	...	...	K..	...	...	...	R.	.R.	...	.C	...
organizes nonancestral religious ceremonies	...	R.	K.C	K..	..C	R.	KR.	.OC	.OC	.OC	..C

Sources: Yang, x, 6-7, 70, 134-138, 141-144, 148, 150-152, 158, 163, 165, 173, 181, 194, 197; Fei, 20-21, 23, 57, 75-76, 84-86, 98-99, 102-106, 114, 129, 204, 216, 223-225, 241, 263, 267, 273; Kulp, xxiv, xxviii, 13, 101, 121, 124, 145-146, 148, 189, 196-199, 202-203, 206-210, 218, 221, 260, 289, 302, 310, 321, 323; Hsu, 16, 24-25, 125, 127-129; Anderson, 37-39, 68, 81-82, 87-90, 92, 101, 120-123, 173; Potter, 12-13, 15, 17-18, 20-21, 27-28, 30, 59, 91, 95-96, 101-104, 106, 108, 111, 115-116, 143, 156, 165-167, 169; Diamond, 22-23, 36-37, 46, 62-65, 68-69, 72, 74-80, 84-86; W.E. Willmott, 1967, 84-87; 1970, 13, 36-37, 44, 49, 55, 65-67, 72-75, 78-79, 81-84, 86-89, 91, 100, 102, 105, 108-112, 114-117; Coughlin, 33-34, 38-45, 47-57, 59, 98-99; D.E. Willmott, 26-28, 50, 53-55, 60, 62, 64-66, 71, 83, 88, 99, 101-102, 115, 119, 122, 129-136, 138-141, 144-145, 167, 170-175, 179, 211-212, 230-234, 247-252, 285-286; Weiss, 80, 88, 90, 92-94, 128, 159-161, 163, 175, 178, 181, 184-188, 190, 192, 194, 201, 203, 211, 214, 221-224, 226, 229, 237; Loewen, 34, 36-38, 83-84, 88-89, 91-93, 109, 112; Ng, 19, 29, 33, 49-60, 65-69, 71-74. Itemized references cited in Serrie, 1976.

reading rooms, media materials, and perhaps courses on or trips to China. In most overseas communities, and in West Town (the large mainland community), benevolent institutions, sometimes including hospitals and clinics, are maintained or supported by organizations for their members and nonmembers—sometimes even non-Chinese—alike.

Concern with education seems fairly universal in Chinese culture. In the mainland and offshore communities the Kuomintang and British governments had established schools. In Phenix Village, which was studied before the government school program got underway, the sole lineage had established a school. In Taitou, the ancestor worshipping P'ans had established a school which subsequently became the government school, while the Ch'en and Yang lineages jointly organized a school for the Christian contingent. A government run school is available to the children of the Boat people, but it is not located within their residential territory, and does not cater to their dialect. Among the overseas Chinese, the functions of preserving ties to China and establishing special Chinese schools serve the Hsu attribute of continuity.

Formalized sociability functions of getting together to talk and of organizing festive celebrations seem widespread in Chinese organizations, and serve the Hsu attribute of inclusiveness. Most of the overseas communities offer formal meeting facilities for sociability purposes. Eating together, casually or at banquets, was reported only for the mainland villages and some of the overseas communities. Cultural and athletic activities were found in a few mainland and offshore villages and all overseas communities. Gambling, a Chinese passion, is only spottily reported as a formal organizational function.

None of the thirteen monographs discuss any sexual functions for any Chinese organization. The absence of this topic implies the Hsu attribute of asexuality. As Hsu has indicated, sex in Chinese life is strictly relegated to private life and to prostitution. When the author was working in Taiwan in 1966 and 1969, and when he was on a study tour of the mainland in 1976, sex was definitely not a proper topic for conversation. Indeed, he witnessed many conversations in which well-intentioned Americans managed to seriously embarrass various Chinese — friends, housekeepers, interpreters, paramedics, officials, etc. — by inquiring about dating, premarital pregnancy, and the like. Chinese clothing and hair styles, patterns of greeting and interaction, and content in advertising, movies, and other media are devoid of sexual content, or at least muted in comparison with American counterparts. Hsu states that it is common in the social organizations of overseas Chinese for men and women to be segregated (Hsu 1984 : personal communication).

Political functions, involving mediating disputes, providing legal assistance, acting for the community, and negotiating with governmental apparati beyond the community level were important in several agricultural villages on the mainland and offshore, and among all overseas communities except Mississippi where they were informal. In that locale, the Chinese community was for several decades heavily engaged in an ultimately successful campaign to reclassify Chinese as "White" rather than "Colored" and to accept them in White schools and other institutions. Various coercions of their own population were deemed necessary by the leaders of the Chinese community to satisfy local White attitudes. These included forcing Chinese males to give up legal or common law spouse relationships with Black women. However, the social and economic sanctions that were applied operated on an informal basis.

In general in Chinese communities, formal legal or political powers of coercion seem far less in evidence than informal means of control. Only some mainland and offshore lineage organizations had formal powers to judge and punish their members. Yet the formal economic controls practised in overseas communities could be employed in much the same way to control people's behavior.

The Hsu attribute of authority is seen in the real political or economic powers of coercion the members give these various organizations in order to enforce the will of the Chinese community on recalcitrant members. The Chinese preference for informal means of control can be seen to express the Hsu attribute of inclusiveness, to the extent that leadership is shared and unobtrusive, and wrongdoers remain integrated in the community. Beyond these considerations, the Hsu attributes of inclusiveness and continuity are seen in the fact that almost all Chinese communities-even the marginal ones in Mississippi and London though not the Boat People-have some semblance of overall community organization.

Ancestor worship seems almost universal in Chinese culture. Formal organizations have assumed responsibility for ancestral ceremonies in all cases except two. Among the Boat People, ancestral concerns, like social organization, go little beyond the extended family level. Among the Mississippi Chinese, however, no evidence of ancestor worship is reported, even at the family level. All three wealthy mainland and offshore communities-Phenix Village, West Town, and Hang Mei- had constructed ancestral temples; and the two that were agricultural villages had set aside land for strictly ancestral purposes. Ancestral temples were also mentioned in passing in the ethnographies on Bangkok and Semarang. In all mainland and offshore communities in the sample, excepting the Boat People, genealogical records were formally maintained. In most mainland and offshore communities formal organizations maintained grave sites and, in several organizations, guaranteed members' funerals.

Ancestor worship is a major expression of the Hsu attributes of continuity and inclusiveness, linking all blood-related mates and their spouses. It binds the living descendants to each other and to the generations of those departed and those yet to come. Genealogies may be stretched into the dim past in order to claim an illustrious personage, real or mythical, as an ancestor; great flexibility is allowed. There are no erotic innuendoes or connotations in ancestor worship, and so it is a major expression of the Hsu attribute of asexuality. Finally, the living owe much to the ancestors as they do to their living patriarchal superiors, which makes ancestor worship a major expression of the Hsu attribute of authority.

Chinese religious needs seem to require more than ancestor worship. Additional involvement with some other religion seems almost universal in Chinese culture, with formal organization of religious ceremonies involving local dieties, Confucianism, Buddhism or Christianity found in all cases. Many of these organizations maintained buildings for their religious purposes, and in one of the wealthy agricultural villages the nonancestral temple also owned land for its own maintenance.

Generally, Chinese people are pragmatic in their religious behavior, taking on additional practices or making changes in accordance with their perceptions of practical benefits. Chinese flexibility regarding the simultaneous practice of two or more religions by the same individual, within the same family, and within the same community is regarded as one of the most important manifestations of the Hsu attribute of inclusiveness in Chinese culture (Hsu 1982 : xiv-xv).

Patterns of Functional Substitution

When the functions in Table 3 are reorganized to show the patterns of substitution with respect to acceptance by different recruitment types of organization in mainland, offshore, overseas, and marginal communities, a general pattern of interchangeability emerges (Table 4). Of 51 functions described in the ethnographies, only 4 are assumed exclusively by one recruitment type. The remaining 47 functions are shared by almost all combinations of kinship, residence, surname, origin, and contractual types of organizations among the thirteen communities in the sample. Eleven functions are served by different combinations of two recruitment types of organization; 14 functions are served by combinations of three, and 8 functions are served by combinations of four. Four functions are served, within one community or another, by all five recruitment types of social organization.

By way of this interchangeability, Chinese social organizations are extremely flexible with regard to accepting multiple or diverse functions and changing functions over the course of time. They seem to be oriented towards retaining a membership of specific persons for life, and disposed to readily take on different functions as the needs of the members change. This functional interchangeability serves the Hsu attributes of continuity and inclusiveness.

In assuming multiple and diverse functions, a Chinese social organization seems to eschew specialization. Instead it resembles the family in a generalized approach oriented towards all or most of the needs of its members. The lineages in Phenix Village and Hang Mei managed land and buildings, coordinated members' labor, offered loans, ran ancestral and other ceremonies, judged and punished members' offenses, mediated disputes, acted for the community as a whole, and negotiated with the government. In the Southeast Asian Chinese communities, the contractual subsistence organizations known as *hui-guan* were heavily involved in political and economic controls, welfare benefits, education, ancestor worship, other religious activity, sociability and recreation, and ties to China.

Sometimes the diversity of functions assumed by a particular organization appears wildly discrepant, as when the K'un Shen temple offered loans; the Bangkok Chinese Chamber of Commerce acted, for many years, as the Chinese Consulate in Thailand; or a Phnom Penh athletic club assisted in the ancestral rituals on Ch'ing Ming. This diversity of functions may even border on or lead into changes in the principle of recruitment, as in the case of the K'un Shen lineages that operated shamanistic cults for an open public; or the former Phnom Penh lineage that doubled as a trade guild for drapers of the community.

Table 4
Patterns of Functional Substitution by Recruitment Types of Secondary Social Organization in Mainland, Offshore, Overseas, and Marginal Chinese Communities

function	MAINLAND (Taitou, Kaihsienkung, Phenix V., West Town)	OFFSHORE (Hang Mei, K'un Shen)	OVERSEAS (Phnom-Penh, Bangkok, Semarang, Sacramento)	MARGINAL (Boat People, Mississippi D., London)
recruitment type of secondary organization				
Global, with Kinship Organizations				
1 owns, maintains ancestral temple	K . .	K . .	SO .	
2 contributes to local school	K . .		S . .	
3 provides legal assistance to members	K . .		S . .	. . C
4 honors successful students	K . .		S . C	
5 contributes to local charities	K . .		SOC	. . C
6 provides charity burials				
7 owns, maintains secular building	K . .	K . .	SOC	. . C
8 negotiates with government				
9 owns, maintains grave site				
10 offers financial aid to students	K . .		. O .	
11 operates, contributes to hospital, clinic		K . .	. OC	
12 guarantees integrity of members' dealings		K . .	. OC	. . C
13 provides welfare benefits to members	K . .	. R .	SOC	. . C
14 owns, maintains nonancestral religious building	K . .	. R .	.OC	. . C
15 acts for community as a whole	K . .	KR .	. . C	. . C
16 mediates disputes involving members	KR .	K . .	SOC	. . C
17 organizes ancestral ceremonies	KRC	K . .	SOC	. . C
18 organizes banquets for members	KRC		SOC	
19 organizes nonancestral religious ceremonies	KRC	KR .	. OC	. . C
20 owns, maintains school	KRC	. R .	. OC	. . C
21 offers loans to members	K . C	KRC	. . C	. . C
22 guarantees funerals of members	. . C	K . C	. OC	
Global, without Kinship, but with Residence Organizations				
23 coordinates members' labor in emergencies	. R .	. R .	. . C	
24 organizes celebrations	. RC	. R .	SOC	
25 members gather for sports	. . C	. R .	SOC	. . C
26 members gather to talk	. RC	. RC	SOC	. . C
27 members gather for music, dance	. . C	. RC	. OC	. . C
28 members gather to eat	. RC		S . C	. . C
29 offers loans at no interest	. RC		. . C	
Global, without Kinship, Residence, but with Contractual Organizations				
30 members gather for games, gambling	. . C		SOC	. . C
31 circulates economic information		. . C	. OC	. . C

Table 4
Patterns of Functional Substitution by Recruitment Types of Secondary Social Organization in Mainland, Offshore, Overseas, and Marginal Chinese Communities

function	MAINLAND (Taitou, Kaihsienkung, Phenix V., West Town)	OFFSHORE (Hang Mei, K'un Shen)	OVERSEAS (Phnom-Penh, Bangkok, Semarang, Sacramento)	MARGINAL (Boat People, Mississippi D., London)
	recruitment type of secondary organization			
Kinship Organizations Only				
* judges, punishes offenses of members	K . .	K . .		
Contractual Organizations Only				
* Offers loans to members at low interest	. . C	. . C		
* contributes to nonancestral religious organization			. . C	
* organizes trips to China for members				. . C
Mainland and Offshore Only				
*32 judges, punishes offences of members	K . .	K .		
33 owns, manages agricultural land	K . .	KR .		
34 owns, maintains genealogical records	KR .	K . .		
35 coordinates members' labor for periodic tasks	KRC	. RC		
36 engages in economic ventures	K . C	. . C		
*37 offers loans to members at low interest	. . C	. . C		
Overseas and Marginal Only				
38 offers assistance to immigrants			SO .	. . C
39 offers reading facilities				
40 offers formal meeting facilities			SOC	. . C
41 members gather for literary, artistic, cultural activities				
42 offers media materials from China			S . C	. . C
43 guarantees quality of members' products			. OC	. . C
44 regulates prices of products, labor				
45 controls business competition				
Overseas Only				
46 serves as employment agency			S . .	
47 provides facilities for storing human remains bound for China			SO .	
*48 contributes to nonancestral religious organization			. . C	
49 organizes outings for members				
50 organizes courses in Chinese language, culture for members				
Marginal Only				
*51 organizes trips to China for members				. . C

*(listed twice)

The best example of functional flexibility in the service of the Hsu attributes of continuity and inclusiveness is that of the Boen Hian Tong in Semarang. This contractual organization started out as a Music Society. After a while, probably following marriage and parenthood and the incorporation of wives and children in the society, it took on mutual aid functions. Years later, when its members had grown old, it converted into a Burial Society. Although a contractual organization, this group of people, who originally came together to enjoy music, commenced to care for each other's material problems and kept this up for the rest of their lives, even to seeing each other past the rituals of death. The addition of mutual aid functions indicate the nurturing aspect of the Hsu attribute of authority as this society increasingly resembled the Chinese family.

This general pattern of interchangeability means that a given Chinese social organization is far more flexible than a Western counterpart in taking on multiple or diverse functions and changing its functions over the course of time. In keeping with the Hsu attributes of continuity and inclusiveness, a Chinese social organization seems to be created around specific persons, in some way familiar if not familial, who more or less assume life memberships in the group. Because the needs of its members change in time, the functions of the organization will also change in response to its members' needs.

Within this general pattern of interchangeability, the recruitment principles of surname and origin serve as substitutes for kinship in Chinese social organization. Of 22 more or less global functions that are assumed by kinship organizations on the mainland or offshore, in overseas communities 13 of these functions are assumed by surname organizations, 17 by origin organizations, and 19 by contractual organizations. Similarly, of 16 more or less global functions assumed by residence organizations on the mainland or offshore, in overseas communities 8 are assumed by surname organizations, 11 by origin organizations, and 16 by contractual organizations (Table 4).

Kinship is the most pervasive principle in the social organization of functions in mainland and offshore communities, with the exception of the marginal Boat People (Table 5). Kinship organizations on the mainland are exclusively responsible for 15 of 34 functions described in the data; and non-exclusively handle an additional 9 to make 24 functions in all, as opposed to 12 functions for residence and 16 for contract. The offshore pattern is almost as strong, with 15 out of 28 functions handled, more exclusively than not, by kinship organizations.

Table 5

Exclusive and Nonexclusive Assumption of Functions by Recruitment Types of Secondary Social Organization in Mainland, Offshore, Overseas, and Marginal Chinese Communities

recruitment type of secondary organization	ALL COMMUNITIES	MAINLAND (Taitou, Kaihsienkung, Phenix V., West Town)	OFFSHORE (Hang Mei, K'un Shen)	OVERSEAS (Phnom-Penh, Bangkok, Semarang, Sacramento)	MARGINAL (Boat People, Mississippi D., London)
		number of functions			
Kinship, Exclusive	1	15	10	—	—
Kinship, Nonexclusive	26	9	5	—	—
Kinship, Total	27	24	15	—	—
Residence, Exclusive	—	1	6	—	—
Residence, Nonexclusive	19	11	7	—	—
Residence, Total	19	12	13	—	—
Surname, Exclusive	—	—	—	3	—
Surname, Nonexclusive	25	—	—	22	—
Surname, Total	25	—	—	25	—
Origin, Exclusive	—	—	—	1	—
Origin, Nonexclusive	31	—	—	30	—
Origin, Total	31	—	—	31	—
Contract, Exclusive	3	5	3	7	30
Contract, Nonexclusive	40	11	5	29	—
Contract, Total	43	16	8	36	30
All Recruitment Types	51	34	28	44	30

Overseas, surname and origin organizations relate, by and large nonexclusively, to 25 and 31 out of 44 functions. Contractual organizations play a much greater role than on the mainland or offshore, relating, largely unexclusively, to 36 out of 44 functions.

Going back to Table 3, there is an interesting feature with regard to the types of social organization responsible for organizing ancestral ceremonies. In six communities kinship organizations are responsible, in four communities surname organizations are responsible, and in four contract organizations are responsible. Ancestor worship is, in fact, the busiest of all 51 functions, in that there are 16 instances (in 11 communities) of organizational types charged with responsibility for it.

This underscores the overall importance of this function in Chinese culture, with clear implications regarding the Hsu attributes of continuity, inclusiveness, authority, and asexuality. Furthermore, it is the clearest indication in the functional data that the surname principle of recruitment is a more preferable substitute for kinship than origin in situations requiring a substitute. A vivid demonstration of this principle occurred in Phnom Penh, when the large Teochiu-speaking dialect association disbanded and divided into eight single-surname associations.

Conclusion

Chinese social organization seems to build outward from the familial to the familiar, with the principle of contract (and its potential for total prior unfamiliarity in recruitment) least preferred. In local village organization on the mainland and offshore, this familial-familiar orientation can be seen in the basic importance of the neighbor groups immediately beyond the bounds of the family, and in the extension of both principles of kinship and residence to the clan or lineage and community-wide organizations. Overseas, this orientation also seems to obtain in the substitution of surname and origin organizations for those based on kinship and residence. Even within organizations based on contract, the members often have prior ties based in real or putative kinship, or in real or putative local origin. Creating or maintaining organizations in which all members have familial or familiar ties to each other requires flexibility and ingenuity in alien locations overseas. Patterns of structural and functional substitution serve to create commonalities for the creation of new social groups, and to allow the nature of the group to chance while retaining members for life.

The familial-familiar orientation and structural-functional flexibility are manifestations of the Hsu attributes of continuity, inclusiveness, authority, and to a lesser extent asexuality. These attributes persist in overseas Chinese communities, despite differences in their internal demographic characteristics or in the external environment of the host culture.

Notes

1 Although these cases comprise some of the variance in Chinese communities, far more must exist beyond them. This research has not attempted to tap changes in dynastic times or under communism. For the precommunist mainland, there is little material available on cities, especially concerning coolies, artisans, factory workers, and the like. Overseas studies, on the other hand, neglected Chinese outside of the cities : in the mines, on the plantations, and in other capacities. There is little or no data on continental Europe, Latin America, Africa, West Asia, South Asia, or the former Soviet Union.

References

Abbott, Kenneth. *Harmony and Individualism*. Taipei, Taiwan: The Orient Cultural Service, 1970.

———. "Cultural Change and the Persistence of the Chinese Personality," in George DeVos (Ed.) *Response to Changes*. New York: D. Van Nostrand, 1976.

Agpalo, Remigio E. *The Political Process and the Nationalization of the Retail Trade*. Quezon City: University of the Philippines Press, 1962.

Amyot, Jacques. *The Chinese Community of Manila: A Study of Adaptation of Chinese Familism to the Philippine Environment*. (Ph.D. Diss., University of Chicago), 1960.

———. *The Manila Chinese*. Institute of Philippine Culture. Ateneo de Manila. Quezon City, 1973.

Anderson, E. N., Jr. *The Floating World of Castle Peak Bay*. Anthropological Studies 4. Washington: American Anthropological Association, 1970a.

———. "Lineage Atrophy in Chinese Society." *American Anthropologist* 72: 2,363-5, 1970b.

Asian American Field Survey. *Summary of the Data*. Washington, DC: Department of Health, Education and Welfare, 1977.

Bandyopadhyay, Raghbab. "The Inheritors: Slum and Pavement Life in Calcutta." *Calcutta, The Living City*. Sukanta Chaudhuri (Ed.), pp. 78-87. Calcutta: Oxford University Press, 1990.

Barth, Fredrik. "Introduction." *Ethnic Groups and Boundaries*. Fredrik Barth, Ed. Boston: Little Brown and Company, 1969.

Bayley, C.A. *Rulers, Townsmen and Bazaars*. Cambridge: Cambridge University Press, 1983.

Beattie, G. "Some Observations Concerning the Integration and Adjustment of the Chinese in Brisbane," *Zealots* 14 (August): 2-14, 1982.

Bentley, G. Carter. "Ethnicity and Practice." *Comparative Studies in Society and History* 29 (1):24-55, 1987.

Berry, Brian J.L.; Rees, Philip H. "The Factoral Ecology of Calcutta." *American Journal of Sociology* 74 (5):445-91, 1969.

Blake, C. Fred. *Ethnic Groups and Social Change in a Chinese Market Town*. Honolulu: University of Hawaii Press, 1981.

Blalock, Hubert. *Toward a Theory of Minority Group Relations*. New York: Wiley, 1967.

Bonacich, Edna. "A Theory of Middlemen Minorities." *American Sociological Review* 38 (October):583-94, 1973.

Boonsangong, Punyodyana. *Chinese-Thai Differential Assimilation in Bangkok: An Exploratory Study*. Ithaca:Cornell University Southeast Asia Data Paper Number 79, 1971.

Bose, Nirmal Kumar. "Calcutta: A Premature Metropolis." *Scientific American* 213 (September): 91-102, 1966.

———. *Calcutta: 1964, A Social Survey.* Bombay: Lalvani Publishing House, 1968.

Carstens, Sharon A. "Form and Content in Hakka Malaysian Culture." *Guest People: Hakka Identity in China and Abroad.* Nicole Constable (Ed.), pp. 124-148, Seattle: University of Washington Press, 1996.

Chakraborty, Satyesh. "The Growth of Calcutta in the Twentieth Century." *Calcutta, The Living City.* Sukanta Chaudhuri (Ed.), pp. 1-14. Calcutta: Oxford University Press, 1990.

Chen, Jack. *The Chinese of America.* San Francisco: Harper and Row, 1980.

Chen, T. *Chinese Migration with Special Reference to Labor Conditions.* United States Bureau of Labor Statistics, 340, 1923.

Cheng, David. *Acculturation of the Chinese in the U.S.: A Philadelphia Study.* Foochow, China, 1948.

Chinatown Study Group Report. New York, 1977.

Choi, C.Y. "Patterns of Migration and Marriage among the Chinese in Australia." *Australian Journal of Social Issues* 7 (July): 141-150, 1972.

———. *Chinese Migration and Settlement in Australia.* Sydney: Sydney University Press, 1975.

Cohen, Abner. *Custom and Polities in Urban Africa.* Berkeley: University of California Press, 1969.

——— (Ed.). *Urban Ethnicity.* Tavistock, London. 1974.

Cohen, Myron. "The Hakka or 'Guest People': Dialect as a Sociocultural Variable in Southeastern China." *Ethnohistory* 15 (3): 237-92, 1968.

Coller, Richard. "A Social-Psychological Perspective on the Chinese as a Minority Group in the Philippines." *Philippine Sociological Review* 8, (Jan.-April), pp. 47-56, 1960.

Constable, Nicole (Ed.). *Guest People: Hakka Identity in China and Abroad.* Seattle: University of Washington Press, 1996.

Coughlin, Richard J. *Double Identity: The Chinese in Modern Thailand.* Hong Kong: Hong Kong University Press, 1960.

Crissman, Lawrence W. "The Segmentary Structure of Urban Overseas Chinese Communities." *Man* 2 (2): 185-204, 1967.

———. "A Discussion of Ethnicity and its Relation to Commerce." *Southeast Asian Journal of Social Science* 5: 96-110, 1977.

Cronin, C. "The Chinese Community in Queensland." *Queensland Heritage* 2 (May): 3-13, 1973.

Diamond, Norma. *K'un Shen: A Taiwan Village.* New York: Holt, Rinehart and Winstom, 1969.

Dumont, Louis. *Homo Hierarchicus.* Chicago: University of Chicago Press, 1970.

Economic Review, 1979-1980. Alipore, West Bengal: Government of West Bengal Press, 1980.

Elvin, Mark. *The Pattern of the Chinese Past*. Stanford: Stanford University Press, 1973.

Fei, Hsiao-Tung. *Peasant Life in China*. London: Routledge & Kegan Paul, Ltd., 1939.

Firey, Walter. *Land Use in Central Boston*. Cambridge: Harvard University Press, 1980 [1947].

Fischer, Michael. *Zoroastrian Iran Between Myth and Praxis*. (Ph.D. Diss., University of Chicago), 1973.

Fitz Gerald, C.P. *China and Southeast Asia Since 1945*. Camberwell, Australia: Longman, 1973.

Freedman, Maurice. "Immigrants and Associations: Chinese in Nineteenth Century Singapore," in L.A. Falters (Ed.), *Immigration and Associations*. Mouton Press, 1967.

———. *Lineage Organization in Southeastern China*. London: The Athlone Press (University of London), 1970.

Gates, Hill. "Money for the Gods." *Modern China* 13 (3): 259-77, 1987.

Geib, Margaret; Ashok Dutt. *Atlas of South Asia*. Boulder: Westview Press, 1987.

Glazer, Nathan and Moynihan, Daniel. *Ethnicity: Theory and Experience*. Cambridge: Harvard University Press, 1975.

Gordon, Milton. *Assimilation in American Life*. New York: Oxford University Press, 1964.

Gould, Julius and William Kolb (Eds.). *Dictionary of Social Sciences*. Glencoe: Free Press, 1964.

Hall, T.D.H. "The New Zealand and Asiatic Immigration." *The Economic Record* 3; 228-239, 1927.

Hamilton, Gary. "Pariah Capitalism: A Paradox of Power and Dependence." *Ethnic Groups* 2:1-15, 1978.

Harrell, Stevan. "Why Do the Chinese Work So Hard? Reflections on an Entrpreneurial Ethic." *Modern China* 11 (2): 203-226, 1985.

———. "The Concept of Fate in Chinese Folk Ideology." *Modern China* 13 (1): 90-109, 1987.

———. "Ethnicity, Local Interests, and the State: Yi Communities in Southwest China." *Comparative Studies in Society and History* 32 (3): 515-548, 1990.

Hayden, Jr. Ralston. *The Philippines: A Study in National Development*. NewYork: Macmillan, 1950.

Hsu, Francis L.K. *Under the Ancestors' Shadow*. Garden City: Doubleday & Company, Inc., 1948, 1967.

———. *Americans and Chinese: Purpose and Fulfillment in Great Civilizations*. Garden City: Doubleday & Company, Inc., 1953, 1970.

———. "The Family in China." Ruth Nanda Anshen (Ed.), *The Family*. New York: Harper and Row, 73-91, 1959.

———. "Rugged Individualism Reconsidered." *Colorado Quarterly* 9:2 (Autumn), 1960.

———. *Clan, Caste and Club.* Princeton: D. Van Nostrand Company, Inc., 1963.

———. "The Effect of Dominant Kinship Relationships on Kin and Non-Kin Behavior: A Hypothesis." *American Anthropologist* 67, 638-660, 1965.

———. "Chinese Kinship and Chinese Behavior." Ho Ping-ti and Tang Tsou (Eds.), *China in Crisis* 1. Chicago: The University of Chicago Press, 1968.

———. *The Challenge of the American Dream.* Belmont, CA: Wadsworth, 1971.

———. *Americans and Chinese: Reflections on Two Cultures and Their People.* New York: American Museum of Science Books, 1972.

———. "Foreword." David Wu, *The Chinese in Papua. New Guinea: 1880-1980*, pp. xi-xvi. Hong Kong: The Chinese University Press, 1972.

———. (Ed.). *Kinship and Culture.* Chicago: Aldine Publishing Company, 1971.

——— and Hu, J.H. "Guild and Kinship among the Butchers in West Town." *American Sociological Review* 10, 357-364, 1945.

——— and Serrie, Hendrick (Eds.). "Family, Kinship and Ethnic Identity Among the Overseas Chinese." Special Issue, *Journal of Comparative Family Studies* 16:2, 1985.

Hsu-Balzer, Eileen; Balzer, Richard J.; and Hsu, Francis L.K. *China Day by Day.* New Haven: Yale University Press, 1974.

Hu, Sien-chin. *The Common Descent Group in China.* New York: Viking Fund Publications, 1948.

Huck, A. *The Chinese in Australia.* Melbourne: Longmans Green and Co. Ltd., 1967.

Hunt, Chester and Houston, Charlie O. "Changing Statutes of Chinese in the Philippines." *Internationales Aseiforum* 10:1-2, pp. 53-66, 1979.

Hunt, Chester, et al. *Sociology in the New Philippine Setting.* Quezon City: Alemars, 1976.

Inglis, C. "Chinese in Australia." *The International Migration Review* 6 (Fall): 266-281, 1972.

International Encyclopedia of Social Sciences. "Economic Growth." New York: Macmillan and Free Press 4:427, 1968.

Isaacs, Harold R. "Basic Group Identity: The Idols of the Tribe." *Ethnicity: Theory and Experience.* Nathan Glazer and Daniel P. Moynihan, (Eds.), pp. 29-52. Cambridge: Harvard University Press, 1975.

Jensen, Khin Khin Myint. *The Chinese in the Philippines During the American Regime, 1898-1946.* (Ph.D. Diss., University of Wisconsin), Madison, 1956.

Jiang, Joseph P.L. "Toward a Theory of Pariah Entrepreneurship." *Leadership and Authority: A Symposium*. Gehan Wijeyewarndene (Ed.), pp. 147-162. Singapore: University of Malaya Press, 1968.

Johnson, Elizabeth Lominska. "Hakka Villagers in a Hong Kong City: The Original People of Tsuen Wan." *Guest People: Hakka Identity in China and Abroad*, Nicole Constable (Ed.), pp. 80-97. Seattle: University of Washington Press, 1996.

Kandel, Denise and Lesser, Gerald. *Youth in Two Worlds*. San Francisco: Jossey-Bass, Inc., 1972.

Kingston, Maxine Hong. *The Woman Warrior*. New York: Random House, 1975.

Kolenda, Pauline. *Caste in Contemporary India*. Prospect Heights, Illinois: Waveland Press, 1985.

Kulp, Daniel Harrison II. *Country Life in South China: The Sociology of Familism 1, Phenix Village, Kwangtung, China*. New York: Bureau of Publications, Teachers College, Columbia University, 1925.

Kung, S.W. *Chinese in American Life*. Seattle: University of Washington Press, 1962.

Lande, Carl H. "The April 7th Election in Manila: A Brief Report." *Philippine Studies Newsletter* 6:1, pp. 1-3, 1978.

Larkin, John A. *The Pampangans*. Berkeley: University of California Press, 1972.

Lee, Rose. *The Chinese in the United States of America*. Hong Kong: Hong Kong University Press, 1960.

Lee, S.E. *The Ecology of the Sydney Chinese*. (B.A Honours Thesis, Department of Geography, University of Sydney), 1963.

Lelyveld, Joseph. *Calcutta*. Hong Kong: The Perennial Press, 1975.

Liang, Yuan. *The Chinese Family in Chicago*. (M.A. Thesis, University of Chicago), 1951.

Loewen, James W. *The Mississippi Chinese: Between Black and White*. Cambridge: Harvard University Press, 1971.

Lubell, Harold. *Calcutta: Its Urban Development and Economic Prospects*. Geneva: International Labour Office, 1974.

Lui, Chi Tien. "The Chinese Point of View: Comments on Events and Institutions." *The Chinese in the Philippines*, Alfonso Felix, Jr. (Ed.), 11: pp. 205-252. Manila: The Historical Conservation Society, Soledaridad Publishing House, 1969.

Lui, Garding. *Inside Los Angeles Chinatown*. Los Angeles, 1948.

Lyman, Stanford. *The Structure of Chinese Society in Nineteenth-Century America*. (Ph.D. Diss., University of California), Berkeley, 1961.

―――. "Contrast in the Community Organization of Chinese and Japanese in North America." *The Canadian Review of Sociology and Anthropology* 5 (2): 51-67, 1968.

Mandelbaum, David G. "The Jewish Way of Life in Cochin." *Jewish Social Studies* 1:423-460, 1939.

Marriott, McKim. "Caste Ranking and Food Transactions: A Matrix Analysis." *Structure and Change in Indian Society*. Milton Singer and Bernard S. Cohen (Ed.), Chicago: Aldine Publishing Company, 1968.

McBeath, Gerlad A. *Political Integration of the Philippine Chinese*. Center for South and Southeast Asia Studies. Berkeley: Monograph 8, 1973.

Mencher, Joan. "The Caste System Upside Down, or the Not-so-Mysterious East." *Current Anthropology* 15: 469-478, 1974.

Mitchison, Lois. *The Overseas Chinese*. London: The Bodley Head, 1961.

New Zealand Chinese Growers Monthly Journal (NZCGMJ), 1949-1971, Translated from the Chinese.

Ng Kwee Choo. *The Chinese in London*. London: Oxford University Press, 1968.

Omohundro, John T. *Chinese Merchant Families in Iloilo: Commerce and Kin in a Central Philippine City*. Ohio University Press: Athens, Ohio, 1981.

Patterson Orlando. "Context and Choice in Ethnic Allegiance: A Theoretical Framework and Caribbean Case Study." *Ethnicity: Theory and Experience*. Nathan Glazer and Daniel P. Moynihan (Eds.), pp. 305-349. Cambridge, Harvard University Press, 1975.

Poa, Dory. "The Molding of an Overseas Chinese as Reflected in the Chinese Language Arts Textbooks." *Lipunan* 1, pp. 69-78, 1979.

Potter, Jack M. *Capitalism and the Chinese Peasant*. Berkeley and Los Angeles: University of California Press, 1968.

Prince, M. *A Study of Ethnicity: The Brisbane Chinese*. Unpublished B.A. Honours Thesis, Department of Anthropology and Sociology, University of Queensland, 1975.

Purcell Victor. *The Chinese in Southeast Asia*, 2nd ed. London: Oxford Press, 1968.

Reynolds, Harriet R. *Continuity and Change of the Chinese in the Ilocos, Philippines*. (Ph.D. Diss., Hartford Seminary Foundation), June, 1965.

Reynolds, Ira Hubert. *Chinese Acculturation in Ilocos: Economics, Politics, Religion*. (Ph.D. Diss., Hartford Seminary Foundation), June, 1965.

Schermerhorn, R.A. *Ethnic Plurality in India*. Tucson: University of Arizona Press, 1978.

Selby, J. "Contemporary Chinese Family Structures in Brisbane." Paper delivered at the Asian Social Studies Conference, University of New England, July 9, 1983a.

———. "Chinese Elderly in Brisbane." Paper delivered at the Conference on the Ethnic Aged, sponsored by the Ethnic Development Welfare Association at Bardom July 27, 1983b.

Serrie, Hendrick. *Constancy and Variation in Chinese Culture: An Analysis of Fourteen Mainland, Offshore, and Overseas Communities in Terms of the Hsu Attributes.* (Ph.D. Diss., Northwestern University), Ann Arbor: University Microfilms, 1976.

Skinner, G. William. *Chinese Society in Thailand: An Analytical History.* Ithaca: Cornell University Press, 1957.

———. *Leadership and Power in the Chinese Community of Thailand.* Ithaca:Cornell University Press, 1958.

———. "Change and Persistence in Chinese Culture Overseas." *Journal of the South Seas Society* 16:86-100, 1960.

———. "Overseas Chinese Leadership: Paradigm for a Paradox." Gehan Wijeyewardene (Ed.), *Leadership and Authority.* Singapore: University of Malaya Press, pp. 191-207, 1968.

Sollenger, Richard. Chinese American Child Rearing Practices and Juvenile Delinquency," *Journal of Social Pscyhology* 74:17, 1968.

Srinivas, M.N. *Social Change in Modern India.* Berkeley: University of California Press, 1966.

Stevens, William K. "Calcutta, Symbol of Urban Misery, Won't Give Up." *The New York Times.* 5/June, Section I, page 10, 1983.

Stonequist, Everett. *Marginal Man.* New York: Charles Scribner's Sons, 1937.

Strizower, Schifra. *Exotic Jewish Communities.* London: Tomas Yoseloff, 1962.

Sung, Betty Lee. *Mountain of Gold.* New York: Macmillan Co., 1967.

———. *Story of the Chinese in America.* New York: Colliers, 1971.

———. *A Survey of Chinese American Manpower and Employment.* New York: Praeger, 1976.

———. *The Adjustment Experience of Chinese Immigrant Children.* Staten Island, NY: Center for Migration Studies, 1979.

———. *Transplanted Chinese Children.* New York: The City College of New York, 1979.

———. *Chinese American Intermarriage.* Staten Island, NY: Center for Migration Studies, 1990.

Suthep, Soonthornpasuch. *Islamic Identity in Chiengmai City: A Historical and Structural Comparison of Two Communities.* (Ph.D. Diss., University of California), Berkeley, 1977.

Szanton, Cristina. "Review of Omohundro, Chinese Merchant Families in Iloilo." *Journal of Asian Studies* 42:1, (Nov,) pp. 229-231, 1982.

Tan, Antonio S. *The Chinese in the Philippines During the Japanese Occupation, 1942-1945.* Quezon City: Asian Center, University of the Philippines Press, 1981.

Teo, S.E. (nee Lee S.E.) "A Preliminary Study of the Chinese Community in Sydney: A Basis for the Study of Social Change." *The Australian Geographer* 2 (September), 579-592, 1971.

Teper, Shirley. *Ethnicity, Race and Human Development*. New York: Institute on Pluralism and Group Identity of the American Jewish Committee, 1977.

Thompson, R. "From Kinship to Class: A New Model of Urban Overseas Chinese Social Organization." *Urban Anthropology* 9 (Fall): 265-293, 1980.

Tobias, Stephen F. "Buddhism, Belonging and Detachment—Some Paradoxes of Chinese Ethnicity in Thailand." *Journal of Asian Studies* 36:2 (February): 303-325, 1977.

Tysen, Frank. "Interest Groups in Calcutta." *Bengal: Change and Continuity*. South Asia Series, Occasional Paper 16. Robert Paul and Mary Beech (Eds.). East Lansing, Michigan: Michigan State University, 1971.

U.S. Census of Population. *General Population Characteristics. Final Report*, PC(1)-B1, United States Summary, U.S. Department of Commerce, 1970.

U.S. Census of Population. *General Social and Economic Characteristics of New York*. U.S. Department of Commerce, 1970.

U.S. Census of Population. *General Social and Economic Characteristics of New York*. U.S. Department of Commerce, 1980.

Viviani, N. *The Long Journey: Vietnamese Migration and Settlement in Australia*. Canberra: Australian National University Press, 1983.

Wagley, Charles and Marvin Morris. *Minorities in the New World*. New York: Columbia University Press, 1968.

Wang, Gungwu. *Community and Nation: Essays on Southeast Asia and the Chinese*. Singapore:Heinemann Educational Books (Asia) Limited for Asian Studies Association of Austrailia, Southeast Asia Publications Series, 1981.

Weber, Max. *Max Weber on Capitalism, Bureaucracy and Religion*. Stanislav Andreski (Ed.), London: George Allen and Unwin, 1983 [1920-21].

Weightman, George H. *The Philippine Chinese: A Cultural History of a Marginal Trading Community*. (Ph.D. Diss., Cornell University), Ithaca, 1960.

———. "A Study of Prejudice in a Personalistic Society: An Analysis of an Attitude Survey of College Students, University of the Philippines." *Asian Studies* 2:1, pp. 87-101, 1964.

———. "The Chinese Family and Sib in the Philippines." *Lipunan* 1:1, pp. 9-16, 1965.

———. "Anti-Sinicism in the Philippines." *Asian Studies* 5:1, (April), pp. 220-231, 1967.

———. "The Philippine Chinese Image of the Filipino." *Pacific Affairs* 40:3-4, Fall and Winter, pp. 315-323, 1968.

———. "The Philippine Chinese in the New Society." Unpublished paper read at Western Conference of the A.A.S, Tucson, Arizona, Oct. 13, 1978.

———. "Changing Patterns of Internal and External Migration among Philippine Chinese." Unpublished paper read at Midwest Conference of Association for Asian Studies, Ann Arbor, Michigan, Oct. 16, 1982.

Weiss, Melford S. "Selective Acculturation and the Dating Process: the Pattern of Chinese-Zancosian Inter-racial Dating." in Sue Stanley and Nathaniel Wagner (Eds.), *Asian-Americans*, Palo Alto: Science + Behavior Books, Inc., 1973.

———. *Valley City: A Chinese Community in America*. Cambridge: Schenkman Publishing Company, 1974.

Wickberg, Edgar. "Some Problems with Chinese Organisational Development in Canada, 1923-1937." *Canadian Ethnic Studies* 11: 88-98, 1979.

Willmott, Donald Earl. *The Chinese of Semarang: A Changing Minority Community in Indonesia.* Ithaca: Cornell University Press, 1960.

Willmott, W. E. *The Chinese in Cambodia*. Vancouver: University of British Columbia Publications Centre, 1967.

———. "Congregation and Associations: The Political Structure of the Chinese Community in Phnom-Penh, Cambodia." *Comparative Studies in Society and History* 11, pp. 282-301, 1969.

———. *The Political Structure of the Chinese Community in Cambodia*. London: The Athlone Press, 1970.

Wolf, Arthur. "Gods, Ghosts and Ancestors." *Religion and Ritual in Chinese Society*. Arthur Wolf (Ed.), pp. 131-182. Stanford: Stanford University Press, 1974.

Wolf, Eric. *Europe and the People Without History*. Cambridge: Cambridge University Press, 1982.

Wolf, Margery. *Women and the Family in Rural Taiwan*. Stanford: Stanford University Press, 1972.

Wong, Bernard. *Patronage, Brokerage, Entrepreneurship and the Chinese Community of New York*. (Ph.D. Diss.) Ann Arbor: University Microfilms, 1974.

———. "Social Stratification, Adaptive Strategies and the Chinese Community of New York." *Urban Life* 5 (1); 33-52, 1976.

———. "Elites and Ethnic Boundary Maintenance: A Study of the Roles of Elites in Chinatown, New York City." *Urban Anthropology* 6 (1): 1-25, 1977.

———. "A Comparative Study of the Assimilation of the Chinese in New York City and Lima, Peru." *Comparative Studies in Society and History* 20 (3): 335-358, 1978.

———. *A Chinese American Community*. Singapore: Chopmen Enterprises, 1979.

———. *Chinatown: Economic Adaptation and Ethnic Identity of the Chinese*. New York Holt, Rinehart and Winston, 1982.

Wu Yuan-li and Wu Chun-hsi. *Economic Development in Southeast Asia: The Chinese Dimension*. Stanford: Hoover Institution Press, 1980.

Wu, Cheng-tu. *Chinese and Chinatown in New York City.* (Ph.D. Diss.) Ann Arbor: University Microfilms, 1958.

Wu, D.Y. "Chinese in New Guinea: A Preliminary Report." *The Bulletin of the Institute of Ethnology.* Academia Sinica 20 (Autumn): 391-416, 1970.

———. "Ethnicity and Adaptation: Chinese Entrepreneurship in Papua New Guinea." *Southeast Asian Journal of Social Science* 5: 85-95, 1976.

Yang, Martin. *A Chinese Village: Taitou, Shantung Province.* New York: Columbia University Press, 1945.

Yorburg, Betty. *The Changing Family.* New York: Columbia University Press, 1973.

Young, C.C.S. "Preliminary Report of the Socio-Linguistic Changes of the Chinese Ethnic Group in Brisbane." University of Queensland, Occasional Papers in Anthropology 6, 1975.

Young, Nancy. "Socialization Patterns among the Chinese in Hawaii," *Amerasia Journal* 1:4, p. 36, 1972.

Index

Page references followed by *t* indicate tables.

aboriginals, 111n2
Act of 1924, 147
Adelaide, Australia: Chinese in, 112n11, 113n13
adolescents, 3, 8
affection, demonstration of, 179-80
Africa, 215n1
aggressiveness, 176
aliens, 65-85
All Saints Day ceremonies, 74, 81
American Chinese, 152, 167; families of, 158-60, 168, 170
American dream, 158, 169
American Exclusion Act, 73
American Legion, 196
Americanization, 162
Amoy, 73, 88
ancestor worship, 54, 81, 166, 208
Ang Men, 84
Anglican Chinese Centre, 133
Anglicans, 124-25, 129
Anglo racism, 7
Annual Sports Tournament, 140*t*
Anti-Asiatic League, 136*t*
anti-Chinese activity, 132
Anti-Chinese League, 135*t*-136*t*
Anti-Communist League, 126, 133, 138*t*, 140*t*, 195
anti-Sinicism, 85
architecture, 78
ascription: by others, 5-6; self, 5-6
asexuality, 190, 206, 214
Asian Americans, 176
Asian investment, 109
assimilation, 7-9; legal, 74; in New York City, 163, 170; in Philippines, 70-75; political, 74-75; social, 74-75; in Thailand, 46, 48-50, 60-61
athletic clubs, 192*t*-193*t*, 196

Auckland, New Zealand, 128-30, 135*t*-140*t*
Auckland Chinese Club, 138*t*
Auckland Chinese Community Centre, 140*t*
Auckland Chinese Hall, 128-29, 139*t*
Auckland Chinese Hall Journal, 129
Auckland Chinese Hui Sor, 125, 128-29, 133, 138*t*, 139, 139*t*
Auckland Chinese Sports Club, 138*t*, 139, 139*t*
Auckland Chinese Young Men's Club, 137*t*
Australia, 83; Asian investment in, 109; boat people in, 113n12; Bureau of Statistics, 105; Cantonese in, 99; census figures, 90-91; Chinese in, 4-6, 36, 88-90, 93-94, 95*t*, 96-97, 98*t*, 99-100, 103-7, 104*t*, 106*t*, 109-10, 112n11; citizenship, 98-100; ethnic clubs in, 99; Hakka Chinese in, 9; Immigration Department, 107; Indo-Chinese refugees in, 105-6; part-Chinese in, 90-91, 112n7. *See also* Brisbane
Australia-China Society, 101-2
Australian Asian Family Association, 100-102
Australian Chinese Association, 102
authority, 189, 207, 212, 214; defined, 190; respect for, 186
Ayutthaya, Thailand: Chinese in, 47

bachelor society, 147, 168
bamboo-joint, 160
bamboo-stick, 160
bananas, 160

228 Index

Bangkok, Thailand, 190-91, 208; Chinese in, 45; contractual organizations in, 195-96; origin organizations in, 194; secondary organizations in, 192*t*-193*t*, 197*t*, 202*t*-205*t*, 210*t*-211*t*, 213*t*
Bangkok Chinese Chamber of Commerce, 209
Bangladesh, 16
BAPERKI, 195
Baptist Church, 101, 125, 138*t*-140*t*
Bene Israel, 40n10
benevolent associations, 93, 192*t*, 195
Bengalis, 17, 19, 27; Hakka interactions with, 22-24, 26-27
bicultural conflicts, 173-88
Biharis, 17, 27
black fellas, 111n2
blood ties (*xue tong xue xiang*), 59
boat people, 191, 198, 200, 207, 212; in Australia, 113n12; contractual organizations, 195; secondary organizations, 192*t*-193*t*, 197*t*, 202*t*-205*t*, 210*t*-211*t*, 213*t*; from Southeast Asia, 91; from Vietnam, 105
bodhisattva, 55
Boen Hian Tong, 212
brain drain, 84; Chinese, 7; Third World, 68
brain exchange, 84
branches (*fang*), 191, 192*t*-193*t*
Brisbane, Australia: Chinatown, 92, 108-10; Chinese in, 8, 87-113, 95*t*, 98*t*, 106*t*; Indo-Chinese refugees in, 107; Vietnamese in, 107-8
Brisbane Chinese Christian Church, 101
British government, 206
brotherhoods, sworn, 166-67
Buddha, 82

Buddhism, 33, 56, 72, 81, 83, 196, 208
burial associations, 192*t*-193*t*, 195, 212
Burma, 8, 49; Chinese from, 48
businesses, 92. *See also* occupations

Calcutta, India, 16, 18-19; Cantonese in, 29, 35; Chinese in, 3, 5-6, 13-41, 39n1; Dhapa (Tangra or Tapsia), 14, 21, 23, 26-30; Hakka Chinese in, 9-10, 13-41; Maidan, 18-19; tanning community, 36
California: Chinese in, 24, 191. *See also* Sacramento; San Francisco
Canada, 83; Chinese in, 9, 109; migrants from, 173
Canterbury Chinese Cultural Society, 138*t*
Canterbury Sports and Culture Center, 140*t*
Canton City, Kwangtung Province, 152
Canton Village Mission, 136*t*
Cantonese: in Australia, 88, 93, 99; in Calcutta, 3, 6, 14, 20, 35, 39n1; Hakka views of, 25; in Manila, 81; in Philippines, 69, 77, 79, 84; in United States, 83
Cantonese associations, 83
Cantonese language, 92, 145
capitalism, 32, 38
castes, 40n6; *chamars*, 21, 27, 41n11; Half-Caste, 88-90; scheduled, 39n4; untouchables, 21, 39n4
Cathay Club, 100, 102
Catholic festivals, 77
Catholics, 70-71, 81-82
CCP. *See* Chinese Communist Party
Cebu, Philippines, 67, 83
chamar caste, 21, 27, 41n11

Index   229

Chambers of Commerce, 83-84, 102-3, 195
Chang association, 167
che (older sister), 153
Chee Kung Tong, 120-22, 132, 136*t*
Ch'en clan, 79; association, 167; lineages, 206
Ch'eung Shin Tong, 135*t*-136*t*
chia (jia), 54, 59, 77-80
chia-chang, 78
Chiang Kai Shek, 137*t*
Chiang Mai province (Northern Thailand), 45
Chiang Rai province (Northern Thailand), 45
children: adolescents, 3, 8; American, 181; Chinese, 156-57, 160, 187; Chinese immigrant, 173-88; Danish, 181
Chin Chien Chi Chia, 153
China, 122-23; Chinese from, 103-4, 104*t*, 105, 110, 187; community structural patterns, 197; Cultural Revolution, 180, 186; diplomatic representation, 119-21, 123-24, 126, 129, 132, 142n13, 209; education, 180; family size, 163; political environment, 175; Russians from, 90; Sino-Indian conflict, 22; war with Japan, 123; wars in, 148. *See also* People's Republic of China; Republic of China
China Society, 101
Chinatown: in Brisbane, 92, 96-97, 108-10; family-name (clan) associations, 166*t*, 166-67; in Kalookan City, 68; in Malabon, 68; in Manila, 68; in New York City, 2-4, 8, 143-70, 177, 182; schools, 177; in Toronto, 37
Chinatown Beautification Project, 76

Chinese: in Brisbane, 87-113; in Calcutta, 3, 5-6, 13-41; foreign-born, 94; in New York City, 3-5, 7-8, 143-71, 173-88; in New Zealand, 4, 6, 115-42; in Northern Thailand, 43-63; overseas, 1-11, 189-215; in Philippines, 65-85; in Southeast Asia, 65
Chinese Americans: families, 143-44, 149; lifestyle, 162
Chinese Anglican Centre, 131
Chinese Anglican Church, 124-25, 128-31, 138*t*, 139, 139*t*-140*t*
Chinese Association, 142n13
Chinese Baptist Church, 138*t*-140*t*
Chinese Building Workers Union, 139*t*
Chinese Chamber of Commerce, 83, 102-3
Chinese Churches, 133, 142n13
Chinese Citizen's Association, 101
Chinese Club, 93, 98-102, 107, 112n9
Chinese Commercial Growers Association, 133, 138*t*
Chinese Commercial Growers Journal, 139*t*
Chinese Communist Party (CCP), 96, 124
Chinese Cultural Society, 133, 138*t*, 140*t*
Chinese Exclusion Law, 146-47, 168
Chinese Grower's Association, 126-28, 131, 140*t*
Chinese Grower's Monthly Journal, 129, 138*t*
Chinese Indians, 5, 22
Chinese New Year, 77, 153
Chinese Progressive Club, 138*t*
Chinese restaurants, 164-65, 191
Chinese Sports and Culture Centre, 140*t*

Index

Chinese Temple Society, 99, 101, 108
Chinese Women's New Life Movement, 195
Chineseness, 91
Ching Ming (Qing Ming), 55, 72, 74, 77, 81, 209
Chino (term), 69
Cholon Chinese, 108
Chong Wah Wui Koon, 120-23, 132, 136*t*-137*t*
Christchurch, New Zealand, 128, 135*t*-136*t*, 138*t*
Christianity, 81, 125, 208; churches, 5, 125; rituals, 167
Christians: Chinese, 4, 70, 82, 108; Indian, 28
Christmas, 77
Christmas Island, 98
Chua (Ts'ai) (surname), 79
Chungshanese, in Australia, 93
Civil Rights movement, 161
clan(s), 67, 69, 77-81, 166-67, 190. *See also* surname(s)
clan associations, in New York City, 166*t*, 166-67
clan name (*hsing*), 79
class consciousness, 161
class model, 109; advantages of, 109-10
Cochin Jews, 40n10
collectivism, 184
Colored (term), 207
Commonwealth Immigration Restriction Act of 1901, 89
Communism, 5, 186; Anti-Communist League, 126, 133, 138*t*, 140*t*, 195; Chinese Communist Party (CCP), 96, 124
community associations, 123; in New Zealand, 135*t*-140*t*. *See also* social organization(s)

community centres, 133
community facilities, 133
community organizations, 116, 119-21, 126-28. *See also* social organization(s)
Confucianism, 10, 186, 208
Confucius, 81, 196
consumption, conspicuous, 182-83
continuity, 106, 194, 196, 199, 207, 212, 214; defined, 190
contractual organizations, 192*t*-193*t*, 195-96; functions of, 213
Cooperative Silk Factory, 195
Cotabato, Philippines, 68, 83
credit, 183
Credit Society, 192*t*-193*t*
criminal associations, 84
Cua-Chua, 80
cultural clubs, 192*t*-193*t*, 196
cultural minority, 65-85
Cultural Revolution, 180, 186
culture: Chinese, 125; definition of, 174; education, 52-56; host environment, 6
customs duty, 121

dacoits (armed robbers), 26, 40n9
Danish children, 181
Darwin, Australia: Chinese in, 112n11
dating, 177-78
De (younger brother), 153
de-alienization, 66
Delta Club, 139*t*
Democratic Clubs, 195
demographics, 49; Australia, 90-91, 109; Brisbane, 87-92; Calcutta, 39n1; New York City, 144, 147, 149; New Zealand, 141n7, 142n10; Philippines, 65-66; Sydney, 109; Yunnanese, 47-48
demonstrative affection, 179-80
dependency, 184-85

deskilling, 107
Di clan, 79
dialect associations, 192*t*-193*t*, 194, 197
dictation test, 94
discrimination, 108
district associations, 192*t*-193*t*, 194, 197
domestic rituals, 54-55
dominant dyads, 2-3, 143-55, 156*t*; father-son, 143-44, 154-55, 164, 169, 190; husband-wife, 144, 155, 159, 164, 169-70; mother-child, 143-44, 154, 169
Dominicans, 70
double identity, 58
Double Seventh, 137*t*
Double Tenth, 122-23, 125, 132, 136*t*-138*t*, 142n14
Double Tenth Annual Sports, 125, 134
Dragon Boat Festival, 153
Dragon Dance, 102
dropouts, 157

East India Company, 16
East Timorese refugees, 112n11
Easter, 77
Easter Sports Tournament, 134, 140*t*
Eastern Club, 125
Eastern Sports and Mui Shuit Club, 133
Eastern Sports Club, 128-29, 138*t*
economic environment, 121, 182-83; Asian investment, 109; credit, 183; Credit Society, 192*t*-193*t*; gold rush, 88-89, 117-18; money, 33; money-hungry, 182; thrift, 153, 182-83; wealth, 28-34
economic family (*chia* or *jia*), 54, 59, 77-80

education, 51-52, 60, 176-77, 180-81, 206; academic standards, 181; Cantonese schools, 83; Chinese culture, 52-56; Chinese language, 52-54, 82-83; Chinese schools, 19, 53, 72, 75-76, 82-83, 177; English schools, 19, 28
el Santo Niño de Cebu, 81-82
elderly, 63n6
employment, 61, 96, 107-8, 157-58. *See also* occupations
endogamy, clan, 79-80
English language, 27, 103-4, 160
English language schools, 19, 28
entrepreneurial ethic, 28-34
ethnic identity, 14-15, 36
ethnicity, 1-11, 43-63, 69, 116; in Calcutta, 16, 18; definition of, 14; in New Zealand, 117, 123-24
ethnocentrism, regional, 161
Europe: Chinese emigration to, 36; Chinese in, 215n1; Hakka Chinese in, 9. *See also* London, England
exclusion, 6, 72-73, 168; American Exclusion Act, 73; Chinese Exclusion Law, 146-47, 168; Oriental Exclusion Act, 84; in Philippines, 72-74; in U.S., 7, 72-73
exogamy, 50; clan, 79-80

false or paper names, 74
familial and familiar, 3, 189-215
families, 77-81, 143-71; American-born Chinese, 158-60; in China, 143-44; Chinese American, 144; conjugal, 148, 150; enlarged, 4, 150; extended, 150, 190; extended or economic (*chia* or *jia*), 54, 59, 77-80; incomplete,

4, 146, 150; intrafamilial relationships, 150-65; mutilated, 146; New Immigrant, 155-58; in New York City, 143-51, 151*t*; nonresidential extended, 2-4, 150, 163-65, 168; nuclear, 148; Old Immigrant, 152-55; of professionals, 160-63; refugee, 149; stranded, 160; Yunnanese, 50-59. *See also* dominant dyads
family restaurants, 164
family-name (clan) associations: in New York City, 166*t*, 166-67. *See also* surname associations
fan gui ("barbarian ghost" or "foreign devil"), 6, 24
fathers, 154
father-son dyad, 143-44, 154-55, 164, 169, 190
Federal Government of Australia, 89
Federation of Chinese Chambers of Commerce, 84
fictive kin, 59
Fiji, 97
Fil-American War, 72
filial piety, 153
Filipinized Chinese, 85
Filipinized Chinese mestizos, 66
Film Club Auckland, 133, 138*t*
Fishermen's and the Farmers' Associations, 195
Fookien Times, 79
former Soviet Union, 215n1
Fort William, 18
Free China, 175
Free China Society, 126, 139*t*-140*t*
friendship, 167
frugality. *See* thrift
Fukienese, 7, 93, 145

gaming or gambling club, den, 192*t*-193*t*
Gandhi, Indira, 37

gardeners, 121
garment factories, 144-45, 164-65
Ge (older brother), 153
ghosts (*gui*), 24
Go clan, 79
Goddess of Mercy (Kuan Yin), 81
gold rush, 88-89, 117-18
government organizations, 192*t*-193*t*, 194
Griffith University, 112n10
Guan Yin (Kuan Yin), 55, 82
Guangdong, 14
Guangfu lao, 25
Guest People, 36
gui, 6
Gujarat, India, 19
Guomindang. *See* Nationalist party (Kuomintang)

habitus, 36
hai ren hai ji, 31
hai ren li ji, 31
Hakka, 3, 5-6, 8, 35-38; in Calcutta, 10, 13-41; in Hong Kong, 34; Indian views of, 22; in Malay, 34; occupations of, 20, 39n1; refugees, 112n11; in Toronto, 37; views of outsiders, 24-28; women's roles, 34-35
Half-Caste, 88-90
Han Chinese, 45, 49, 63n4
Hang Mei, Hong Kong, 190, 194, 197, 207, 209; contractual organizations in, 195; secondary organizations in, 192*t*-193*t*, 197*t*, 202*t*-205*t*, 210*t*-211*t*, 213*t*
haw, 48
hen you qian (very wealthy), 31
heroes and heroines, 186-87
hill tribes, 49
Hindi language, 17, 27; schools, 19
Hinduism, 5
Hindus, 6, 13, 16-17, 23, 27

Hispanics, 78, 180
Ho Ah Mei, 135*t*
Hokkienese: in Australia, 111n5; in Philippines, 69, 74, 77, 79-81
Hong Kong, 5, 175, 180, 186, 190; Hakka in, 34
Hong Kong Chinese: in Brisbane, 94, 97-98, 103-7, 104*t*, 106*t*, 109, 112n10, 187; immigrants, 37, 110, 173
Hong Kong Student's Association, 101-2
Hong Men, 84
Honolulu, Hawaii, 144
households (*hu*), 78; in New York City, 151, 151*t*
Hsieh association, 167
hsing (clan name), 79
Hsu association, 167
Hsu attributes, 189-90, 199, 214
Huang Association, 167
Hubeinese, 3, 6; in Calcutta, 14, 20, 39n1; Hakka views of, 25
hui-guan, 209
husband-wife dyad, 144, 155, 159, 164, 169-70
Hwang Hou Cheng, 136*t*

identity, 91; double, 58; ethnic, 14-15, 36; Hakka, 13-41; Yunnanese, 48
illegal aliens, 67
illegally illegal, 73
illegally legal, 73
Iloilo, Philippines: Chinese in, 67-68
Ilokos, Philippines: Chinese in, 73
immigration, 94, 145-51, 152*t*; to Australia, 36, 107, 112n11; of children, 173-88; to Europe, 36; illegal aliens, 67; illegally illegal, 73; illegally legal, 73; kinship, 143-71; labor, 38; New Immigrants, 3, 149-50, 155-58, 168; to New York City, 145-51, 152*t*, 168, 173-74; to New Zealand, 118-19, 121, 123; Old Immigrants, 150, 152-55, 168; restriction, 89, 109; to Thailand, 45; to Toronto, 36; to U.S., 146-50, 168; of war brides, 146-48. *See also* exclusion
Immigration Act of 1924, 146
Immigration and Nationality Act Amendments of 1965, 149
Immigration Law, 168
Immigration Restriction Act, 94
impurity, 21
inclusiveness, 194, 196-97, 199, 206-7, 212, 214; defined, 190
India: caste system, 21, 27, 39n4, 40n6, 41n11, 88-90; Chinese in, 8, 27; non-Hindu minorities in, 28; Sino-Indian conflict, 22. *See also* Calcutta
Indians: Chinese, 22; Christians, 28; definition of, 40n8; Hakka interactions with, 22-25, 27-28; Jews, 40n10; Muslims, 28
individualism, 183-84
Indo-Chinese refugees, 102; in Australia, 105-7, 106*t*
Indonesian Chinese, 5; in Brisbane, 97; Peranakan, 10, 70
industrialization, 164
innovation, 115-42
integration, 87-113
intermarriage, 7-9, 45-46, 48, 50, 69, 74, 90, 105, 121, 162-63
Irrigation Cooperative Society, 195
Islam, 5, 81

Jai-li ren, 59
Japan: anti-Chinese propaganda, 7; war with China, 123
Jews, 29; Indian, 40n10

jia (*chia*), 54, 59, 77-80
jobs. *See* employment; occupations
John An Tong v Ah Foo, 135*t*
Jolo, Philippines, 73, 81; Chinese in, 78-79
judo, 99
Juk Kak, 160
Juk Sing, 160

Kaihsienkung, Kiangsu, 190, 194; residence organizations in, 194; secondary organizations in, 192*t*-193*t*, 197*t*, 202*t*-205*t*, 210*t*-211*t*, 213*t*
Kalookan City, Philippines: Chinese in, 68
Kampuchean Chinese, 105, 112n11, 113n13
ke tou, 55
kinship, 43-63, 164; fictive, 59; patrilineal, 2-3, 59, 165-66, 190; pseudo, 167; wider, 165-67; Yunnanese, 50-59
kinship organizations, 3-4, 191, 192*t*-193*t*, 212
kinship terminology, 153, 162
KMT. *See* Nationalist party (Kuomintang)
Korean War, 124, 133, 138*t*
Kuan Yin (Guan Yin), 55, 82
K'un Shen, Taiwan, 190, 209; contractual organizations in, 195-96; residence organizations in, 194; secondary organizations in, 192*t*-193*t*, 197*t*, 202*t*-205*t*, 210*t*-211*t*, 213*t*
kung fu, 178
Kuo association, 167
Kuomintang. *See* Nationalist party
Kwangtung province: Chinese from, 7, 198
Kwong Chew Association, 121, 141n9

labels, 180
Lady Mayoress' Charitable Fund, 99
Lady of Grace Church (Kalookan City), 82
language, 123, 174; Cantonese, 92, 145; Chinese, 41n12, 52-54, 82-83, 103-4, 104*t*, 160; dialect associations, 192*t*-193*t*, 194, 197; English, 103-4, 104*t*; Hindi, 17, 19, 27; mandarin (or *kuo yu*), 74, 96, 102, 108, 145; Toysanese, 145, 152-53
lao (fellow), 6, 25
Laos, 49; refugees from, 105
Latin America, 173, 215n1
Leather Research Institute, 41n11
legislation: anti-Chinese, 121. *See also specific acts*
"Letter of Instruction" (No. 270, April 11, 1975) (Philippines), 68
Li association, 79, 167
li ren hai ji, 31
li ren li ji, 31
Lim (surname), 79
Lima, Peru: Chinese in, 6-7, 163, 167; family-name associations in, 166
Lin association, 79, 167
lineage(s), 166, 206, 209
lineage associations, 4, 192*t*-193*t*
lin-li system, 194
literacy, 52-54, 57
Liu association, 167
local government organizations, 194
locality, 116
London, England, 190, 198, 200-201, 207; contractual organizations in, 195-96; secondary organizations in, 192*t*-193*t*, 197*t*, 202*t*-205*t*, 210*t*-211*t*, 213*t*

Los Angeles, California: Chinese in, 144
Lu-Co-Kho-Dhu-Kee, 80
luuk ciin, 10, 45, 48, 50

Ma association, 79, 167
Macao, Philippines, 73
Macaos, 69
macho, 176
Malabon, Philippines, 68
Malaysian Chinese, 5; in Brisbane, 94, 97-98, 100, 103-7, 104*t*, 106*t*, 109-10, 112n10
Mandarin (or *kuo yu*) language, 74, 96, 102, 145; instruction, 108
Manhattan Savings Bank, 182
Manila, Philippines: Chinese in, 4, 7, 67-68, 70-76, 78, 80-84, 163, 166-67; General Chamber of Commerce, 84
Maoris, 121, 141n6
Marawi, Philippines, Chinese in, 68
Marcos, Ferdinand, 68, 76, 83-85
Marcos, Imelda, 76
marginal men, 187
marginality, 187-88
marriage, 49-50, 69, 159; endogamy, 79-80; exogamy, 50, 79-80; intermarriage, 7-9, 45-46, 48, 50, 69, 74, 90, 105, 121, 162-63; interracial and interethnic, 162-63; Yunnanese, 56-57
martial arts, 99, 178-79
Marwaris, 17
Masons, 72, 84
Mei (younger sister), 153
mei you qian (poor), 31
Melbourne, Australia: Chinese in, 88, 93, 96, 98, 112n11; Indochinese refugees in, 113n13

men: Australian-born Chinese, 90; bachelor society, 147, 168; fathers, 154; marginal, 187
mestizos, 66, 69-72, 82; citizenship, 74; Filipinized, 66; Sinicized, 66, 71, 82; Sinified, 10
Mid-Autumn Festival, 55
migration, 75, 187; from Calcutta, 36-37; Cantonese, 84; family, 77. *See also* exclusion; immigration
minorities, cultural, 65-85
Mississippi Delta, 190, 198, 200-201, 207; contractual organizations in, 196; secondary organizations in, 192*t*-193*t*, 197*t*, 202*t*-205*t*, 210*t*-211*t*, 213*t*
money, 33, 182
Moon-cake Festival, 153
morality, 51-52
mother-child dyad, 143-44, 154, 169
multisurname associations, 79-81, 166, 191, 192*t*-193*t*
music associations, 84
Music Society, 212
Muslims, 13, 17, 23, 27, 63n4; Chinese, 45, 80; Indians, 6, 28

name(s), 74; clan (*hsing*), 79; false or paper, 74; last, 111n2; real or stone, 74. *See also* surname(s)
nationalism, 72; in New Zealand, 123-24; Philippine, 7, 76
Nationalist party (Guomindang) (Kuomintang or KMT), 45, 48, 52, 75, 84, 96, 120, 126, 132-33, 136*t*, 140*t*, 194, 206; embassy, 79, 84; government, 102; in New Zealand, 122, 124
nationalization, 66

236 Index

native place, 48-49
naturalization, 77, 85
neighborhood associations, 192t-193t, 194
Nepalese, 16-17, 27
New Guinea Chinese, 91, 100, 103, 105, 110; language use by, 103-4, 104t
New Immigrants, 3, 149-50; families, 155-58, 168
New Society, 66
New South Wales, Australia: Chinese in, 89
New Year, 72, 77, 153
New York City, New York: Chinatown, 2-4, 8, 143-70, 182; Chinese immigrant children in, 173-88; Chinese in, 3-5, 7-8, 143-71, 151t; political environment, 175; public schools, 181
New Zealand, 125; anti-Chinese organisations in, 119; Chinese commissions to, 119-20; Chinese Consul, 120, 132; Chinese in, 4, 6, 115-42, 135t-140t, 141n7, 142n10; European society in, 118, 121; immigration policy, 118-19, 121, 123; legislation and government activity, 124, 135t-140t, 141n6; racial consciousness in, 119; residence status, 142n14; Select Committee, 118, 135t
New Zealand Anglican Church, 130
New Zealand China Society, 140t
New Zealand Chinese Association, 120-21, 123, 126, 128-30, 132-33, 137t-140t; rules, 120
New Zealand Chinese Weekly (Wellington), 137t

Northern Names, 80
Northern Soccer Club, 125
Northern Territories, Australia, Chinese in, 88
Northern Thailand, 51; Chinese in, 43-63. *See also* Thailand
number game, 67

occupations, 89, 92, 96, 107-8, 121, 157-58; in Calcutta, 15-18, 20; Chinese restaurants, 164-65, 191; clan and, 79; gardeners, 121; garment factories, 144-45, 164-65; of Hakka, 20, 39n1; of Hubeinese, 20; specialization, 80; tanning, 20-21, 23, 41n11
Oceania, Chinese students from, 112n10
Old Immigrants, 150; families, 152-55, 168
Old Irish Association, 102
Old World influence, 168-69
Ong (Wang) (surname), 79
organizations. *See* social organization(s)
Oriental Exclusion Act, 84
orientations, psychocultural, 2-3
origin organizations, 192t-193t, 194
overseas Chinese, 1-11, 189-215; in Thailand, 63n1; women, 59-60
Overseas Chinese Communities, 92

Pacific, Chinese from, 91
P'ans, 206
pao-chia system, 194
paper names, 74
paper sons, 148
Papua New Guinea Chinese, 5; in Brisbane, 97-100, 105-7, 106t, 112n10
parenthood, 167
Parent-Teacher's Association, 196

Parsis, 29, 40n10
patrilineal kinship, 2-3, 59, 165-66, 190
Peninsulares, 71
Pentecost, 77
People's Republic of China (PRC), 5, 76, 85, 102, 124-25, 133; diplomatic representation, 68, 126, 133-34, 140*t*; immigrants from, 173; travel between Thailand and, 46
Peranakans, 10, 70
peripherality, 18-19, 21
persistence, 115-42
person (*ren*), 24
Perth, Australia: Chinese in, 113n13
Peru: Chinese in, 10, 163, 165. *See also* Lima
Phenix Village, Kwangtung, 190, 197, 206-7, 209; contractual organizations in, 195; secondary organizations in, 192*t*-193*t*, 197*t*, 202*t*-205*t*, 210*t*-211*t*, 213*t*
Philippine Airlines, 77
Philippine Bureau of Private Schools, 83
Philippines, 66-77, 197; Cantonese in, 80; Chinese in, 6, 10, 65-85, 165; citizenship, 68-69, 74-75, 80; colonial period, 70-75; Commonwealth Constitution of 1935, 74; Constitution of 1972, 83; educational system, 76, 83; exclusion, 72-74; Hispanics in, 6; independent, 75-77; institutional structures in, 77-84; Japanese in, 67, 75; nationalism, 7; New Society, 84; Presidential Decree No. 176, 76; Sinified mestizos in, 10; War of Independence, 70

Phnom Penh, Cambodia, 190-91, 209; contractual organizations in, 195-96; origin organizations in, 194; secondary organizations in, 192*t*-193*t*, 197*t*, 202*t*-205*t*, 210*t*-211*t*, 213*t*
Ping Shan Kung So, 195
political environment, 175
political organizations, 192*t*-193*t*, 195
poll tax, 119
Poon Fa Association, 121, 128, 135*t*-136*t*, 139*t*, 141n9
population. *See* demographics
poverty, 34
PRC. *See* People's Republic of China
prejudice, 108
Presbyterian Church, 135*t*, 138*t*, 142n13
primordial identifications, 9-11, 36
professionals, 161; families of, 160-63, 168; first-generation, 161-62; stranded, 4
Progressive Club, 125
Protestants, 81-83
pseudo kinship, 167
psychocultural orientations, 2-3, 189
PTA, 160
Pukekohe, New Zealand: Chinese in, 139*t*
Punjabis, 17
purity, 21

Q Sing Times (Auckland), 137*t*
Qing Ming (Ching Ming), 55, 72, 74, 77, 81, 209
qinqi, 59
Queensland, Australia: Chinese in, 87-89, 91-92, 95*t*, 96-99, 98*t*, 106*t*, 106-7, 111n3; part-Chinese in, 112n7

racial consciousness, 119
racism, 7
real or stone names, 74
Refugee Act, 149, 153, 168
refugees: Chinese, 112n11, 149; East Timorese, 112n11; Indochinese, 113n13; Indo-Chinese, 105-7
religious institutions, 81-82; churches, 125; contractual organizations, 192*t*-193*t*
ren, 6
Republic of China (ROC), 102, 125, 134; diplomatic representation, 140*t*; Economic Council, 139*t*; Treaty of Amity, 82
Republic of the Philippines: Treaty of Amity, 82. *See also* Philippines
Republican Clubs, 195
residence organizations, 192*t*-193*t*, 194
restaurants, 164-65, 191
Returned Servicemen's Association, 121
Rewi Alley, 139*t*
rituals, 52, 54-57; Christian, 167; domestic, 54-55
Rizal, Jose, 71
ROC. *See* Republic of China
Rotary club, 196

Sacramento, California, 190-91, 201; contractual organizations in, 195-96; origin organizations in, 194; secondary organizations in, 192*t*-193*t*, 197*t*, 202*t*-205*t*, 210*t*-211*t*, 213*t*
Saint James or Santiago, 81
San Francisco, California: Chinese in, 144

San Zi Jing (*Three Character Classic*), 54
savings. *See* thrift
scheduled caste, 39n4
scholars: stranded, 148-49. *See also* students
schools. *See* education
secondary social organizations: assumption of functions by, 213*t*; functional substitution by, 210*t*-211*t*; functions of, 202*t*-205*t*; recruitment types, 197*t*
secret societies, 192*t*-193*t*, 196-97
segmentation: in Brisbane, 87-113; in Calcutta, 25; in New Zealand, 116-17, 130-31, 134
self ascription, 5-6
self-definitions, 39n2
self-gratification, 184
self-hatred, 176
self-identification, 38
self-interest, 184
self-reliance, 183
Semarang, Indonesia, 190-91, 197, 208; contractual organizations in, 195-96; origin organizations in, 194; secondary organizations in, 192*t*-193*t*, 197*t*, 202*t*-205*t*, 210*t*-211*t*, 213*t*
semi-legal or criminal associations, 84
Sen, Lin, 137*t*
sexuality, 176-78; asexuality, 190, 206, 214
Seyip Association, 128, 137*t*, 139*t*
Seyip Youth Club, 138*t*
Shan women, 48
Shanghainese, 145
shemoi kharap (times are bad), 26
Shen Temple (Jolo, Philippines), 81
Shen (spirit) worship, 72, 81

Shih association, 167
Siam, 70
Sikhs, 17, 27, 37
Sin You She, 195
Singapore Chinese, 5; in Brisbane, 94, 97, 100, 103, 105-7, 106*t*, 109-10, 112n10
Singapore Society, 101
Sinicized mestizos, 66, 71
Sinified mestizos, 10
Sino-Filipinos, 66
Sino-Indian conflict, 22
Sino-Japan War, 147
Sinophobia, 85
Small Mutual Aid Clubs, 195
social clubs, 192*t*-193*t*
social organization(s), 189, 192*t*-193*t*, 196-97, 214; assumption of functions by, 213*t*; in Brisbane, 102; differentiated formations of, 15; functional substitution by, 208-14, 210*t*-211*t*; functions of, 201-8, 202*t*-205*t*; global, 199; kinship-oriented, 3-4; in New Zealand, 135*t*-140*t*; recruitment types, 192*t*-193*t*, 197*t*, 202*t*-205*t*, 213*t*; secondary, 192*t*-193*t*, 197*t*, 202*t*-205*t*, 210*t*-211*t*, 213*t*; semi-legal or criminal associations, 84; structural substitution by, 199-200, 214; types of, 192*t*-193*t*, 196
social ostracism, 181
socialization patterns, 185
Societat, 196
sociopolitical organization, 4-5
sojourners, 93, 115, 200
Solo, Philippines, Chinese in, 68
South Asia: Chinese in, 215n1

Southeast Asia: Chinese in, 65, 191, 209; refugees from, 91, 173
space: role of, 39n5
Spain, 71-72
speech groups, 73-74, 92, 116
spirit (*Shen*) worship, 72, 81
sports, 123, 125, 178-79
sports organisations, 124, 131; athletic clubs, 192*t*-193*t*, 196
stereotypes, 45
stone names, 74
Straights of Malacca, Chinese from, 100
stranded Chinese, 148-49, 161
stranded families, 160
students: Chinese, 94, 95*t*, 96-98, 101, 112n10, 122; stranded Chinese scholars, 148-49
subsistence organizations, 192*t*-193*t*
Sugar Manufacturing Association, 195
Sulu, 70
surname(s), 111n2, 165, 167; in New Zealand, 116; in Philippines, 79; in South China, 79; writing of, 167
surname associations, 92, 191, 192*t*-193*t*, 193, 197; functions, 213; multiple surname, 79-81, 166, 191, 192*t*-193*t*
sworn brotherhoods, 166-67
Sydney, Australia: Chinese in, 88, 91, 93, 96, 98, 109, 111n5; Indochinese refugees in, 113n13
Szeyap, 93

Tagalog, 83
T'ai P'ing Club, 195
Tai Tung Opera Club, 133, 138*t*-139*t*

T'ai-chi Ch'uan, 102
Taitou, Shantung, 190, 194, 206; residence organizations in, 194; secondary organizations in, 192*t*-193*t*, 197*t*, 202*t*-205*t*, 210*t*-211*t*, 213*t*
Taiwan, 175, 180, 186; Chinese from, 33, 105-7, 106*t*, 173, 187
Tan (clan), 79
Tang ren (people of the Tang [dynasty]), 24
tanners and tanning, 20-21, 23, 41n11
Tan-Oh-Yao-Chan-Ghu, 80
Taoism, 72, 81
tattling, 181-82
taxes: customs duty, 121; poll tax, 119
Teochiu, 111n5, 112n11
Terry, Lionel, 136*t*
Thailand: Chinese in, 7-8, 10, 43-49, 57; citizenship, 63n7; education, 52-53, 63n7; employment, 58-59; Kampuchean border camps, 112n11; *luuk ciin* in, 10; overseas Chinese in, 49, 63n1; stereotypes, 45; travel between PRC and, 46; Yunnanese Chinese in, 10, 49, 59-61, 63n1. *See also* Northern Thailand
Third World Brain Drain, 68
Three Character Classic (San Zi Jing), 54
thrift, 153, 182-83
ties of blood (*xue tong xue xiang*), 59
Timor, Chinese from, 97
Ting association, 167
Toisanese, 93
Tong Wars, 148
tongs, 196

Toronto, Canada: Chinatown, 37; Hakka Chinese in, 9, 36-38
Toysanese language, 145, 152-53
trade relationships, 126
transients, 95*t*, 96
Treaty of Amity, 82
Triad Temple, 91, 93, 99
Triads, 84, 91
Ts'ai association, 79, 167
tsu, 191
Tung Jung Association, 121, 128, 136*t*, 141n9
T'ung Meng Hui, 119-20, 132, 136*t*

United Nations, 147
United NZ Chinese Action and Advisory Council, 140*t*
United States, 162; Cantonese in, 83; Chinese in, 6, 96, 109, 165; colonial rule, 65, 70, 72-75; Deep South, 191; exclusionist policies, 7, 72-73; immigration policies, 146-50, 168; relations with China, 149-50. *See also* California; Mississippi Delta; New York City; Sacramento
University of Queensland, 97, 101, 112n10
untouchables, 39n4; definition of, 21
urbanization, 164

values, 11, 162; Confucian, 186
Veterans of Foreign Wars, 196
Victoria, Australia, Chinese in, 88-89
Vietnamese: in Australia, 113n13; in Brisbane, 107-8; refugees, 8, 105
Vietnamese Chinese, 5; in Australia, 113n13; in Brisbane, 107-8, 110; refugees, 8

Wacol Migrant Centre, 106-7
Wang (surname), 79
War Bride Act of 1945, 147-48, 153, 168
weakness, 176
wealth, 28-34
Wellington, New Zealand: Chinese in, 118, 122, 124, 128-30, 133, 135*t*-140*t*; City Council, 129
Wellington Chinese Sports and Cultural Centre, 129, 133
West Asia, 215n1
West Town, Yunnan, 190, 206-7; residence organizations in, 194; secondary organizations in, 192*t*-193*t*, 197*t*, 202*t*-205*t*, 210*t*-211*t*, 213*t*
Westerners: definition of, 40n8; Hakka views of, 25-26
White (term), 207
White Australia policy, 94
white fellas, 111n2
White New Zealand League, 121, 137*t*
White Race League, 136*t*
women: aboriginal, 111n2; in Australia, 89-90; Biharis, 27; Chinese, 89-90, 142n10, 195; elderly, 63n6; Hakka roles, 34-35; immigration of, 146; in Northern Thailand, 51; overseas Chinese, 59-60; Shan, 48; war brides, 147-48; Yunnanese, 50-60
Women's Liberation Movement, 164
World War I, 45
World War II, 4, 7, 91
wu cai you de (a woman without talents is virtuous), 52
wu gui (black ghosts or black devils), 6, 25

xue tong xue xiang (ties of blood), 59

Yang (surname): association, 167; lineages, 206
yella fellas, 111n2
youth clubs, 133
Yu (clan), 79
Yuan Hsi Kai, 121
Yung, Joe, 136*t*
Yunnan. *See* West Town
Yunnanese, 7; in Northern Thailand, 44-60; in Thailand, 10, 49, 59-61, 63n1

Zealots, 101
Zhong Qiu Jie (Mid-Autumn Festival), 55

DATE DUE

	APR 2 6 2001		
	FEB 1 2 2002		
	MAR 1 4 2002		
	APR 1 6 2002		
GAYLORD			PRINTED IN U.S.A.